Cook's Sites

Mark Adams is one of New Zealand's most distinguished documentary photographers. His work on Samoan tattooing, Maori-Pakeha interactions around Rotorua, and historic sites around the South Island has been extensively exhibited within New Zealand, as well as in Europe, Australia, South Africa, and Brazil. His previous publications include *Land of Memories* (1993).

Nicholas Thomas is an anthropologist and historian. His influential books include *Entangled Objects* (1991), *Colonialism's Culture* (1994), and *Possessions: Indigenous Art/Colonial Culture* (1999). He is Professor of Anthropology at Goldsmiths College, University of London.

Cook's Sites
Revisiting History

Mark Adams and Nicholas Thomas

University of Otago Press
with
Centre for Cross-Cultural Research,
Australian National University

Published by the University of Otago Press
PO Box 56/56 Union Street, Dunedin, New Zealand
Fax: 64 3 479 8385
Email: university.press@stonebow.otago.ac.nz

First published 1999

ISBN 1 877133 82 5

Mark Adams acknowledges the assistance
of Creative New Zealand

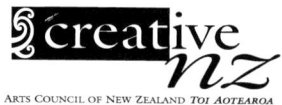

ARTS COUNCIL OF NEW ZEALAND *TOI AOTEAROA*

University of Otago Press thanks the
Centre for Cross-Cultural Research,
Australian National University,
for assisting this publication

research towards this publication
has been supported by:

the centre for cross-cultural research
AN AUSTRALIAN RESEARCH COUNCIL SPECIAL RESEARCH CENTRE
THE AUSTRALIAN NATIONAL UNIVERSITY, CANBERRA, ACT 0200
www.anu.edu.au/culture

Special thanks to Sharon Marson and Martin Schänzel
of GP Print Ltd who scanned the images and printed the book

Printed in New Zealand by GP Print Ltd, Wellington

Contents

Acknowledgements

In the six years since this project was conceived, we have incurred many debts to individuals and organisations. The Queen Elizabeth II Arts Council and subsequently Creative New Zealand provided Mark Adams with three major grants. The Photography Department at the School of Fine Arts, University of Auckland, provided support and technical facilities; particular thanks to John Turner, senior lecturer in Photography. Some of the work was done while Mark Adams was supported by a residency at Southland Art Gallery and Museum and at Southland Polytechnic. Nicholas Thomas's travel and research were supported by a grant from the Australia-New Zealand Foundation, by the Australian Research Council, and most particularly by the Centre for Cross-Cultural Research at the Australian National University, which has also provided a generous subsidy towards the production of this book. We are grateful also to Ron Brownson for his encouragement regarding the development of an exhibition arising from the project.

We should thank staff at the Staatsbibliothek, Berlin; the Institute of Ethnology, Göttingen; the Pitt Rivers Museum, Oxford; and the Royal Botanic Gardens, Kew, for their co-operation and assistance. We are also grateful to: Dick and Kathy of the *Pembroke* who enabled us to spend three weeks in Dusky Sound in 1995; Ian Leedon, Ian MacDonald, Andrew MacDonald, and Darren Glass, who accompanied us on the 1995 trip, as did Haru Sameshima who has provided a great deal of ongoing support and encouragement. Mark Adams would also like to thank Tony, Nash and Roger of the *Marine Countess* of Bluff for facilitating his second trip to Dusky Sound; Jenny Bramley, Wayne Marriott, Maree Frewen, David and Victoria Moore, and Joanne and Murray Fuller in London, Beverley and Mike Lear in Wiltshire, Peter and Takutai Beech in Picton, Jane Kominik of the Ministry of Cultural Affairs, and Jeanne Lomax and Eymard Bradley in Wellington. Special thanks also to Kerry Robertson, John and Linnea Adams, and Ana, Benjamin and Dante.

Ann McGrath provided Nicholas Thomas with helpful comments on a draft of the text. He would also like to thank Annie Coombes for her support. We are very grateful to Wendy Harrex at University of Otago Press for her commitment to the project, and those involved in the realisation of the exhibition linked with the book at Te Papa Tongarewa, the Museum of New Zealand, particularly Paul Thompson, Alison Preston, Nigel Cox, and Eymard Bradley.

Auckland
July 1999

Introduction

The voyages of Captain Cook remain tremendously significant in public historical imaginings in New Zealand, Australia, and Britain. Many people continue to celebrate the navigator's accomplishments for their maritime heroism and for their foundational place in the beginnings of colonisation. Others condemn the voyages for a related reason: they inaugurate a violent history of intrusion. This book tries to come to terms with the burden of this history in a new way. Through images and texts, we revisit the voyages, aiming to avoid the certainties of celebration and condemnation alike. We have literally revisited sites of contact between Cook and Indigenous peoples, specifically the Maori of southern New Zealand. In a few particular places, we have examined the traces of the past and the ways in which the places and traces have been imaginatively refashioned at various times since the 1770s. We do not simply record these successive historical imaginings, but have ourselves re-imagined the sites and their histories in ways that seem appropriate to the present. We also document and respond to certain European sites in which relics of the voyages are kept. 'Relics' is not the usual word for the sorts of documents, botanical specimens, and ethnographic artifacts we have in mind – and it may be the wrong word, even an offensive word, if it implies that such artifacts are no more than dead memorials. From an Indigenous viewpoint, or some Indigenous viewpoints, they are treasures and heirlooms that retain a vital force, which is why associating them with the notion of the relic, with its implications of sacredness and efficacy, may not be so inappropriate.

Of the many places Cook visited in the south and north Pacific, we revisit only two in New Zealand, both in the South Island, Te Wai Pounamu. One is near the southern extremity of the South Island, and the other is at the northern end. Cook, in the *Resolution* on his second voyage, visited the first of these places, Dusky Sound, once only, in April and May of 1773, for rest and refreshment after an extended cruise in Antarctic waters. The period was notable for a brief but highly singular encounter with one Maori family, or rather with a group of people who apparently constituted a family but did not behave quite like one, perplexing the observers of Cook's party. This was a peaceful encounter and one replete with mutual surprises, but also one later believed to have led to the massacre of the 'family' at the hands of another Maori group. One of the stories attached to this site, then, is a sort of murder mystery.

Queen Charlotte Sound was, in contrast, visited five times over Cook's three voyages. There was evidently a good deal of movement and conflict in the area, and different Maori groups were encountered on each occasion, but there was nevertheless some accumulation of mutual understanding and misunderstanding, marked particularly by violence in which more European sailors' lives were lost than during any other skirmish in the course of the Cook voyages. The so-called Grass Cove massacre overshadows other elements of the contact experience in this area, and arguably had vital longer term ramifications for Cook's attitudes towards the peoples of Oceania. We therefore juxtapose one fleeting encounter with a succession of others; and one that was mainly peaceful with one that was notably violent.

Whereas Tamatea, or Dusky Sound, is now wholly uninhabited – and is visited regularly only by fishing boats and small chartered vessels carrying hunters and tourists – Queen Charlotte Sound is a popular holiday spot, being immediately north of Picton and the ferry route between the North and South Islands. Although Ship Cove, the bay in which Cook's ships routinely anchored, is not accessible by road, there are many tourist lodges, backpacker hostels, and holiday houses along the sound. These are connected by walking tracks and by launch and water taxi services. If many New Zealanders visit the area for the fishing and walking, rather than for its heritage aspects, much is nevertheless made locally of the Cook connection. Whereas Dusky Sound appears to be much as it was, Queen Charlotte Sound is dramatically transformed; yet it is in the latter area that Cook's visits are most extensively marked and commemorated. In one place we encounter the traces of the past; in the other we find the signs of a national history.

~

The joint authors of this book, a photographer and a writer, are conscious of the artifices of image-making and history-making. Much contemporary writing on art, photography, anthropology, and history is dedicated to exposing such artifice, to deconstructing critically representations, invented traditions, myths of nationhood, and stereotypes of other peoples. This literature has become repetitive, but it has brought some vital truths to our attention. No image is an innocent transcript of nature, and no account of the past can be a simple reconstruction that lacks a grounding in the present. One's stance may be acknowledged or covert, explicit or implicit, but either way it shapes the images and narratives one produces.

To adopt this view is to recognise the partiality of all accounts of the past. Every telling is doubly partial: in being selective and incomplete, and not being disinterested. This is to say more than that there are many histories, all as good as each other, all equally true or equally contrived. The notion that everything is a fiction is not a new postmodernist insight but simply an old-fashioned relativist cliché, and one that goes nowhere in helping us to account for the murk of truth and mystification that characterises cross-cultural histories in countries such as New Zealand and Australia. It is true that Cook's encounters with Maori have been narrated in different ways with markedly different inflections, but we consider it important that we go beyond this observation. Some of these histories are more contrived than others; some are absurd. We are not after a singular truth behind the contacts of the 1770s, but we do want to point out that some ways of representing these meetings, which inaugurated the history of a colonial nation, are fanciful.

If all histories are politicised, this is so in a special way in settler-colonial nations. In states of this kind – admittedly a diverse range, including Canada, Australia, New Zealand, Mexico, and South Africa – settlers have displaced native peoples, and have generally fashioned myths of national foundation that in some way ennoble or justify both dispossession and the creation of settler or creole societies on another people's land. As we have already noted, the moral values of the foundational moments of these histories can only be deeply contentious: for some, Cook will be a heroic figure; for others, he will be an invader. Both the positive and negative hagiographies are motivated by national narratives: the one celebrating European colonisation, the other a charter for a counter-colonial Indigenous nationalism.

We attempt to come to grips with the ways in which Cook's intrusions indeed inaugurated a colonial history. But we insist that little is gained by turning the heroes into villains. It is a striking feature of the Cook voyages that the participants themselves were preoccupied with the morality of their encounters with native peoples. Though they were resolutely committed to the business of maritime discovery, the writers of the various journals often acknowledged the injustices of petty transactions, the regrettable excesses of members of the crew, and the prospective tragedy of the spread of venereal disease. For Cook himself, for John Hawkesworth (the editor of the journals of Cook's first voyage) and for Johann Reinhold Forster and his son George (the remarkable natural historians we refer to extensively here), these were grievous consequences that tarnished the whole endeavour. The radical Forsters, in particular, were drawn into a confused and contradictory rhetoric. They lurched between lyrical celebrations of the liberality of scientific discovery, which conformed with Providence's larger scheme for the improvement of the human species, and the observation that the health, morality, and happiness of the peoples they called 'South-Sea Islanders' would be permanently damaged by contact with Europe. This antinomy is often exhibited, and is in no way resolved, in the extensive writings from the voyage. But it is bleached out of the history that was composed later, in the nineteenth and twentieth centuries. And this contradiction in the European culture of the voyaging eighteenth century has again been bleached out, in a different way, by postcolonial scholars of recent years who have simply not acknowledged the many dimensions, and the uncertainties and inconsistencies, in travel writings that are conflated under the rubric of 'colonial discourse'.

In drawing attention to these confusions, we are trying to discover the past, to see past public histories. We reveal the loose ends that are inconsistent with both the positive and negative moralising narratives. We aim to draw attention to the ways in which the business of discovery, and the effort to understand and respond to unfamiliar peoples and places, were invariably double-sided. On the one hand there were possessive declarations; on the other there was a licentious or promiscuous engagement with a sheer plurality of novel and curious objects. Likewise, on the one hand there were moments of cross-cultural empathy, exchange, and a sense of human sameness; on the other, there were efforts to make the absolute superiority of civilisation manifest, and to impose quasi-racial hierarchies. And there was also the desire, the violence, and the unequal exchange of promiscuity in the most literal sense.

If nearly all social relationships entail both reciprocity of some sort and asymmetry or exploitation, this double-sidedness is surely magnified in cross-cultural relations. If it has to be acknowledged that the asymmetries, and the scope for sheer exploitation, were and are conspicuous, reciprocity is often, in any case, an unstable and unpredictable relation. If there was much to be gained at certain moments in cross-cultural transactions, there was much also to be risked or lost. In revisiting these sites, we are concerned to move away from the sense of inevitability that pervades much writing in colonial history, and rediscover the risk and possibility that was in fact vital to these early meetings. If there were multiple potentialities in cross-cultural relations, if other things could have happened then, those other things may happen now. An engagement with history may not enable us to anticipate the future, but it should make the past less predictable.

~

Any enquiry into a cross-cultural history confronts the question of how one can do justice to the perspectives of both parties – or, perhaps, rather to the many perspectives, given that neither foreigners nor natives, neither colonisers nor colonised, are ever homogeneous blocs. With respect to Tamatea, the people we are talking about are not 'Maori' but Ngatimamoe,[1] and were probably best known to themselves not by that tribal name, but by a more local term that is not known to us. No doubt the most desirable approach would aim to reconstruct and represent both sides – or as many 'sides' as can be found. And over the last forty years this has essentially been the project of scholars working on history and culture in the Pacific. Initially such enquiries were confined to the rubric of 'ethnohistory', a subdiscipline marginal to both political and economic history, and to anthropology, which was then oriented more to the ahistorical study of supposedly traditional societies. Over time, the concerns with change, encounters, colonialism, and Indigenous historical understandings shifted to almost encompass both disciplines, so that in place of a simple overlap there is now a wide-ranging genre of cultural enquiry that is increasingly indifferent to old boundaries between history, anthropology, and related fields such as archaeology and art history.

This fertile area has produced many studies that have attempted, with varying degrees of success, to move beyond accounts of change from the European point of view, and detail the ramifications of early contacts, Christianity, and colonialism, on and in Indigenous societies. The ways visitors were perceived, the ways Indigenous peoples responded, the ways Indigenous socialities and cultures were transformed, and the ways these changes are registered in Indigenous rites, myths, and historical imaginings, have been traced and reconstructed. The sources have ranged from oral information collected recently, vernacular accounts recorded at various times in the past, and the quotations and traces of Indigenous voices that are preserved in the interstices of colonial sources. These histories have broken open the lineaments of one-sided narratives; if the idea of a balanced, two-sided history is likely to be elusive, for all kinds of reasons, they have nevertheless introduced a partial representativeness, a cross-cultural history.

This book does not attempt to reconstruct the Maori point of view, or to tell the history from two sides. There are several reasons why we have adopted what might seem a constrained approach, even an out-of-date one, and limited ourselves to an enquiry into European and Pakeha (white settler) historical imaginings in this joint work. The principal reason is not that we take the view that 'the' Maori side of the story can only be written by Maori. Although Maori may well have particular insights that outsiders are likely to lack, we do not presume that it is impossible for outsiders to produce valuable, and indeed culturally sensitive, accounts of Indigenous history. Maori and other Indigenous peoples are certainly equipped, conversely, to produce insightful accounts of European and colonial histories. That said, we suggest that Indigenous understandings of the contacts in Tamatea and Totaranui lie substantially beyond the visual and textual evidence we have worked from. Rather than map out an alternative history from the other side, we do not presume that there is an Indigenous counterpart to this history, in the sense of a narrative that shadows, or opposes, the narratives we describe. It may be that Indigenous historical imaginings have different beginnings, and acknowledge different happenings.

It has seemed better to say less rather than more for another, essentially practical, reason. Were this a work of empirical ethnohistory, rather than an imaginative response to certain sites, images, narratives, and histories, we would moreover have been compelled to address the problem that there is negligible information concerning Indigenous history in Dusky Sound relevant to the period or the events in question. This is so partly because the small groups in the area were highly mobile. Subsequent depopulation meant that little information could be obtained by the late date when ethnologists began recording myths and oral histories for southern New Zealand in general. The rich tribal histories and histories of contact and colonial experience that can be produced for the more densely and continuously populated regions (on the basis of both Maori and Pakeha documents and living knowledge) for many parts of the North Island, for instance, are simply not available here. Though Anne Salmond has done a remarkably thorough job in reconstructing Indigenous social relations and responses in the places visited by Cook, the paucity of material for the far south, and for this early period, is striking in comparison with the later histories, for which both sides (or several) can be told in a more nuanced and satisfying way.[2]

⌒

Cook's Sites arises from a conjuncture of visual and verbal enquiry. We do not aim to theorise explicitly the much-debated issues around the differences between words and images, but rather seek to exemplify a way in which the literary and the visual might work in a complementary fashion to evoke a richer sense of the past, and of argument about the past, than either could alone.

The book therefore tries to avoid the biases of conventional historical and theoretical writings (in which images are generally no more than illustrations), and those of art and photography catalogues (in which texts merely serve as introductions or captions). It consists rather of both photographs and words: through both we revisit and reinterpret the sites, encounters, and histories that are central to our concerns. Both are individually authored, but arise from the closest possible dialogue and collaboration. We travelled together to Dusky Sound and Queen Charlotte Sound, and to Berlin and Göttingen, though Mark Adams worked alone in the United Kingdom, and made return visits on his own to some of the key sites in Dusky Sound. The images published here emerge from these visits, from shared responses to places, from discussions about environments and specific sites. The texts were written by

Nicholas Thomas in Canberra without Mark's direct input, but were shaped also by shared preoccupations and many long conversations about the voyages and their histories.

Each chapter in the book is both visual and textual. Each engages with particular places and with the issues that arise from them, from the archive of texts and images that emerged from Cook's encounters, and from the photographs we produced. In only a few cases do the texts provide a direct commentary on the images. We have preferred to let those images make their visual statements without literal explication, while developing an argument that resonates with the photographs, proceeding in parallel, or perhaps in productive tension, with them. The photographs and texts are both moreover like historical conglomerates, new formations that incorporate old matter: the pictures incorporate monuments, and images within images; the texts quote from the voyage narratives, and discuss sketches, paintings and engravings that we reproduce. Hence the idea of parallel but distinct paths is perhaps less apt than the suggestion that there are two bodies of representations and reflections here. They differ in their media, they sometimes merge in direct mutual commentary, and they present distinct facets of the same objects and arguments. Yet they could also be seen to work in essentially different registers; the one conveying significances and responses that fall between the lines, or beyond the vision, of the other. It is probably not productive to attempt to spell this relation out further: it cannot emerge from our efforts of definition, but only from an audience's viewing and reading. *Cook's Sites*, then, is not only a collaboration between a photographer and a writer, but one between the two of us and you. This is true to the ways histories are always made and remade, not in isolated gestures of acting and writing, but in the imagining of acts and the reception of texts. To revisit history is to engage, for better or worse, in exchange.

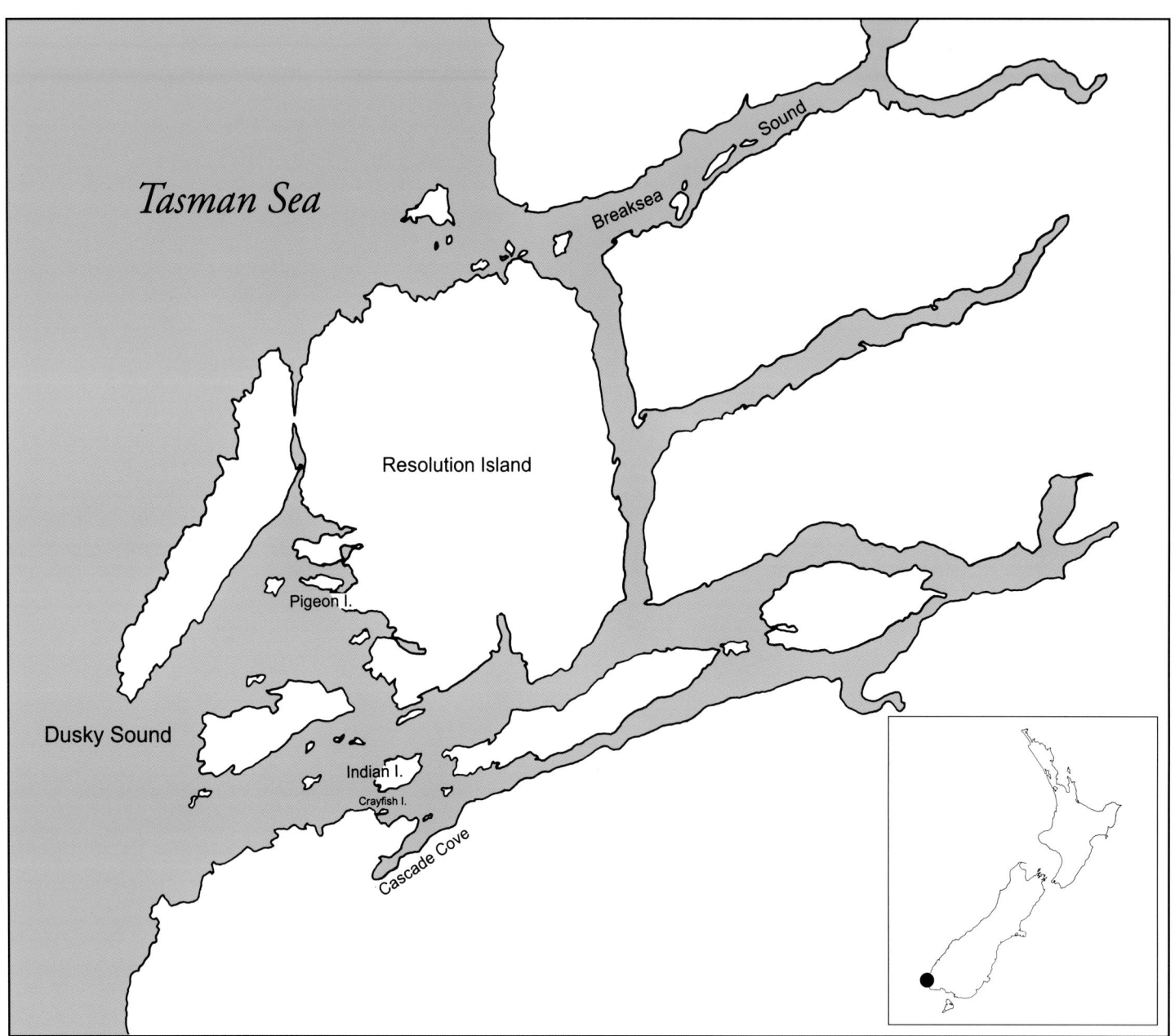

South-west Fiordland, visited by the Resolution *in 1773.*

1. Astronomers Point

It had rained overnight. In the morning, the water was limpid; there was not much heat in the sun, but wet rocks high on the mountains that surround Tamatea, or Dusky Sound, glittered. On Sunday 28 March 1773, Cook's *Resolution* was worked or towed through a narrow gap between Crayfish Island and the mainland, into a small cove where that afternoon the vessel was moored. There was, as Cook wrote, a convenient gangplank 'which nature had in a manner prepared for us by a large tree which growed in a horizontal direction over the Water so long that the Top of it reached our gunwale.'[3] The area, thickly and variously forested and apparently uninhabited, was extremely attractive, especially to those who had spent one hundred and seventeen days out of sight of land. They had not only been at sea, but passed this time in harsh conditions among huge and grotesque icebergs in the Antarctic, in pursuit of an imagined southern land or prospective continent for European settlement. The utopia that had been lacking in the far south was, however, almost realised here. Wood and 'a fine stream of fresh Water' were convenient, 'every place abounded with excellent fish', there were fowl in the woods; in short, as Cook put it, 'we expected to injoy with ease what in our situation might be call'd the luxuries of life.'

Today, in the southern autumn and winter months, you can join a group of ten or twenty on one of several boats, and cruise through Doubtful and Dusky Sounds and possibly also Preservation Inlet, still farther to the south. You might go simply because these places are beautiful and remote, but the trip will nevertheless be in part an historical one. Your vessel will almost stop, and take you carefully through that narrow gap between Crayfish Island and the mainland – ignoring, like Cook, the much wider opening available on the other side – around Astronomers Point, and into the small cove. Your party will all be standing around the boat's bow, because this is a special moment in the course of the tour, a high point that you have been alerted to in advance. Your engine will throb through an awkward manoeuvre; there will be a fine trail of fuel on the water; the cruise boat will come about and nuzzle the shore, as the *Resolution* did. You and your companions will reach out and grasp the horizontal tree that is still there, that extends itself from the thick and wet land like a greeting. It is a dead, hard tree; fragments of bark and grey-green lichen will come away on your fingers. History is suddenly tactile.

⌁

This engagement with a history has itself a history. In the Auckland Art Gallery, there's a photograph album from the turn of the century with a series of views of this area, the work of Russell Duncan, who photographed extensively in the South Island. The photographs are carefully arranged and captioned so that places are seen in the order in which they were encountered by members of Cook's party. And in the mid-1960s, two Dunedin doctors, Charles and Neil Begg, published their book *Dusky Bay: In the Steps of Captain Cook.* The dust jacket features a William Hodges painting that admittedly has 'A View in Dusky Bay' inscribed on its frame, but in fact depicts, beyond any doubt, a waterfall in Tahiti that Hodges visited on 4 May 1774. The Beggs went to considerable lengths to locate the particular spots at which various events occurred during the *Resolution*'s six-week stay in the area. They had brought with them a plaque, which they cemented into rock on the point by Pickersgill Harbour. Their book describes these activities, and imagines the fatal impact of the voyage upon the Maori with whom the crew trafficked. It also traces events in the area after Cook's visit.

The most remarkable chapter of this subsequent history is a different tale altogether, that of the naturalist Richard Henry. Born in 1845, he grew up in rural Victoria, underwent some training as a carpenter, got to know local Kooris (Aboriginal people) well, and developed a preoccupation with natural history and birds in particular. After moving to New Zealand, he failed both in sheep farming and in a suicide attempt which the Beggs do not mention. In 1894 he became the keeper of New Zealand's first bird sanctuary on Resolution Island, a precipitous and daunting massif that separates Dusky Sound from Breaksea Sound. Henry lived on a small adjacent island for some years, underfunded and in almost total isolation. He attempted to preserve birds such as kakapo that were threatened by ferrets among other introduced pests on the mainland, but found time to write a few papers, later collected in a monograph on the *Habits of the Flightless Birds of New Zealand*. In 1900 stoats were discovered on Resolution Island, so it appeared that the isolation of the sanctuary had been breached, and the effort was abandoned.[4]

For Viscount Cobham, who wrote the preface to *Dusky Bay*, the Beggs' book breathed 'the very essence of New Zealand'. He added, somewhat perplexingly, of the unhappy Irish-Australian, 'Richard Henry could have been a man of no other race.' Whatever the character of this national essence, it is something that your cruise should put you in touch with. Perhaps the day before or the day after visiting Astronomers Point, you'll walk around Pigeon Island and see the remains of Henry's bird-house and the site of his own residence – without information panels, signs, or plaques. If you rummage around, you may find some of his glass negatives, broken among the ponga tree ferns. This site is managed somewhat ambivalently by the Department of Conservation: Henry's efforts to redress the disorder produced by introduced species resonate awkwardly, perhaps, with the packaging of wilderness. This site tells a story that does not have a particular beginning or ending, a story of a perhaps hopeless effort to contain the ecological effects of colonisation, of settler animals gone wild. This seems all too symptomatic, given the numbers of rabbits, among other feral creatures in New Zealand (and Australia). This kind of history is in fact all too foundational; it is perhaps not surprising at all that Henry's Pigeon Island is not treated as an historic site, unlike Astronomers Point, which seems to inaugurate a national narrative.

⁓

Let us imagine ourselves back at that point. The boat has nudged the horizontal tree. Never mind that this is obviously not the same tree mentioned by Cook and painted by Hodges. We will use some kind of dinghy to get to shore. Even in these protected waters there is a little swell, so this is slightly more difficult than it at first appears. Our approach to the site is arranged partly by topography and partly by the New Zealand state, through the Department of Conservation. There is an obvious rock shelf on which to land, and a newer metal plaque behind this point, featuring a view of the ship in the cove loosely based on Hodges' view, together with a text explaining the significance of the voyage. From here a boardwalk keeps us out of the mud, and prevents us from trampling delicate ferns. It zigzags onto the low hill that forms the point, and a path circumscribes the area that Cook's men cleared in March 1773.

If the 1773 visit is now understood, officially and unofficially, by government agents, tour operators, photographers, and anthropologists as an historical moment rather than merely as an incident, it was also seen in these terms at the time. How it was seen then, by Maori whom we would now presume were Ngatimamoe, I do not know, and for the moment will not speculate. But one European, at least, chose later to present the visit as a microcosm of human progress:

> The superiority of a state of civilization over that of barbarism could not be more clearly stated, than by the alterations and improvements we had made in this place. In the course of a few days, a small part of us had cleared away the woods from a surface of more than an acre, which fifty New Zeelanders, with their tools of stone, could not have performed in three months. This spot, where immense numbers of plants left to themselves lived and decayed by turns, in one confused inanimated heap; this spot, we had converted into an active scene, where a hundred and twenty men pursued various branches of employment with unremitted ardour:
>
> > Quales apes æstate nova per florea rura
> > Exercet sub sole labor.
> > VIRGIL.
> > Such was their toil, and such their busy pains,
> > As exercise the bees in flowery plains,
> > When winter past and summer scarce begun,
> > Invites them forth to labour in the sun.
> > DRYDEN.
>
> We felled tall timber-trees, which, but for ourselves, had crumbled to dust with age; our sawyers cut them into planks, or we split them into billets for fuel. By the side of a murmuring rivulet, whose passage into the sea we facilitated, a long range of casks, which had been prepared by our coopers for that purpose, stood ready to be filled with water. Here ascended the steam of a large cauldron, in which we brewed, from neglected indigenous plants, a salutary and palatable potion, for the use of our labourers. In the offing, some of our crew appeared providing a meal of delicious fish for the refreshment of their fellows. Our caulkers and riggers were stationed on the sides and masts of the vessel, and their occupations gave life to the scene, and struck the ear with various noises, whilst the anvil on the hill resounded with the strokes of the weighty hammer. Already the polite arts began to flourish in this new settlement; the various tribes of animals and vegetables, which dwelt in the unfrequented woods, were imitated by an artist in his noviciate; and the romantic prospects of this shaggy country, lived on the canvas in the glowing tints of nature, who was amazed to see herself so closely copied. Nor had science disdained to visit us in this solitary spot: an observatory arose in the centre of our works, filled with the most accurate instruments, where the attentive eye of the as-tronomer contemplated the motions of the celestial bodies. The plants which clothed the ground, and the wonders of the animal creation, both in the forests and the seas, likewise attracted the notice of philosophers, whose time was devoted to mark their differences and uses. In a word, all around us we perceived the rise of arts, and the dawn of science, in a country which had hitherto lain plunged in one long night of ignorance and barbarism!
>
> George Forster, *Voyage Round the World*, I, p. 177–9

In Forster's lyrical account, the business of cultivation and the improvement of nature suggests a radical contrast between the barbarism of the place and the state of society exemplified by the visiting Europeans. This evocation is in many ways untypical of George Forster, who has a good deal more to say about the barbarism of British sailors than that of any Pacific Islanders. He denounced common seamen for their promiscuity, their alcoholism, and for being cruel to pet monkeys, for example; he often commended the neat and extensive gardens in the Society Islands, Tonga, and Vanuatu among other places. In most of the places visited on Cook's second voyage, there was little scope for denouncing the lack of environmental modification. It was the nomadism of the people of the far south of Te Wai Pounamu that licensed the comments here on the attainments of the inhabitants in general, and this negative evaluation was moreover at odds with Forster's positive response to them as individuals. They were not at all like those other nomads encountered on this voyage, the inhabitants of Tierra del Fuego, who were, to Cook, Forster, and much later Darwin, evidently stupified by a harsh climate. The 'family of Dusky Bay', described on a number of occasions and depicted in a number of William Hodges' works, are dignified, intelligent, and attractive people.

A flow of gifts had both resulted from and given substance to temporary human proximity. But Forster, when it came to the moment of hindsight, wrote these paragraphs, and denied the meeting, denied what had been shared. He insisted on a gulf between European and Maori – a distance that seems conflated with the time between primeval nature and civilisation itself. Though there is much talk elsewhere in his book of the unity of the human family and the scope for improvement at all places and times, here the note is pessimistic. Forster proceeds:

> But this pleasing picture of improvement was not to last, and like a meteor, vanished as suddenly as it was formed. [Here Forster's translation of his own book into German even adds 'Sic transit gloria mundi!']. We re-imbarked all our instruments and utensils, and left no other vestiges of our residence, than a piece of ground, from whence we had cleared the wood. We sowed indeed a quantity of European garden seeds of the best kinds; but it is obvious that the shoots of the surrounding weeds will shortly stifle every salutary and useful plant, and that in a few years our abode no longer discernible, must return to its original chaotic state.
>
> Forster, *Voyage Round the World*, I, p. 179–80

Astronomers Point is an extraordinary place, for the drama of its turbulent weather and rapidly changing light, and because the 1773 visit seems so strangely close. This is partly because the forest and the sound and the basic surrounds remain undeveloped; one feels that nothing has changed. There are many small resonances, too: just as Cook's crew remarked on the fearlessness of the many tiny birds, the visitor today will be struck by the way tiny wrens and robins flit about the bushes within an arm's length, at once seemingly curious and indifferent to the human presence. The stream takes the same course; the same route that the Forsters among others took can be followed up to Lake Forster; the same types of fish are abundant in the waters of the sound and can be caught and 'broiled *à l'indienne*' as Forster put it, though finding sufficient dry wood to get a fire going and keep it going is difficult. These affinities between now and then enable an embodied mimicry of the past; we didn't need to be told by a tour guide to re-enact exploration, we found ourselves doing so. If hiking and camping experiences often recapitulate the frontier experiences of explorers, pioneers, and early settlers in a more comfortable and suitably abbreviated register, wilderness tourism in Dusky Sound enables engagement with a foundational historical moment of first contact. And this engagement inevitably compounds tawdry and contrived re-enactment with fortuitous and unexpected affinities.

A visitor suspicious of the business of travelling in the steps of Cook, who may even assume that any such project glorifies colonialism, will experience the passage between Crayfish Island and the mainland, towards Astronomers Point, with a combination of scorn, estrangement, and repressed curiosity. Yet this same visitor may well find himself or herself inadvertently delighted to recognise a plant or rock described by Cook or some other voyager. I, at least, was astonished by these recognitions, and by how precisely William Hodges captured the mist, bright sunlight, and heavy cloud that are so often anomalously co-present in Dusky Sound. At a time when almost all 'students of culture and history' take it for granted that representations are elaborately contrived social and ideological constructions, one can travel to the end of the world and be caught off one's guard by an appearance of the truth that critical scholarship in the humanities has laboured for so long to deconstruct. Here, so far from the West, Western mimesis retains its deceptively uncomplicated magic.

If a trip 'in the steps of Cook' has elements both of critical mockery and unexpected recognition, neither of these are straightforward: the mockery may be a little too deliberate, even dishonest, while moments of recognition are, on reflection, unsettled. Hodges was not consistently an empirical artist. His naturalism was nearly always united with the imaginative construction of moralised scenes – scenes that were moralised in a historical sense, that is, rather than a merely judgemental one. This is to say that his scenes incorporate social and political problems, which loom surprisingly large, even among the few inhabitants of Dusky Sound, as we shall see.

~

At Astronomers Point, we are close to the events of 1773 for another reason, because Forster was wrong about the local ecological impact. The low hill that forms the point has not 'returned to its original chaotic state'. Forster could not have known how slowly trees decayed and grew in this temperate forest, which is further south than Tasmania, as far south as Patagonia. The stumps of some of those then felled can be discerned now, like obscure monuments shrouded in kidney fern.

More arresting is the contrast between the vegetation on the point and the pristine forest that surrounds it. Away from that microcosm of civility, the ground is clear but for bracken and small ferns. Huge rimu and totara, beleaguered by strange epiphytes, are widely spaced, six hundred, eight hundred, perhaps a thousand years old. It is possible to stand back from any one tree and admire its enormity, even if its higher branches are interlocked and confused with those of others. There is almost a natural architecture, a visual coherence, in the glens apart from the space of intrusion. On the point itself, though, there are no great trees. Instead you encounter secondary forest, regrowth that is not especially thick, but is optically bewildering: the tangle of saplings precludes any open view. Seeing this, and particularly seeing it through a camera, you are confronted with the problem of depth of field. Are you trying to look at the trees in the foreground, or through them? There is no object, prospect, or perspective on offer here, except one which an extension of the boardwalk leads you down to. There, on the point itself, is a small platform, and you can look back to Crayfish Island and the gap the ship was towed through. You are provided with a sort of visual retrospect on the route of arrival; the site that is so manifestly historic itself bears that history's legacy in exhibiting no view. Forster supposed that the cleared area would degenerate again into chaos, but the disorder that strikes us now is not a primeval condition but the upshot of contact. It figures not as a marker of a lack of civilisation, but as historical evidence for the beginnings of civilisation, as an organic monument to first efforts to deforest this area, and the first European efforts to deforest any part of New Zealand.

~

Forster's ready identification of clearing trees with civilising reaches us awkwardly, in fact simply badly. While he could associate the removal of vegetation with honest labour and with the preconditions for the emergence of science and art, we are accustomed to regard the destruction of trees as vandalism in the name of progress, and indeed as ultimately life-threatening, via the destruction of the ozone layer and the greenhouse effect.

If these environmental issues are at once serious in a global sense and the raw material for various self-congratulatory moralisms that need not concern us here, they assume special resonance in New Zealand, because clearing was such a conspicuous aspect of the country's development, particularly in the late nineteenth century. William Hodges' *View in Pickersgill Harbour* (p. 30), which centres upon a clearing for a temporary settlement, is in this sense a seminal painting for New Zealand art. Hodges' painting ironically anticipates many nineteenth and twentieth century works depicting the business or the results of deforestation. If early examples, such as Charles Heaphy's *Kauri Forest, Wairoa River* (1839), are often matter-of-fact, by the late nineteenth century artists like Alfred Sharpe and photographers like Josiah Martin were recording the great forests for melancholy posterity. The dead tree subsequently became a motif, and rapidly something of a visual cliché, though the tendency was to evoke the stark and sombre in general, rather than the historical process of clearing. This genealogy of dead trees can be traced back to these original ancestors on Astronomers Point.

These days, it is often suggested that modernity engenders its opposites: civilisation creates not only the ideal of the primitive, but also supposedly freezes dynamic societies on its periphery into static traditional communities. Likewise, globalisation makes localities visible and prompts people to affirm their distinct identities. Whether or not these broad-brush propositions are more than half true, they are exhibited in the microcosm of the civilising process at Astronomers Point. The shock of dense regrowth is evident in contrast to the surrounding forest, but the condition of that forest is in fact no less an upshot of contact. The majestic clarity of the tall trees and low bracken arises from a later colonisation: that of deer. The introduced game are said to browse the undergrowth, which seems not quite the right word: a decent historian will no doubt 'browse' equally voraciously, but we conventionally imagine that the book or the archive is still there after he or she has finished.

Which is to say that this recognition of Tamatea, or Dusky Sound, might bring us to the end of a cultural tradition, both Western and antipodean, that had one of its beginnings in the Forsters' writings and Hodges' paintings of the area. I mean the appreciation of nature in the form of wilderness, in all its romantic specificity. George Forster's *Voyage* inspired the great German naturalist Alexander von Humboldt, who cited it (with William Hodges' paintings of India, rather than of the Pacific) among a few key stimuli that aroused his interest in natural history. And when one reads Forster's impassioned and embodied accounts of mist, water, strata and plant life, it is easy to understand why his voyage narrative was profoundly influential for scientific romanticism. What is beautiful and remarkable, in his perspective and in that of successors, lies not in ideal or standard forms, but in the magnificent variety and particularity of nature. I am not suggesting that we should now eschew this aesthetic – it seems strange, today, that anyone would not be impressed and delighted by the trees and waterfalls here – but that we must begin to appreciate history in the form of wilderness. As the mist moves off the still and transparent water, as a seal splashes, as a nondescript stump is regarded as a monument, what is enchanting is not original harmony, but a site and its successive mediations, a site and its confusions of perspective.

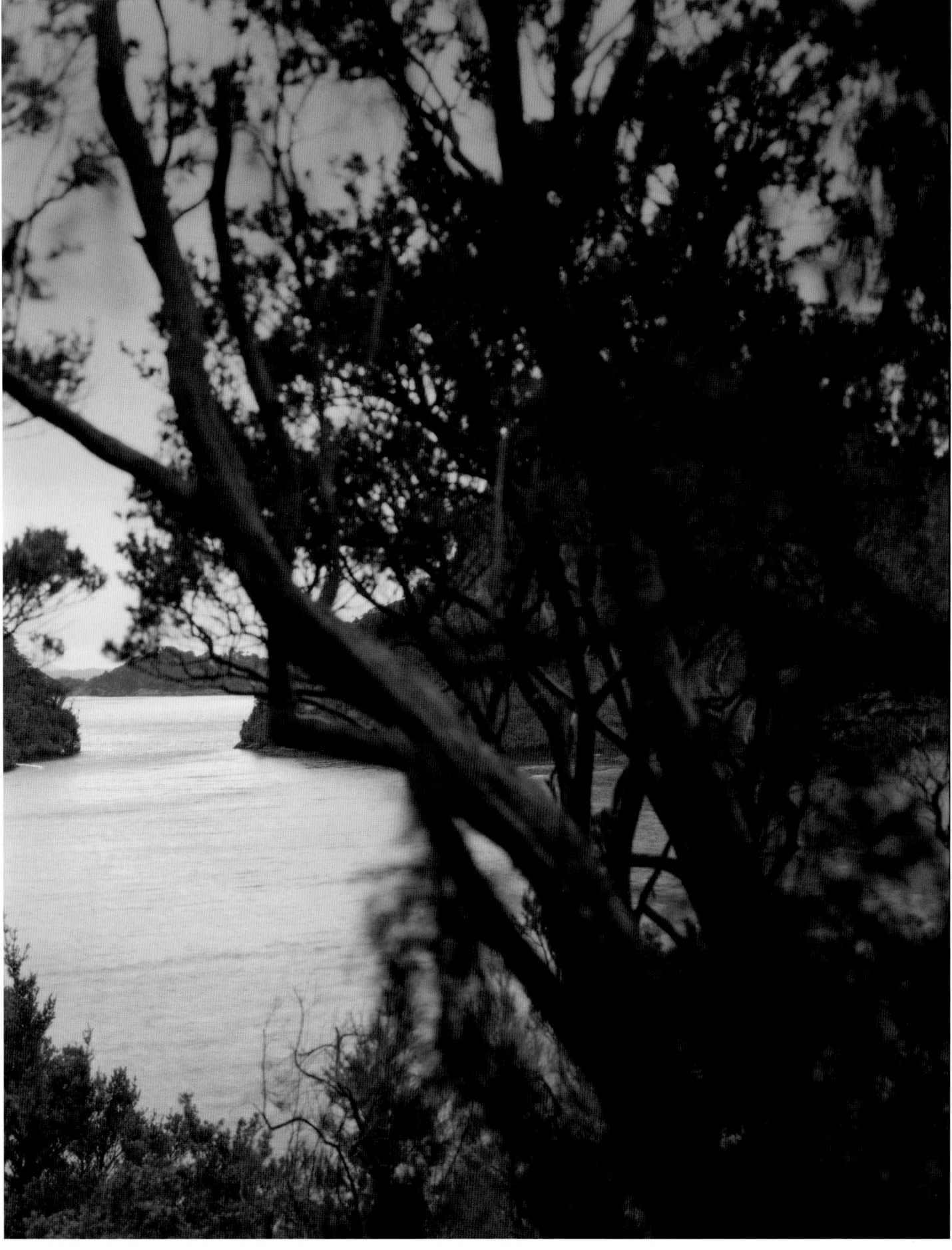

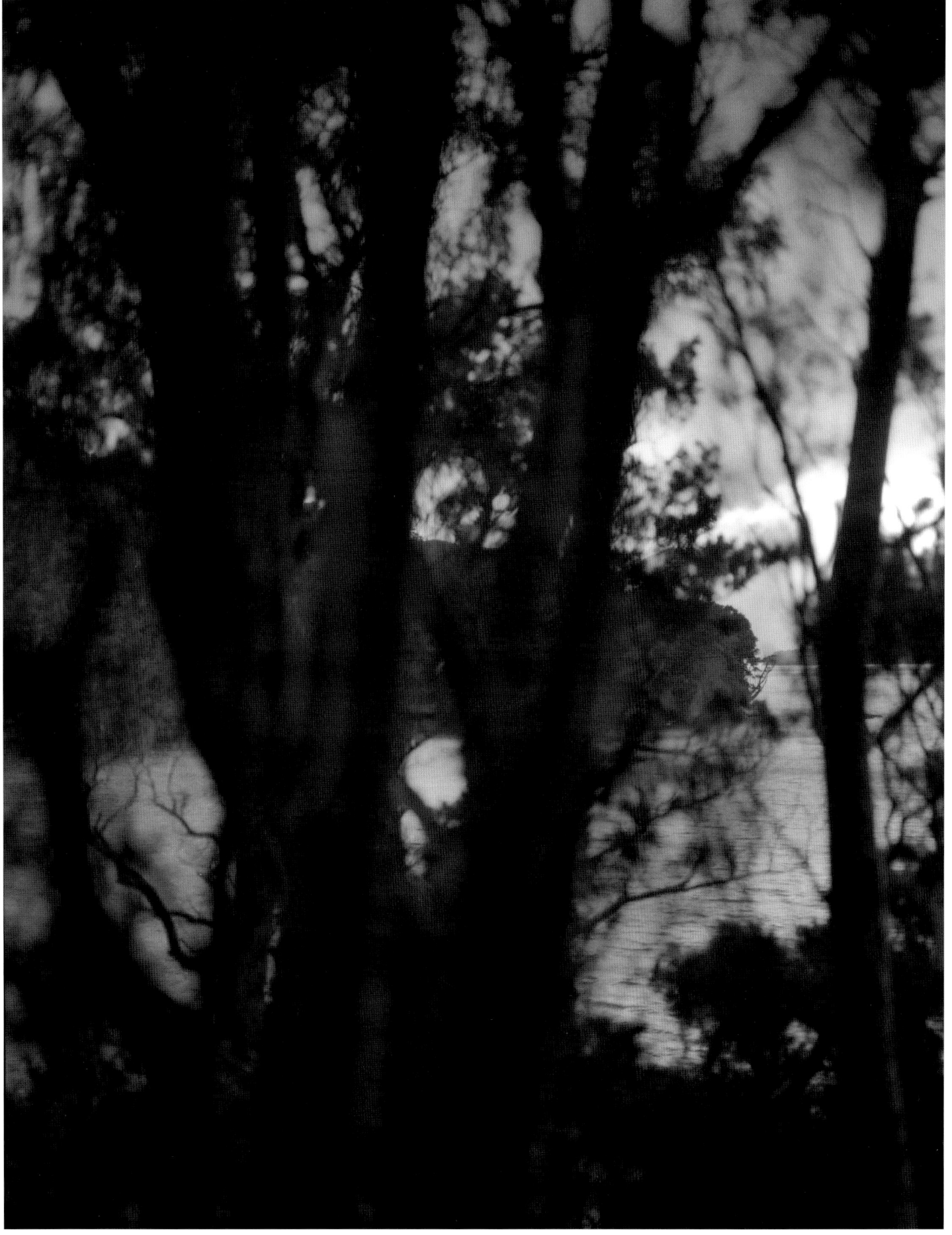

1 (a,b,c)
Views from Astronomers Point, 15 May 1995

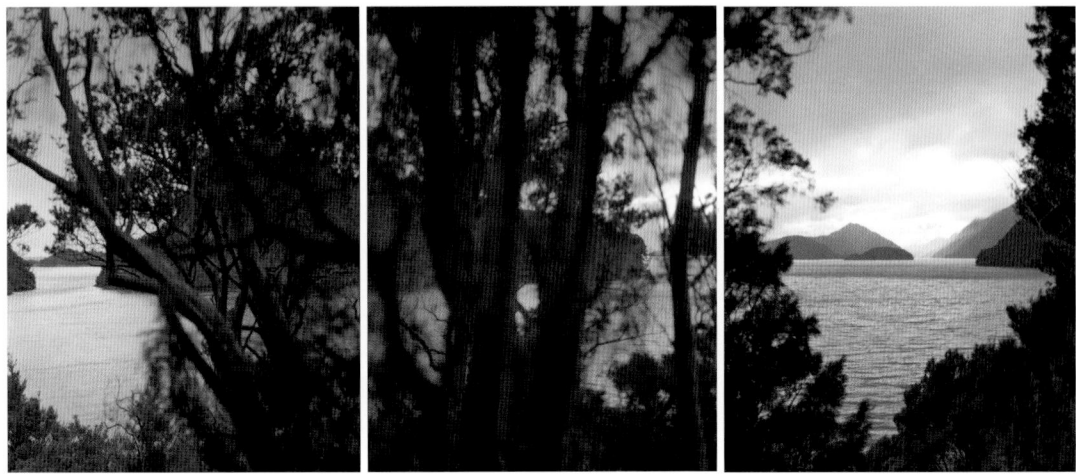

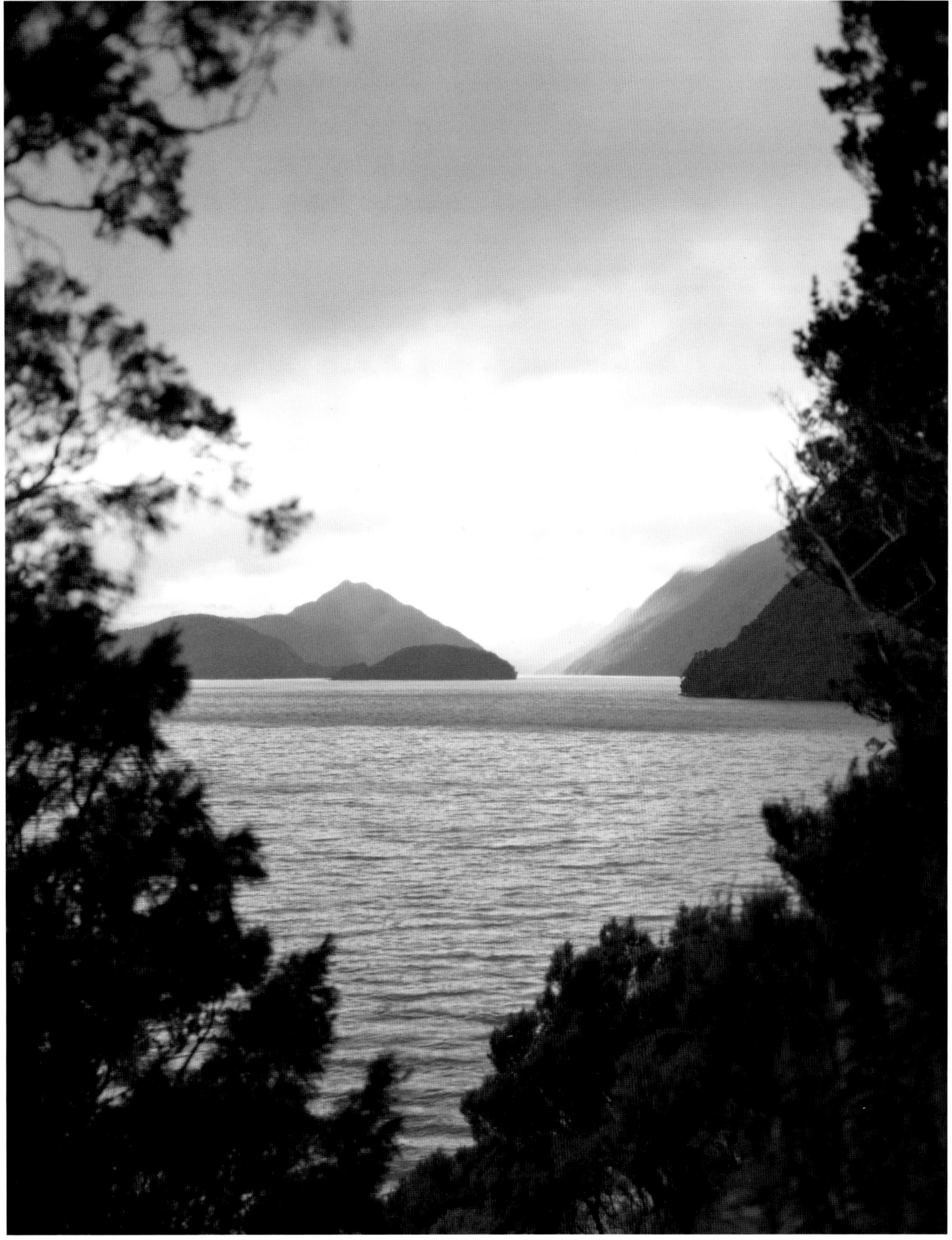

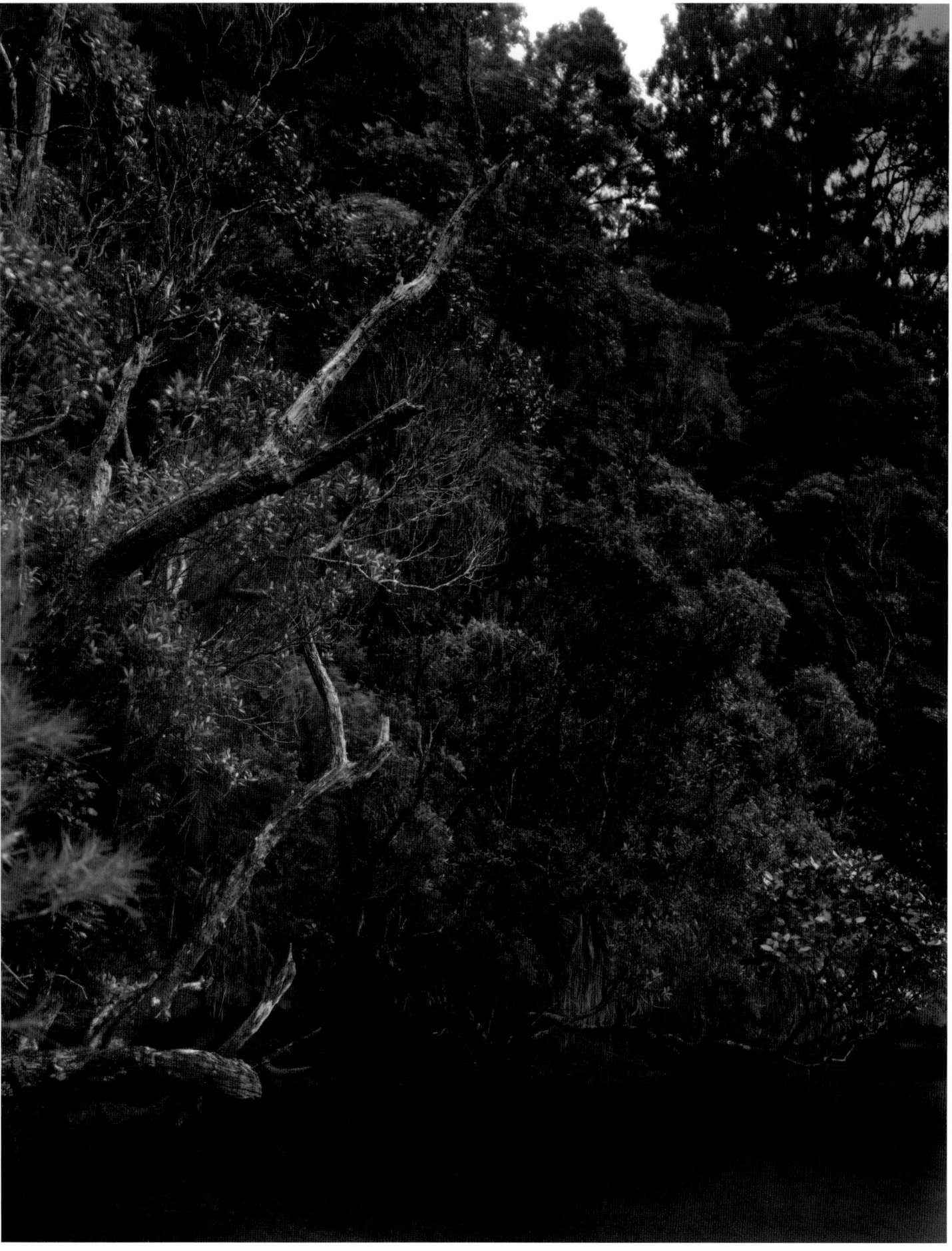

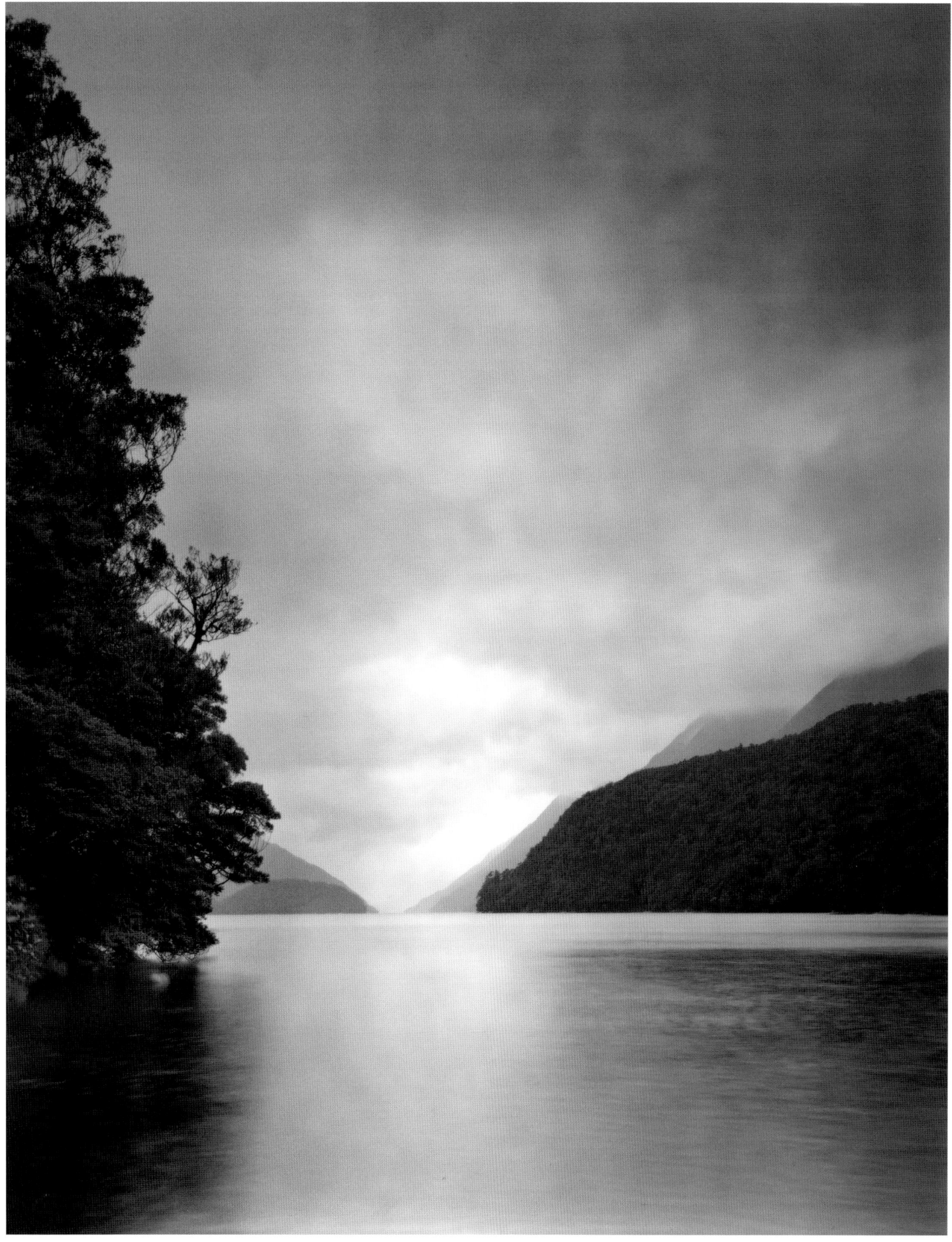

2 (a,b,c)
View in Pickersgill Harbour after William Hodges, 17 May 1995

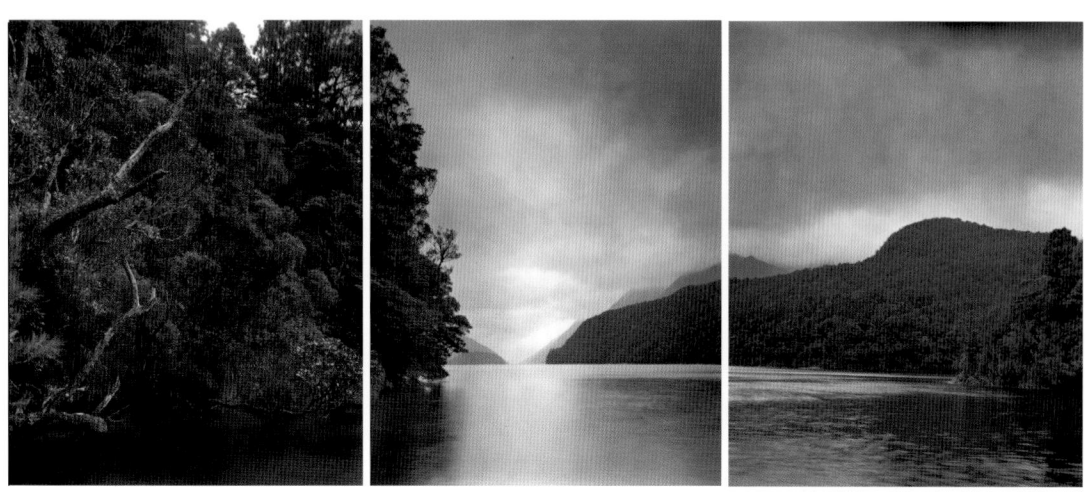

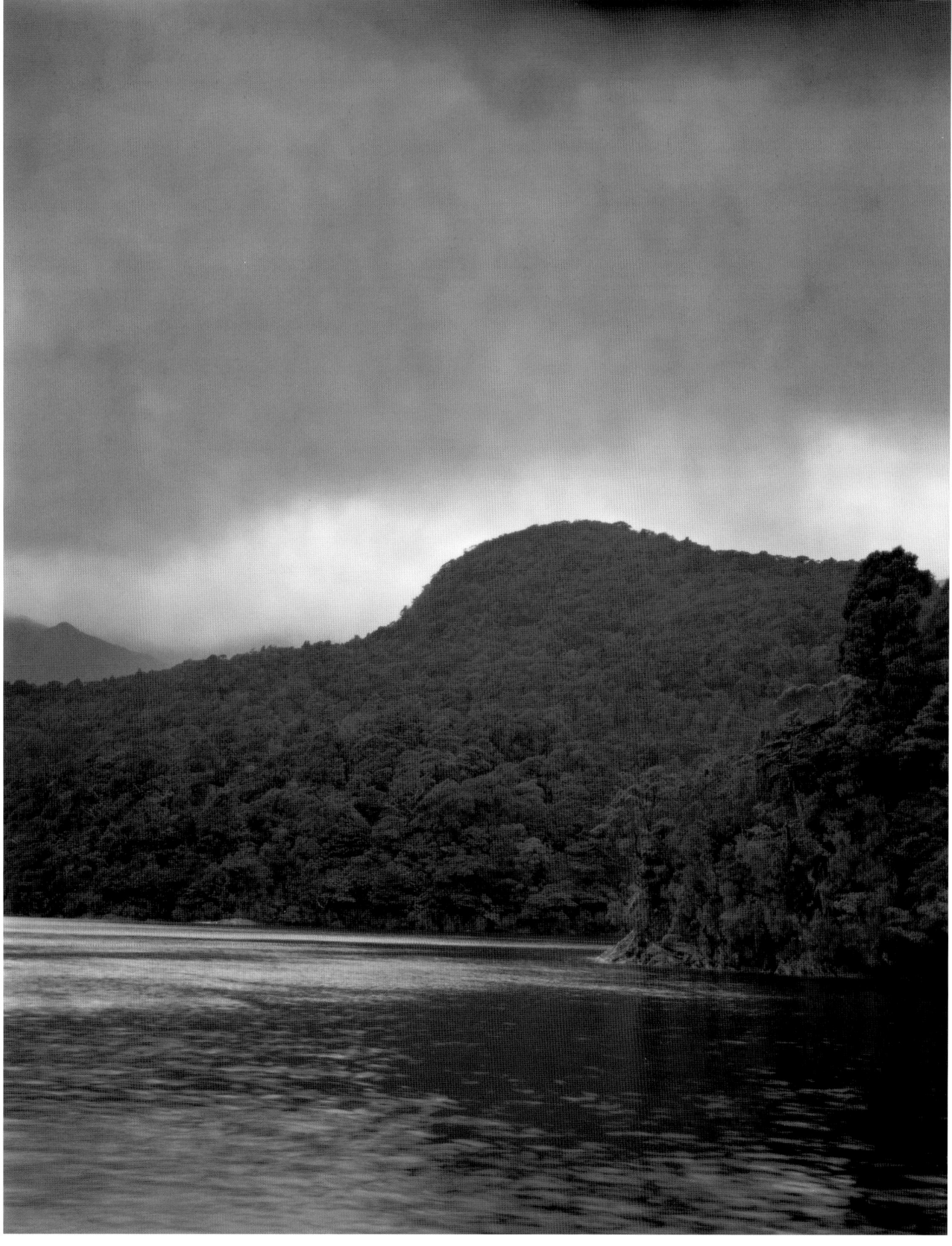

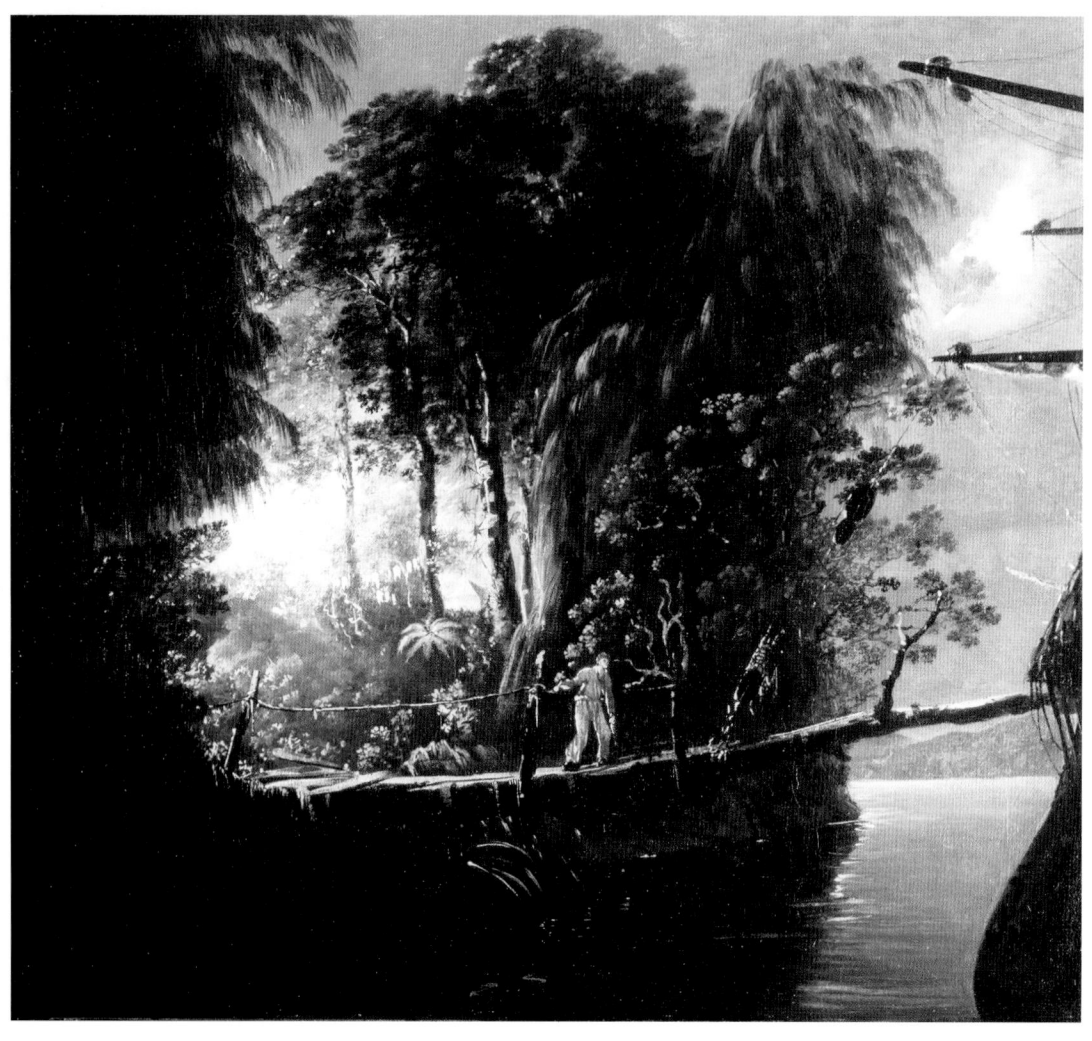

William Hodges, *A View in Pickersgill Harbour, Dusky Bay, New Zealand, 1773*, oil, 65.4 x 73.1 cm. National Maritime Museum, London

3 Astronomers Point, Department of Conservation boardwalk, 23 May 1995

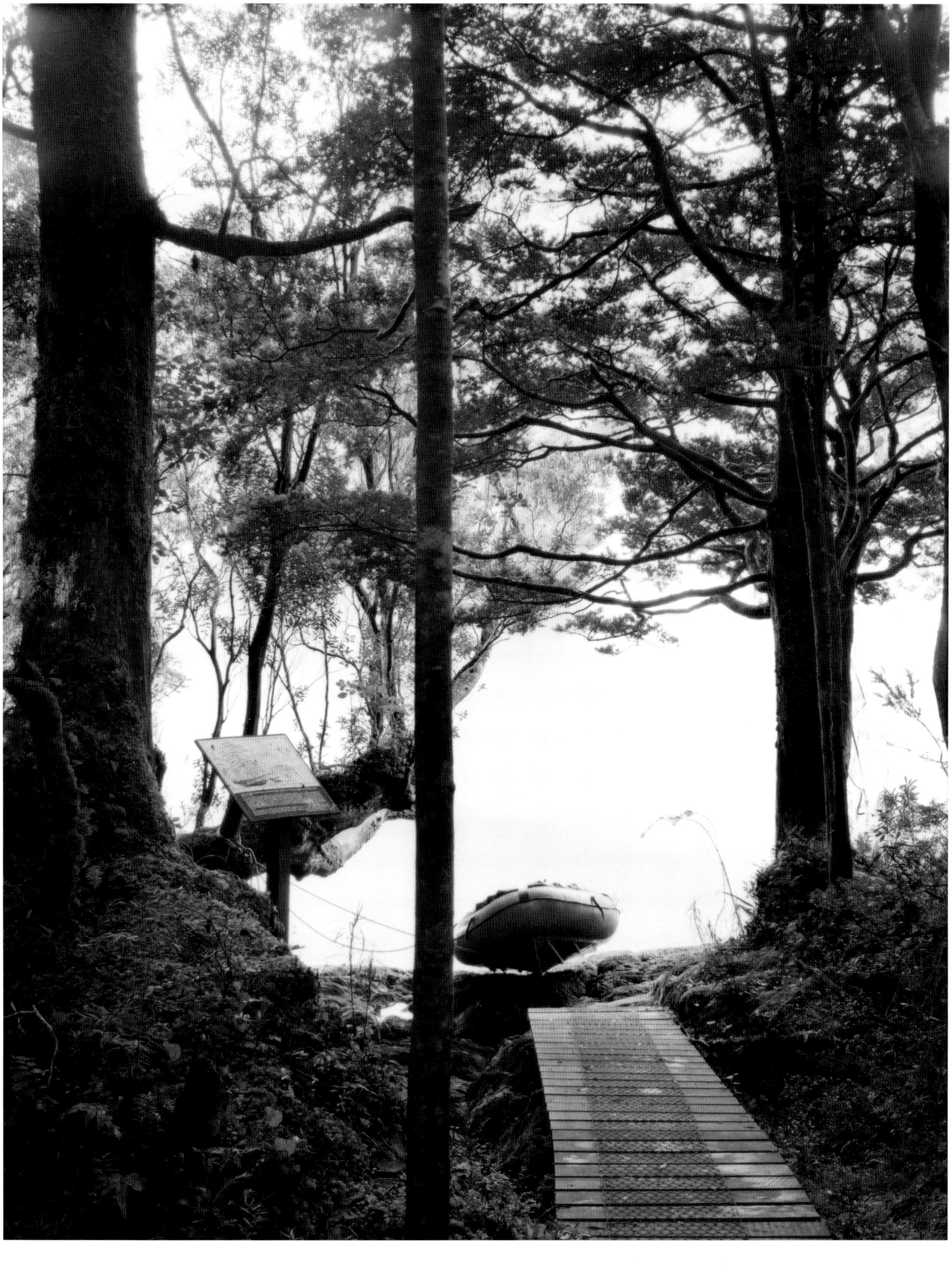

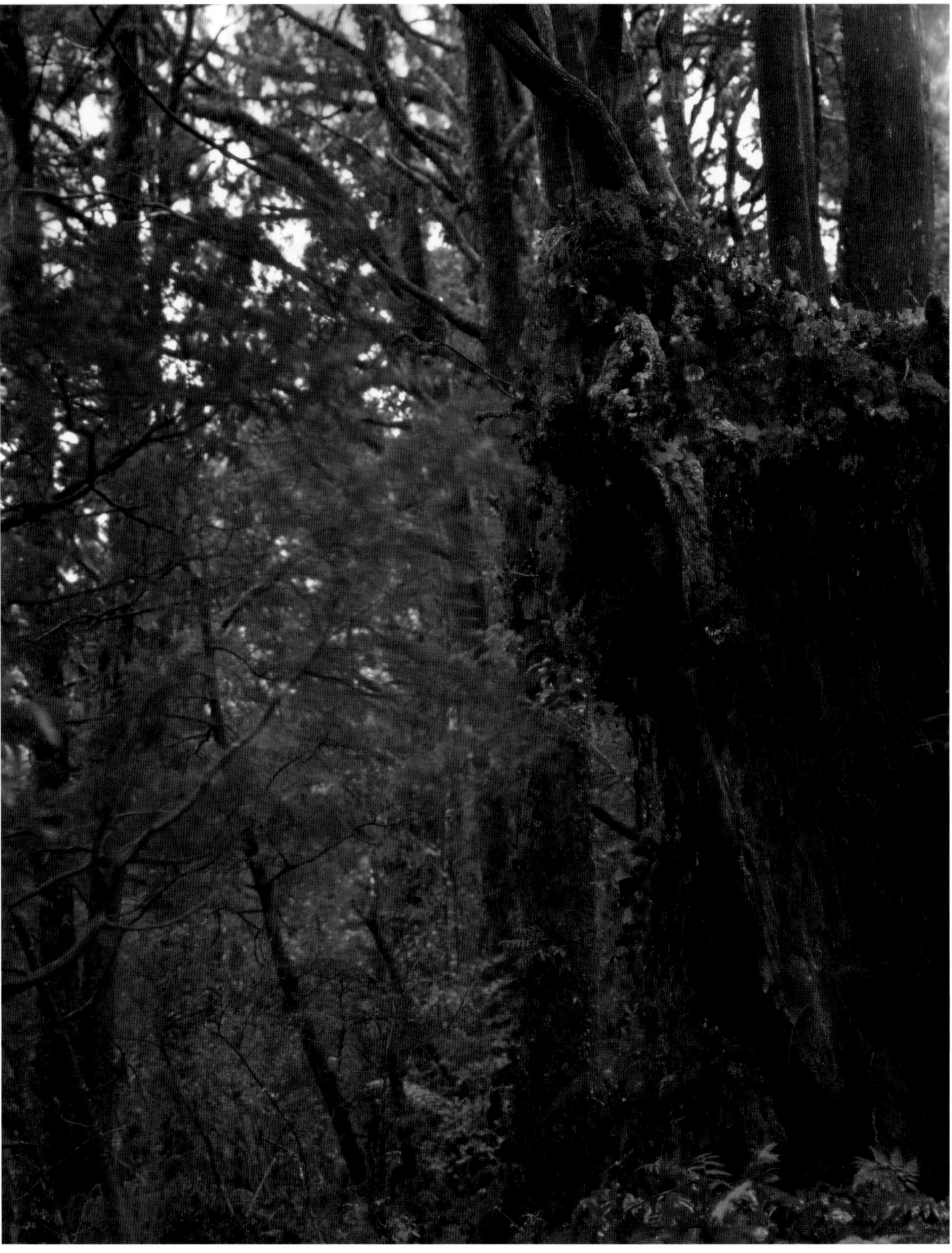

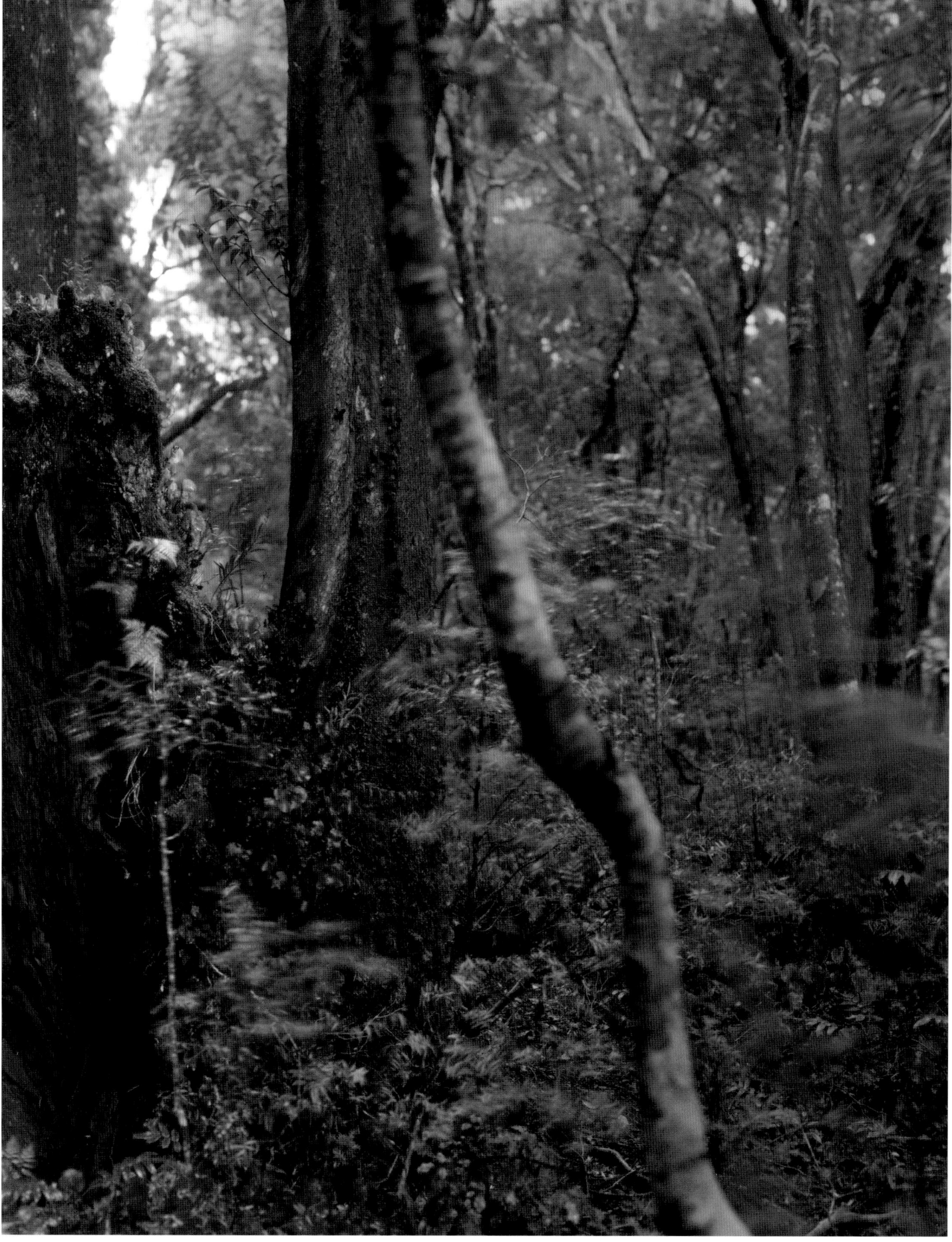

4 (a,b,c)
Astronomers Point. Stump of tree chopped down in 1773, 15 May 1995

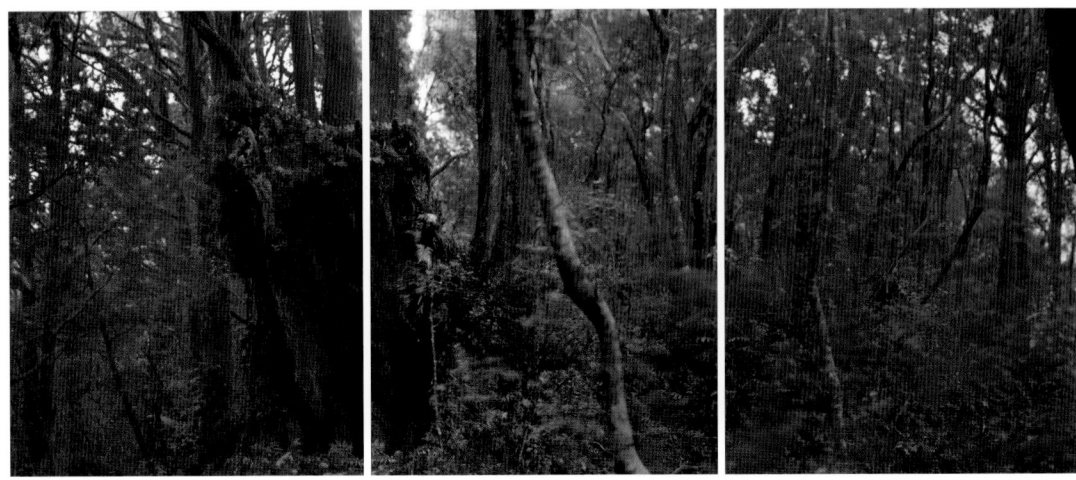

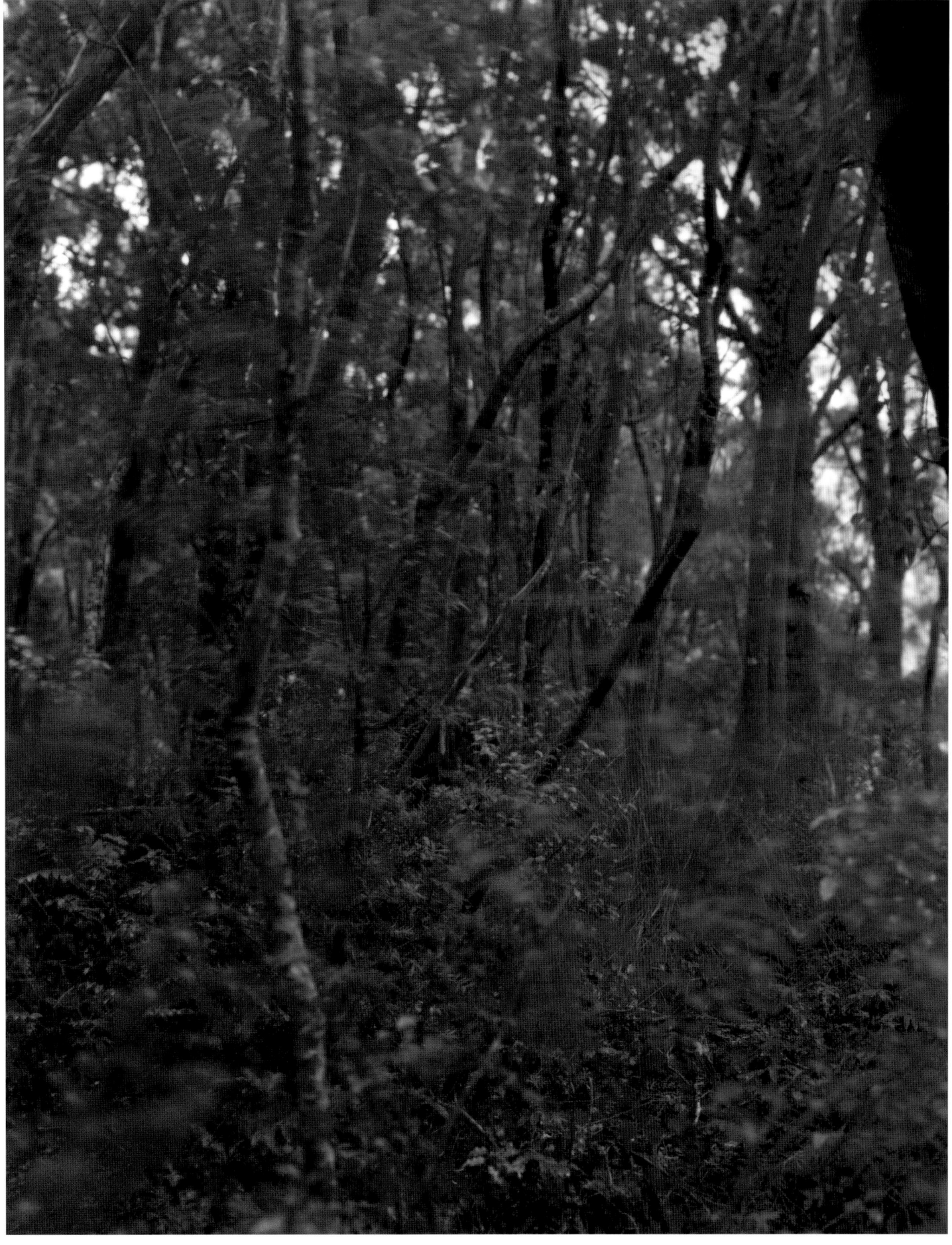

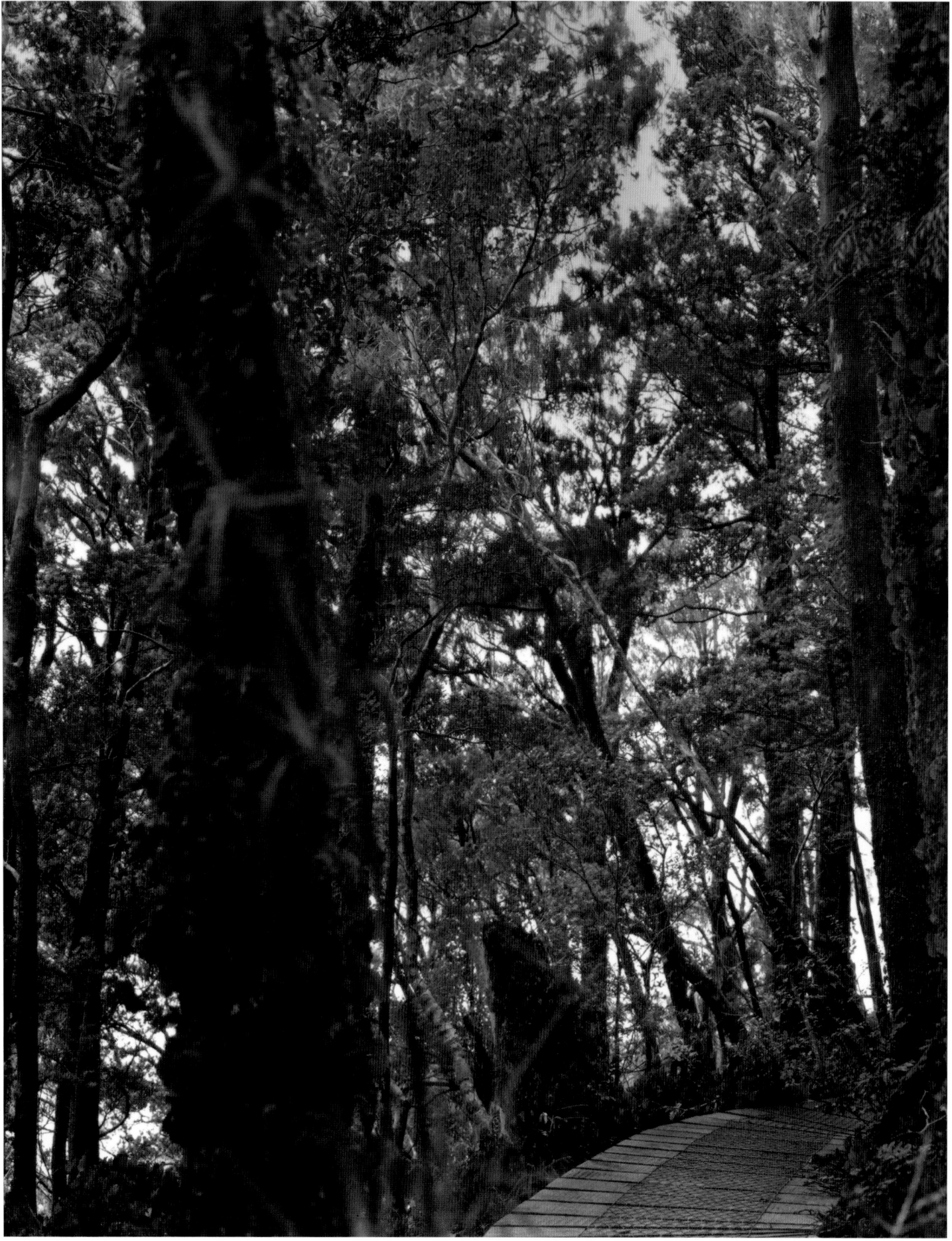

5 (a,b,c)
Astronomers Point. Stumps and regenerating forest, 25 May 1995

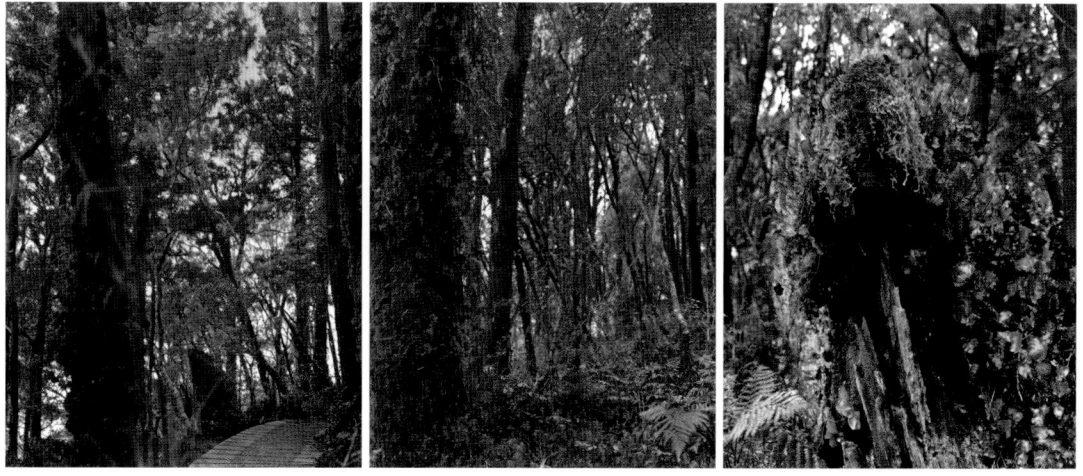

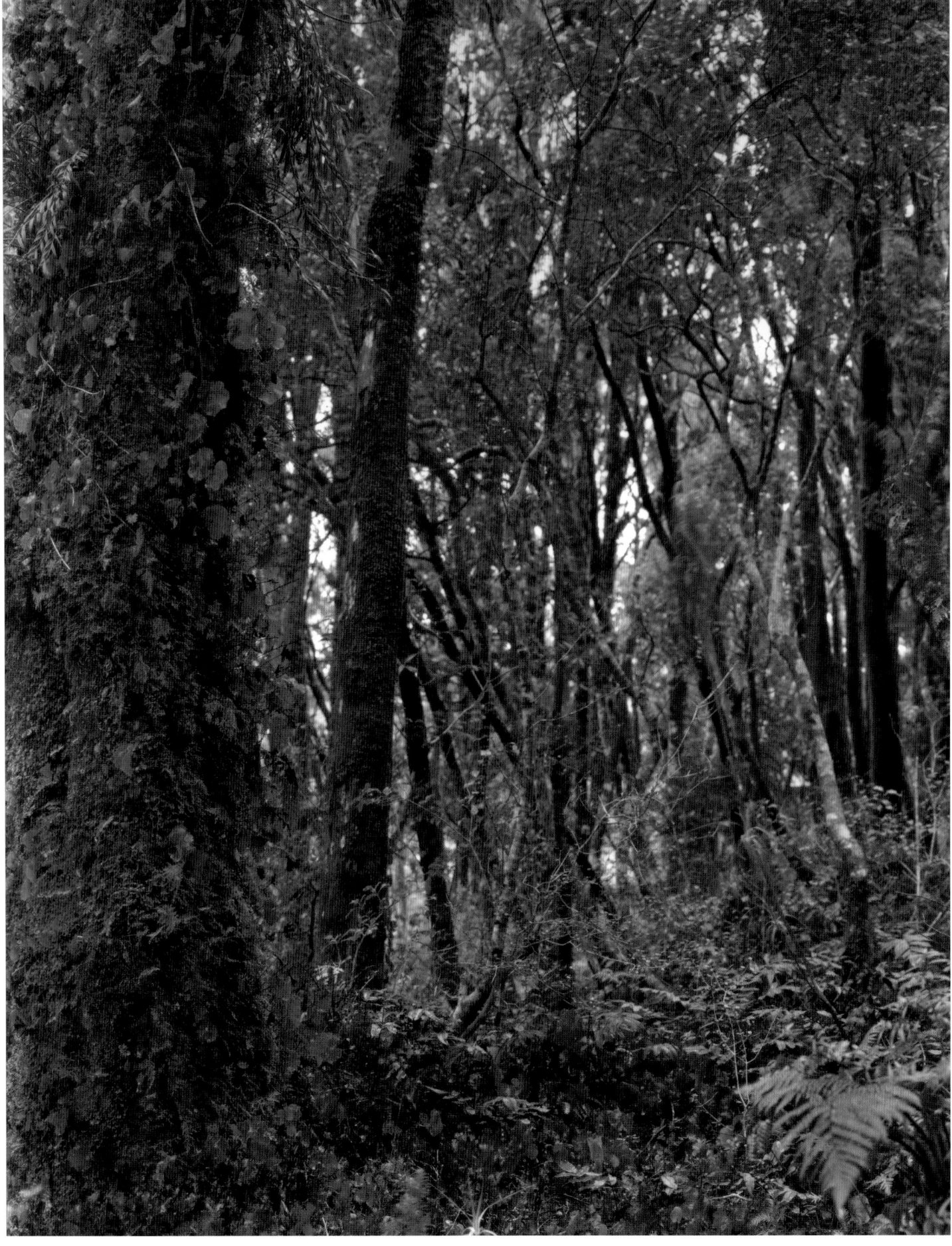

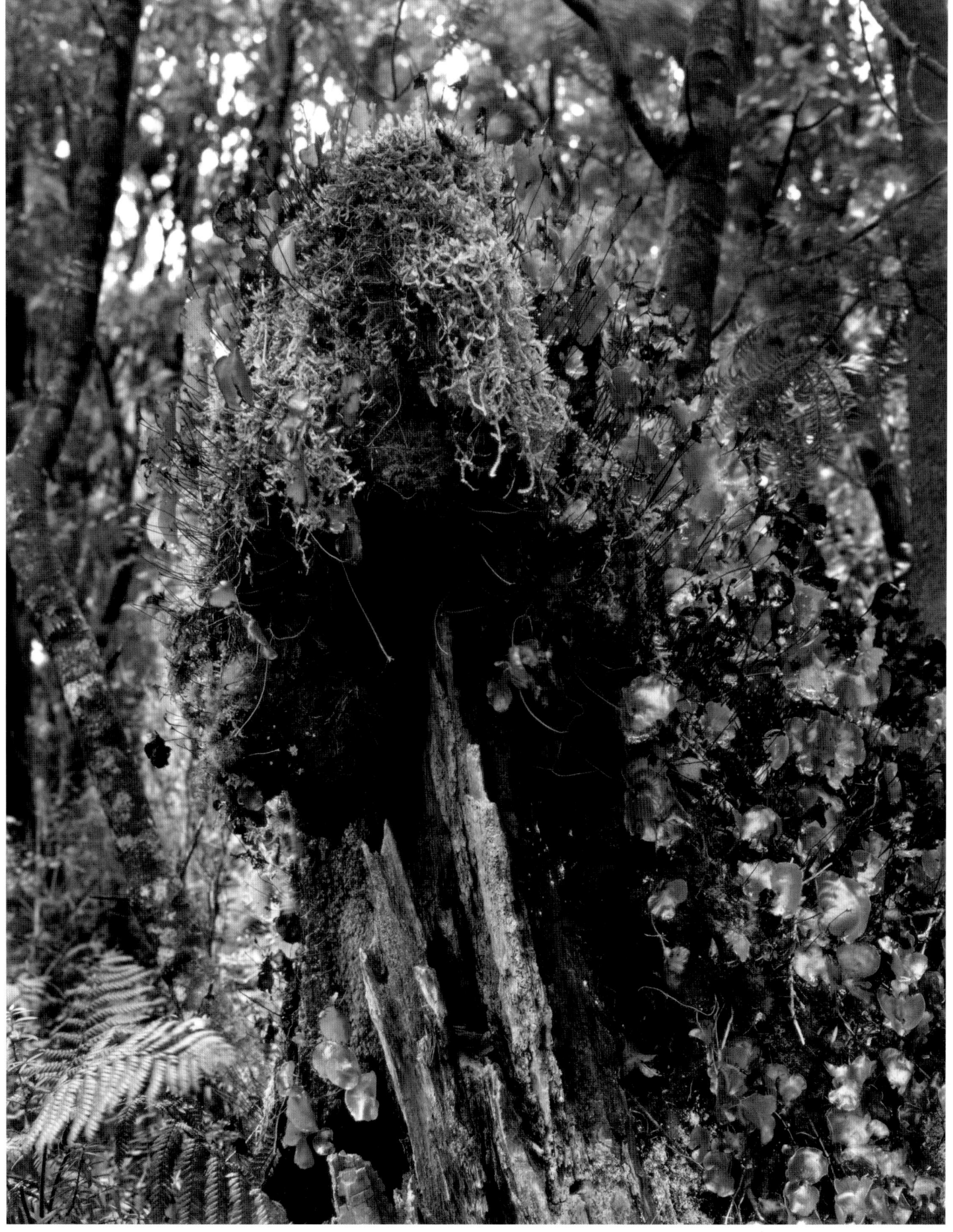

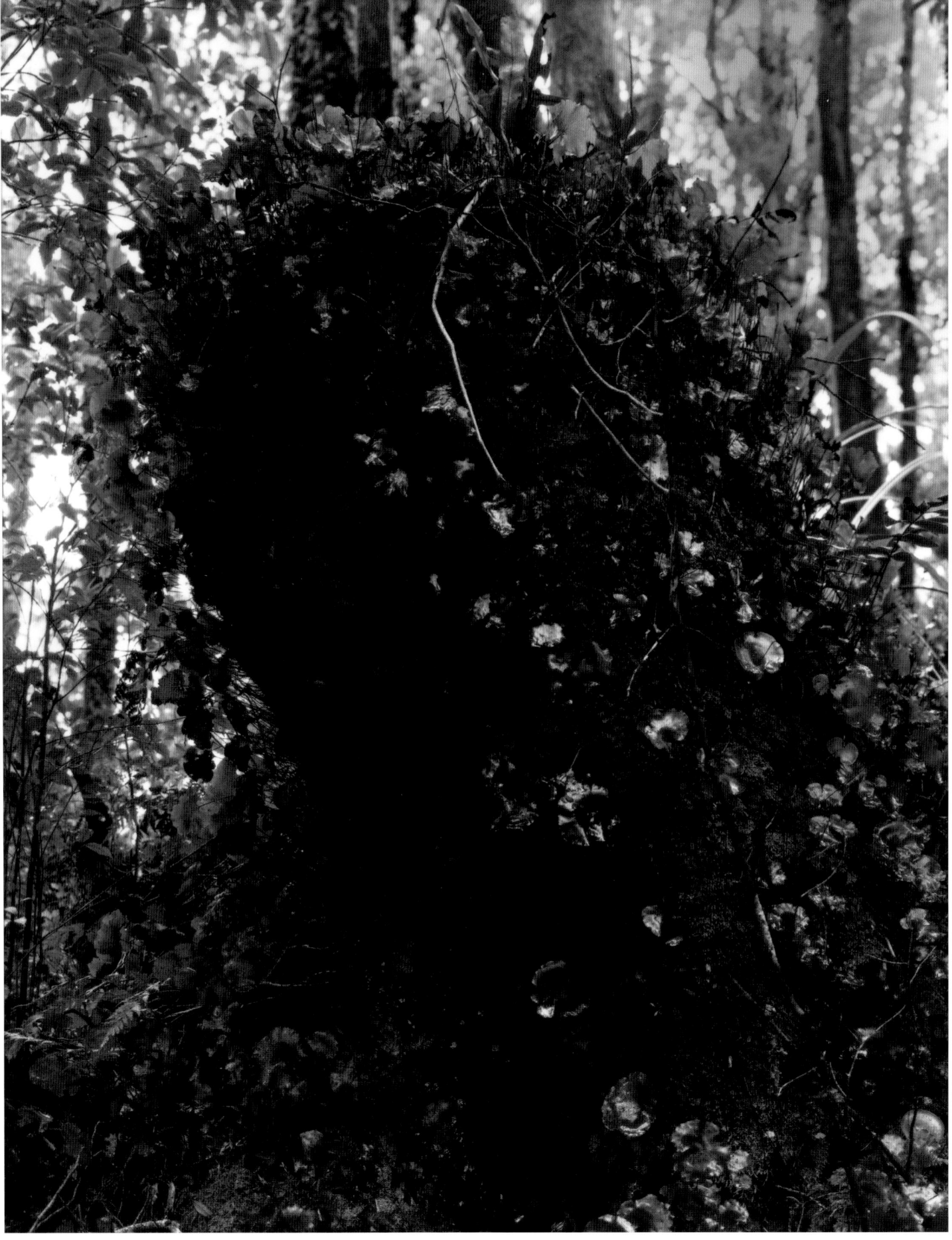

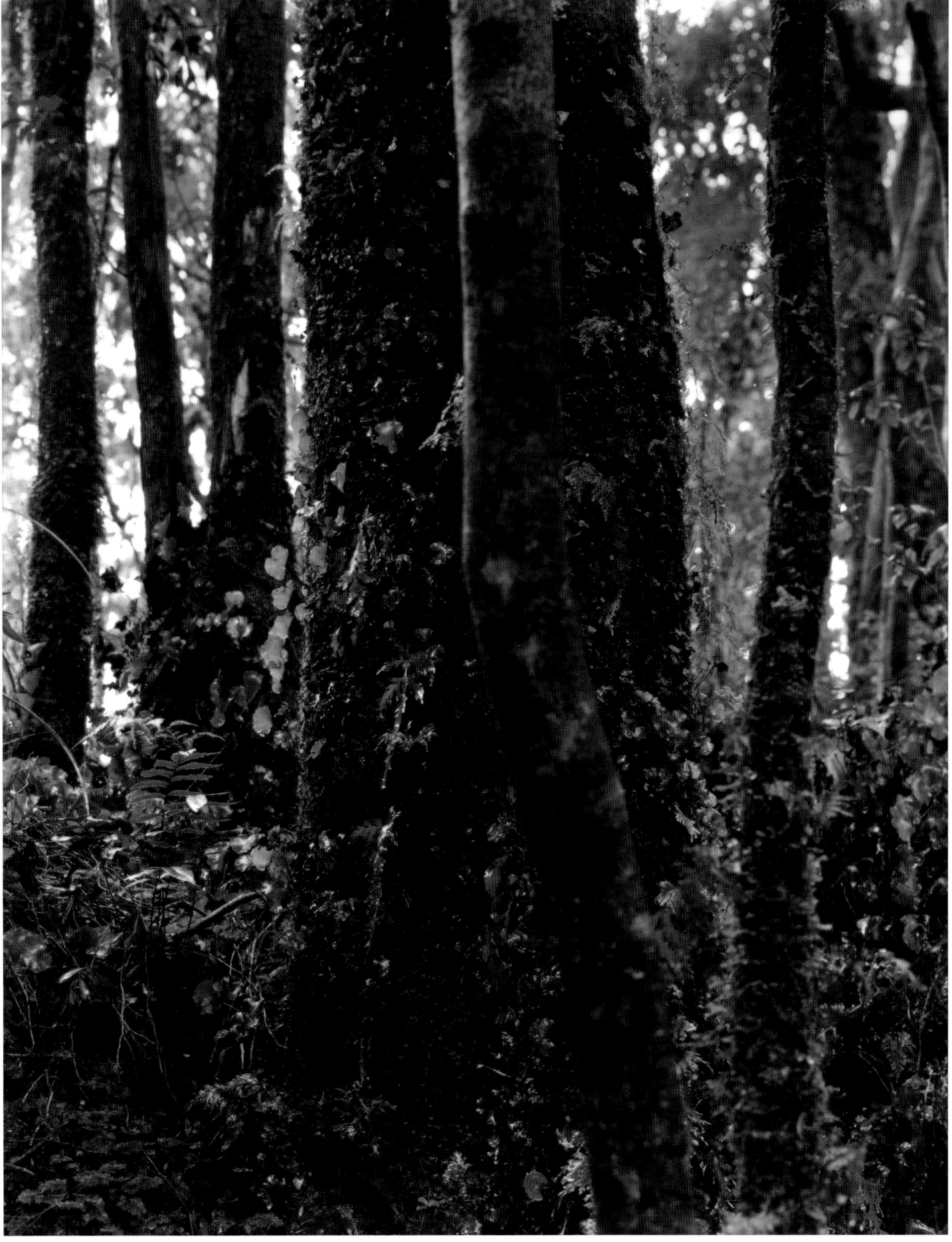

6 (a,b,c)
Astronomers Point. Stumps and regenerating forest, 25 May 1995

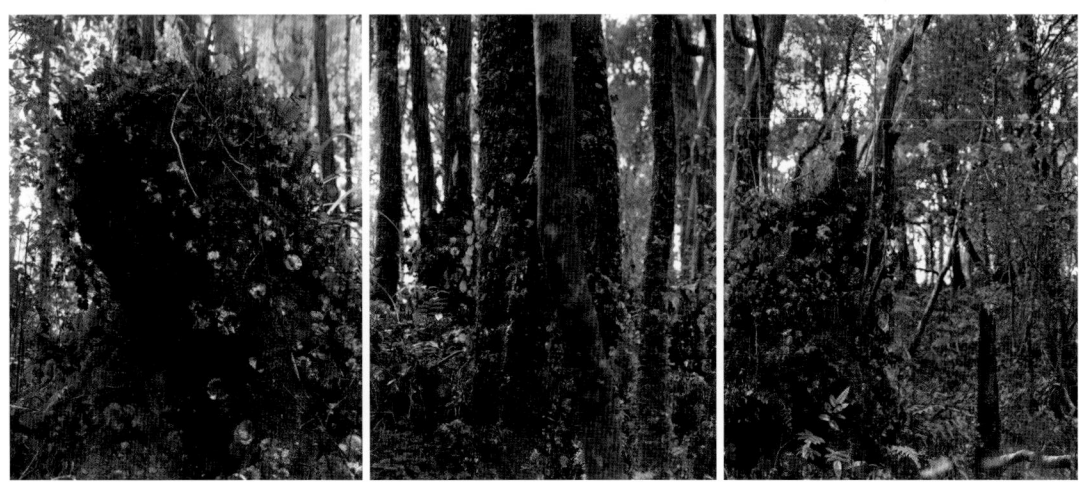

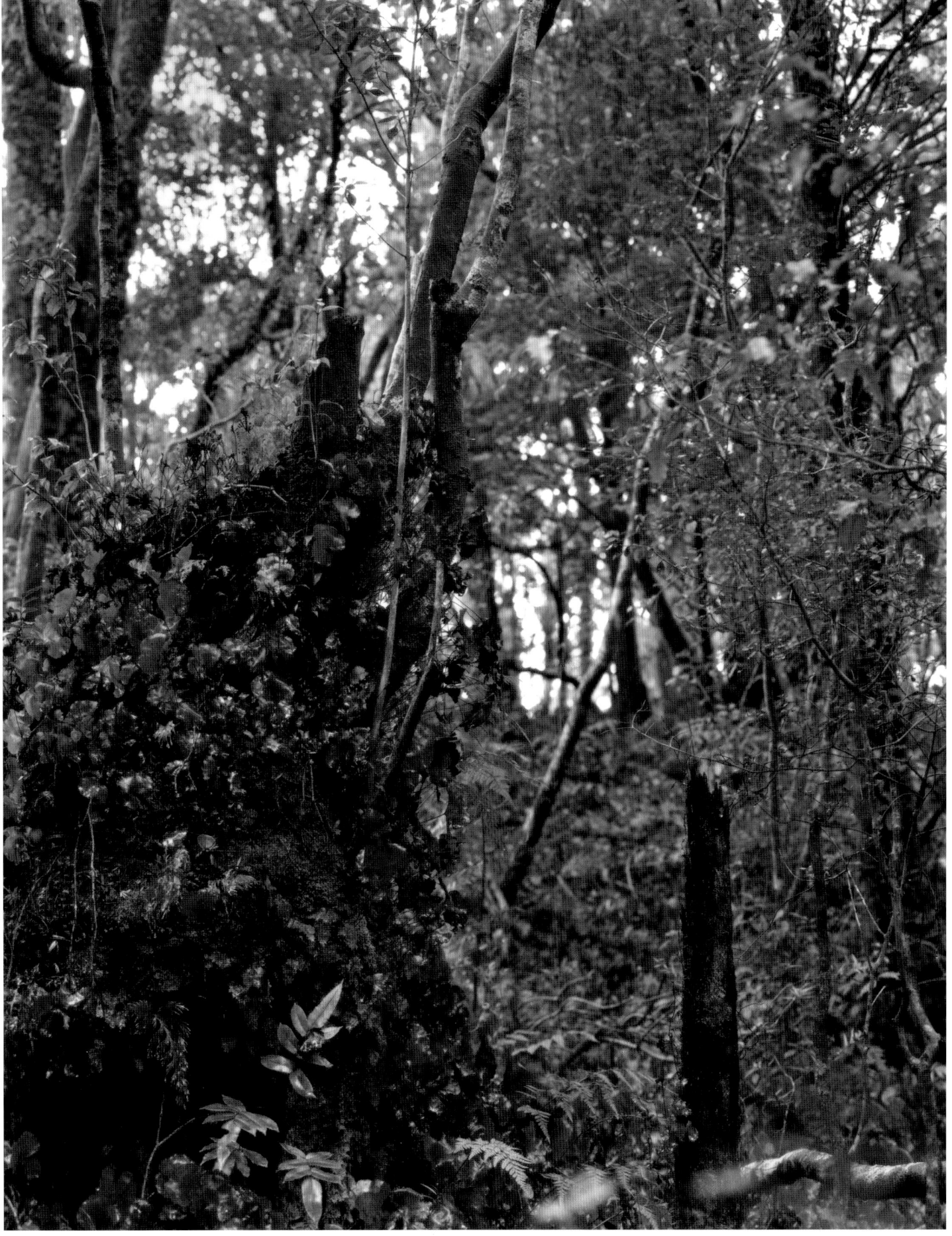

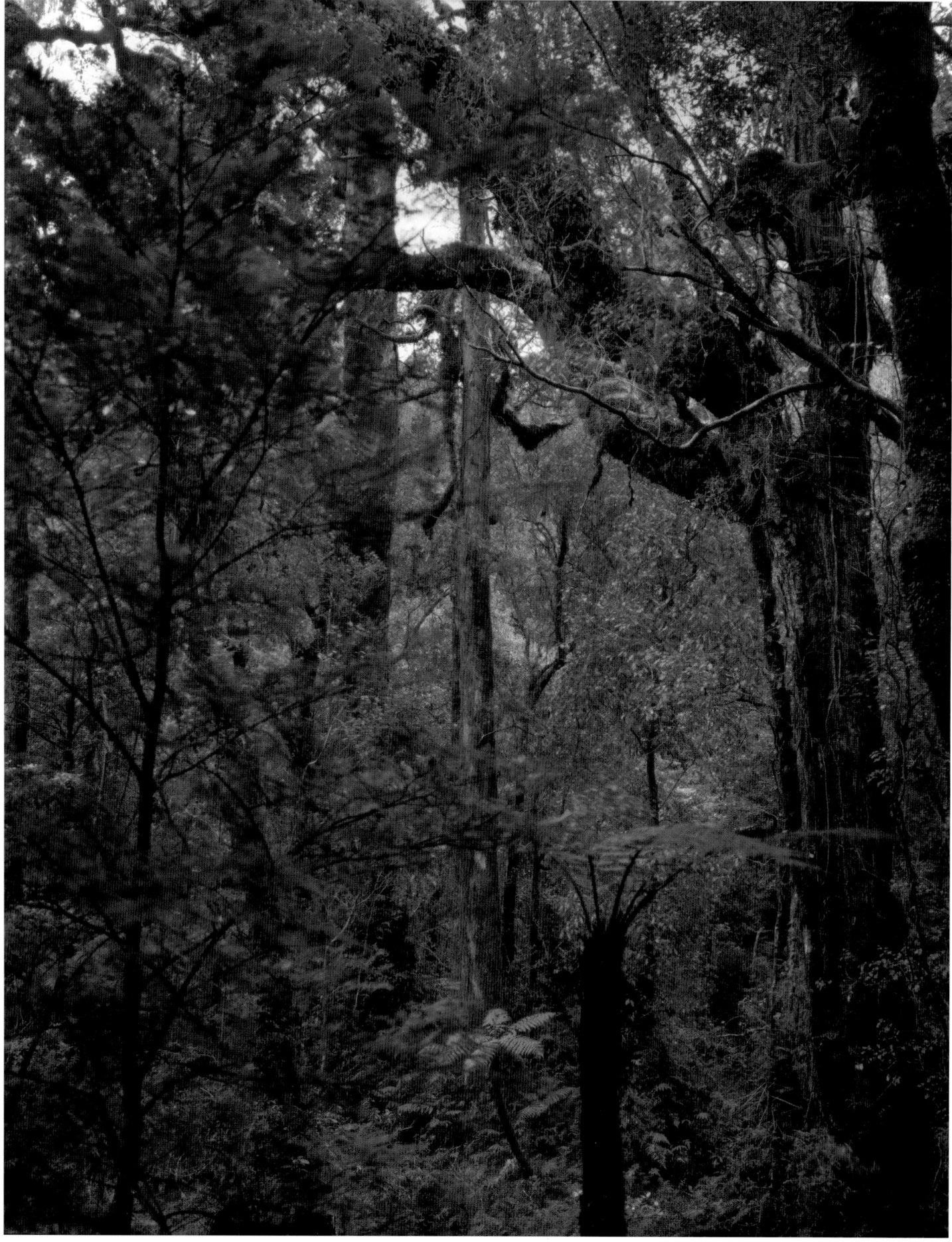

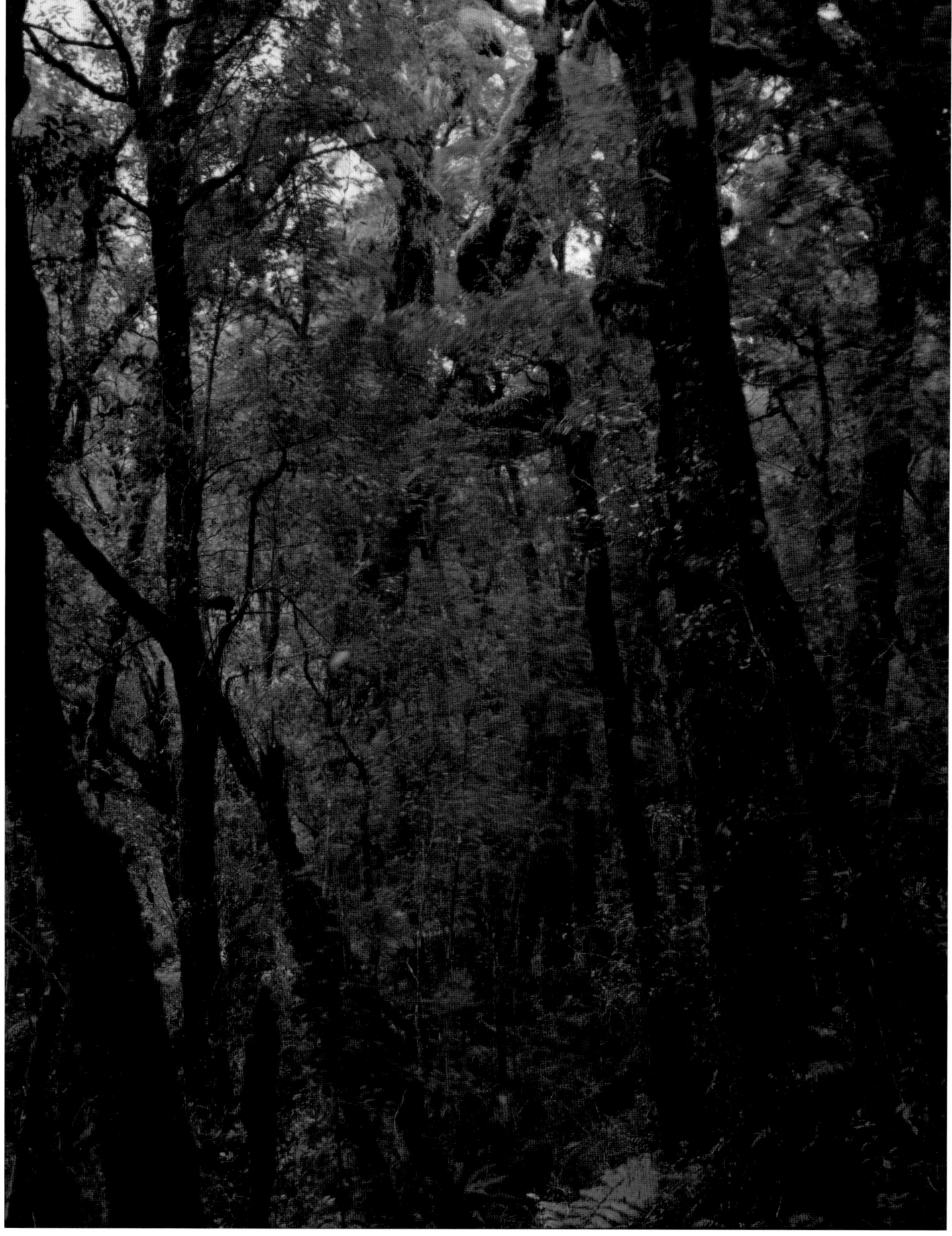

7 (a,b,c)
Podocarp forest behind Astronomers Point, 29 July 1998

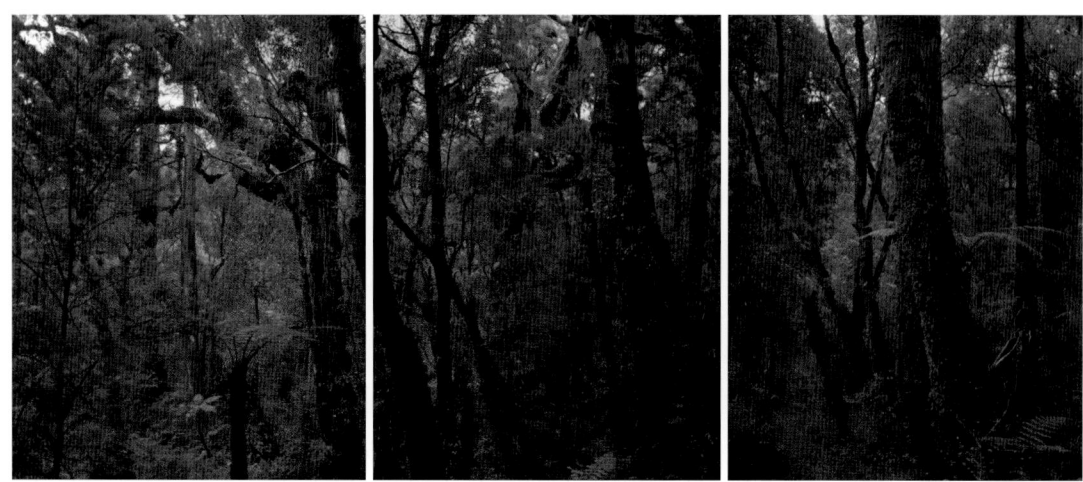

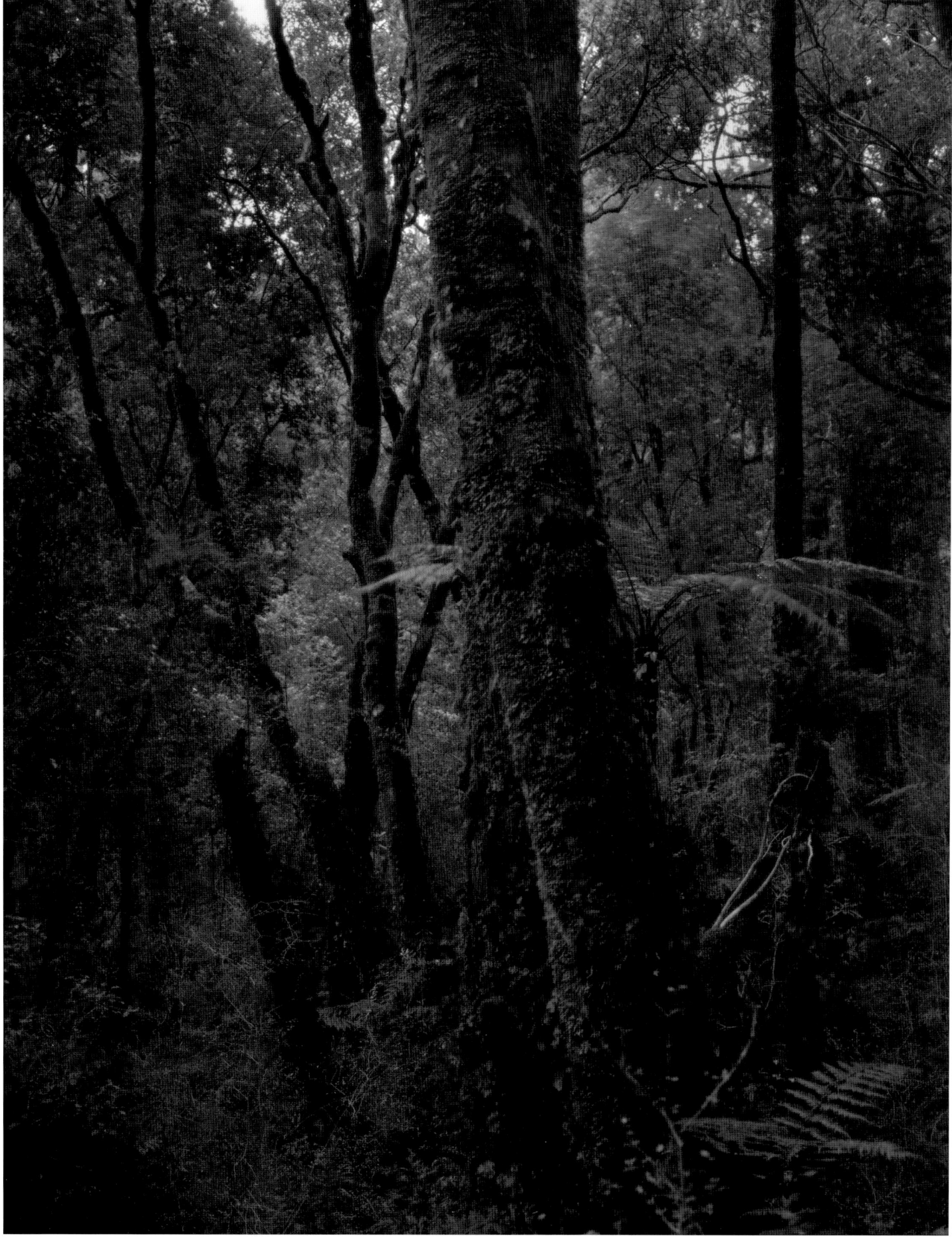

8 (a-d)
View, SE to SW from the site of the observatory, 19 May 1995

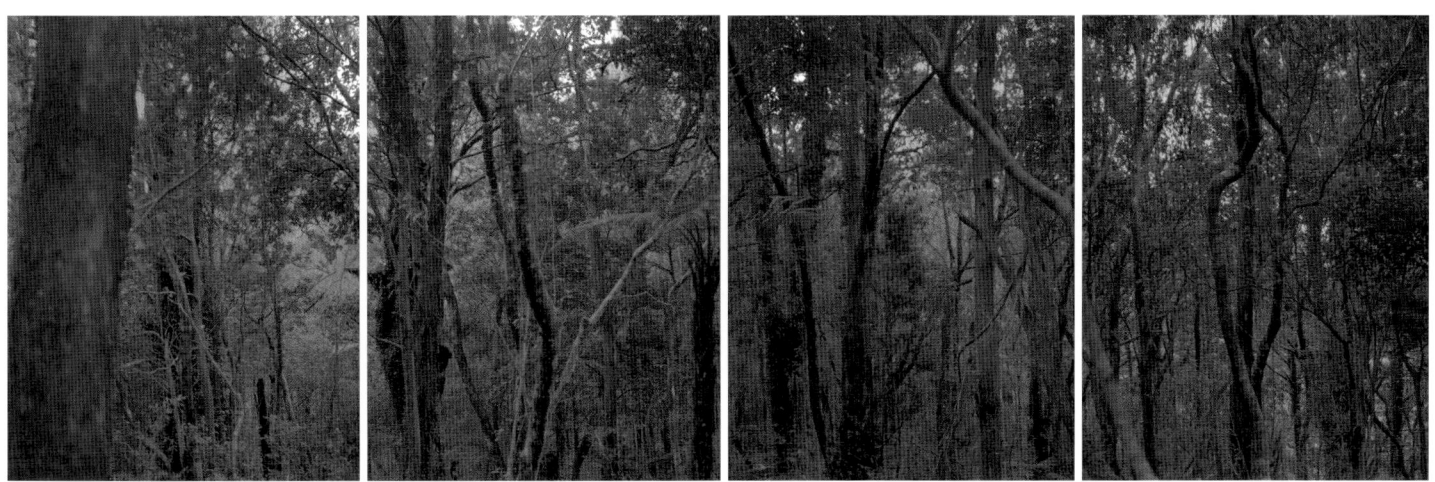

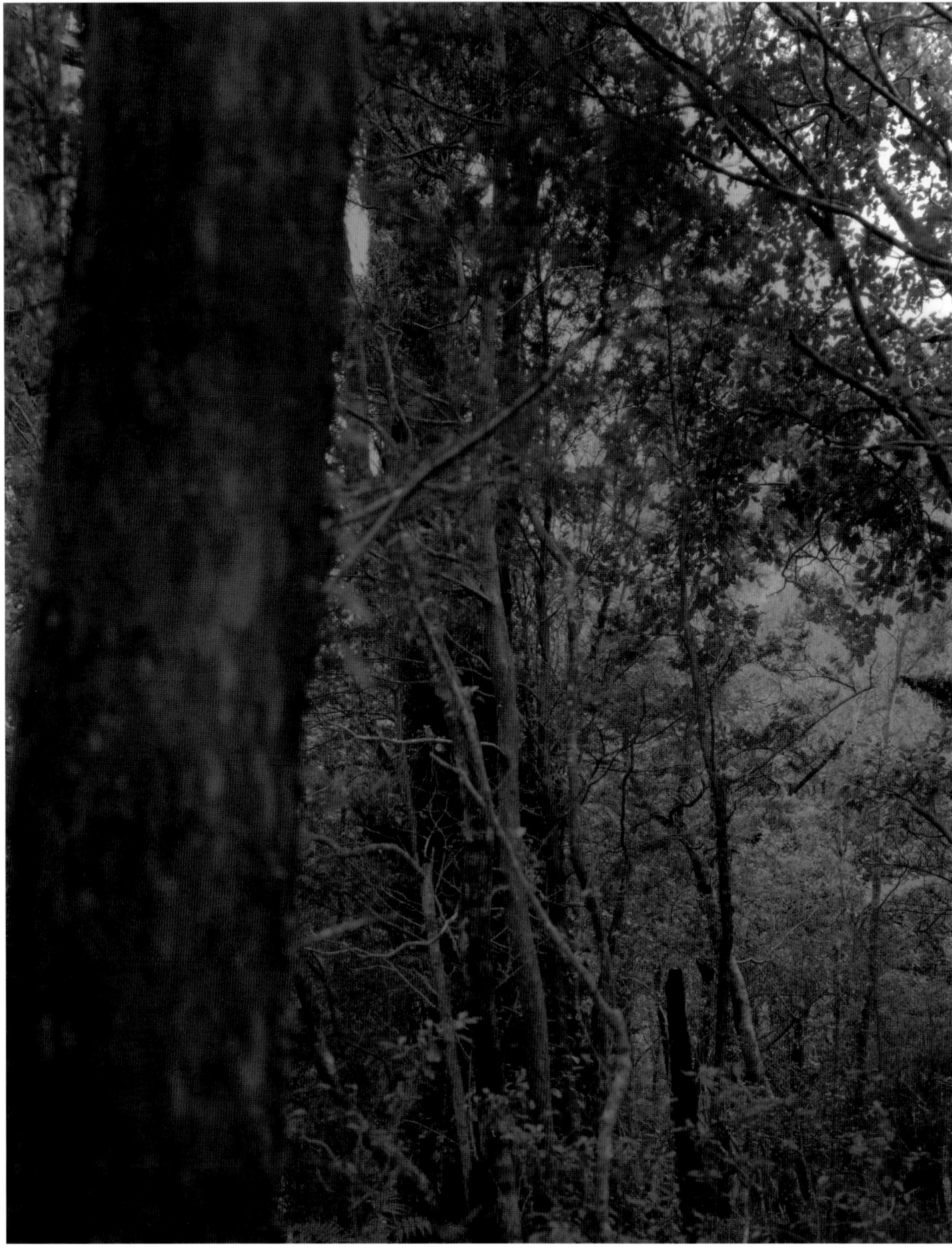

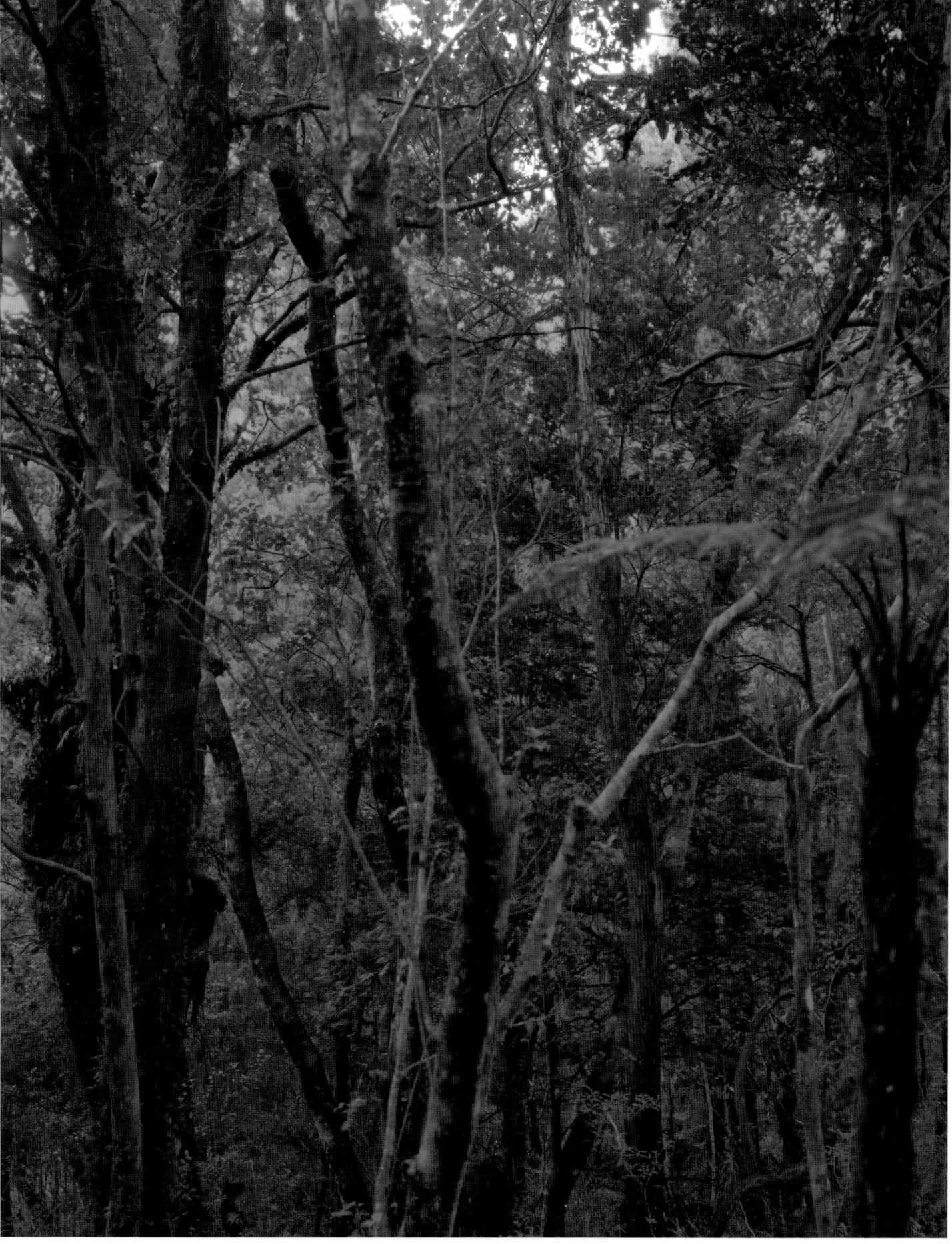

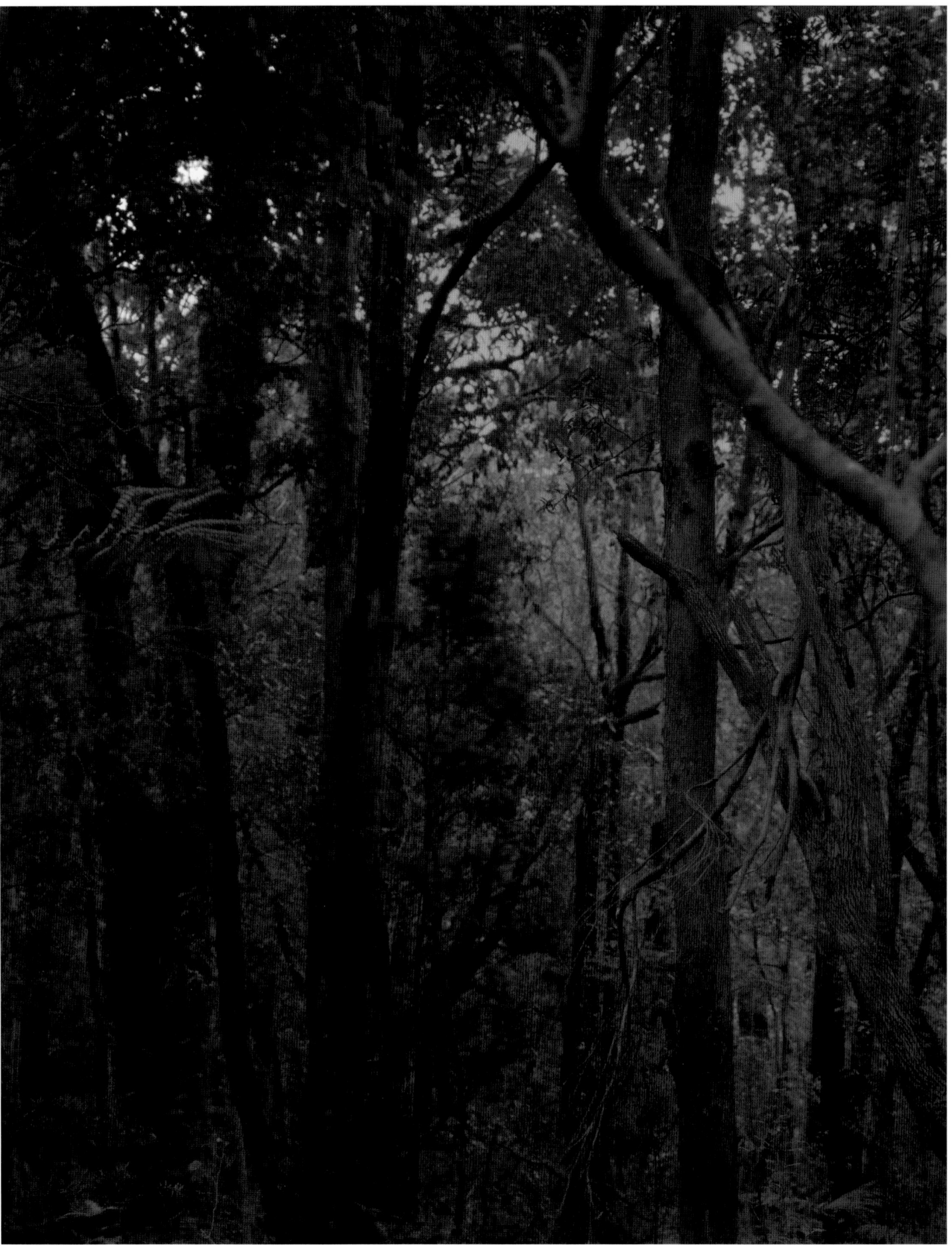

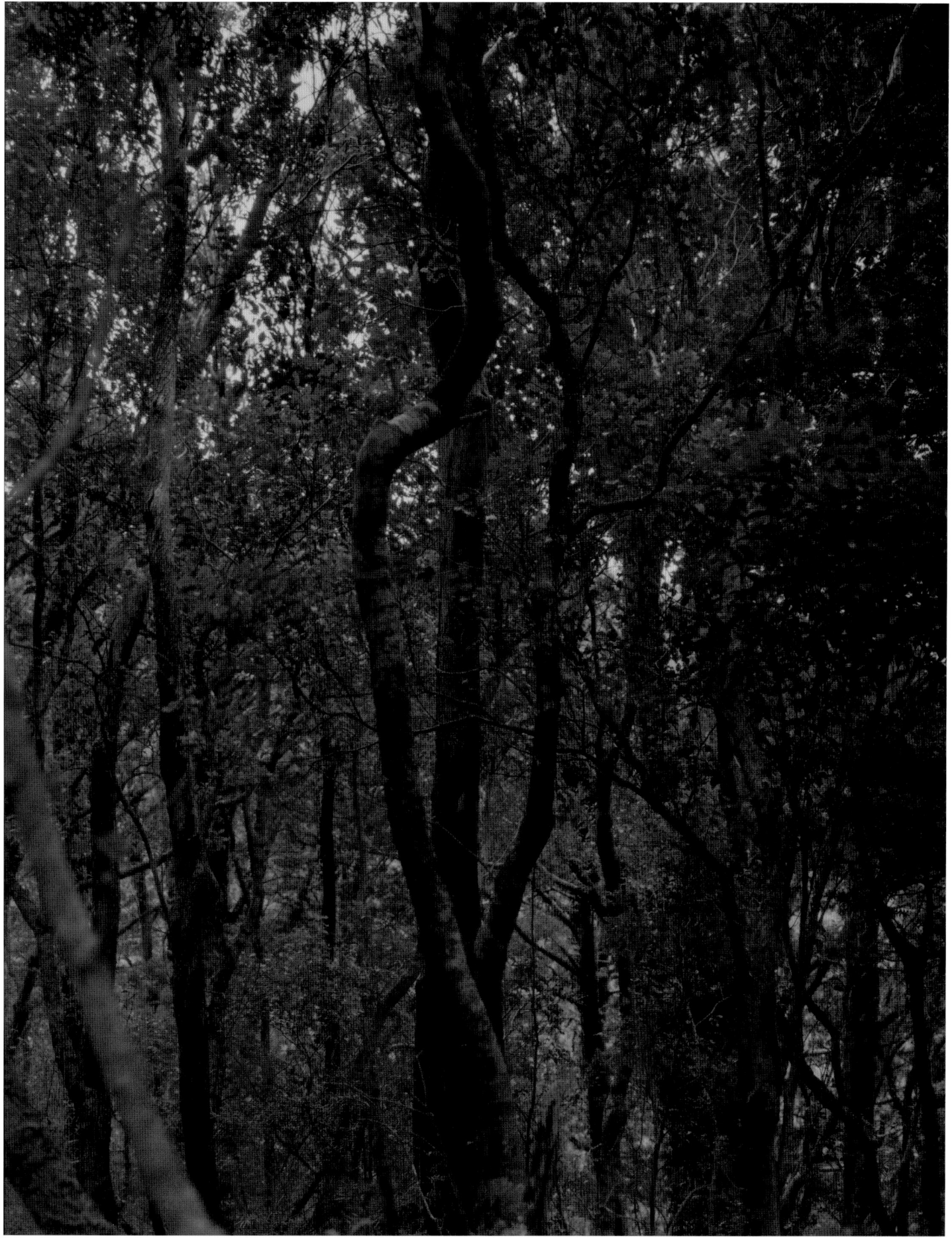

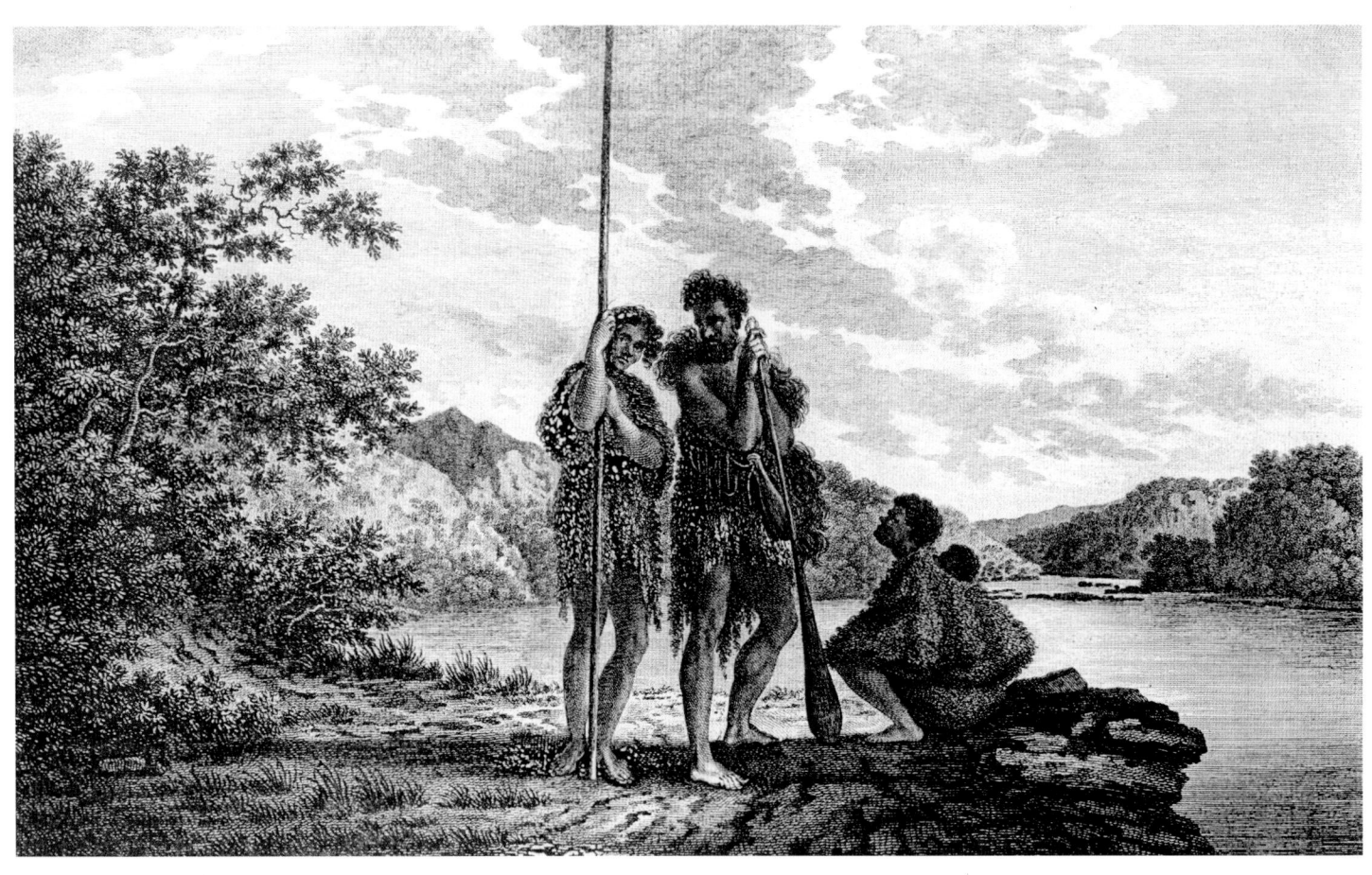

Family in Dusky Bay, New Zealand, engraving by D. Lerpernière after William Hodges,
from James Cook, *A Voyage Towards the South Pole and Round the World* (London 1777), II, plate 63

2. Indian Island

William Hodges was the first professional European artist to visit the Pacific – and for that matter the Antarctic, and later India. Tamatea, or Dusky Sound, was his first Pacific landfall, though he had produced atmospheric views of the Funchal port at Madeira and Cape Town, and some more extraordinary sketches of ice and water, in which the *Resolution* and its boats often look highly vulnerable on the frigid ocean's surface, before louring clouds.

We know this artist through images rather than words. If he kept a journal of any kind on the *Resolution*, it is not known to us, and not much that is not matter-of-fact is said of him in other diaries or narratives. Yet his pictures speak in many registers; they exhibit a characteristic combination of immediacy and idealisation, and make much later art associated with travel and colonisation seem bland. On the one hand Hodges approaches the unfamiliar in a conventional way, on the other he presents an undomesticated exoticism.

The island is small; large enough, no doubt, to spend the better part of a day struggling around the rocks and dense brush above its shoreline; but it is nevertheless inconsiderable, the sort of size one imagines Arthur Ransome's Swallows and Amazons transforming into a theatre of exploration and contact, into an imaginary geography. The names given to the sites of Dusky Sound in 1773 sound like those of a British or colonial children's story – Indian Island, Cascade Cove, and Astronomers Point – and that is because this sort of voyage provided the model for stories of that kind. Yet, even at the beginning, all the uncertainty and contention did make real exploration a matter of make-believe.

On the eastern point of this island is a small rocky point. Though this is not at all high above the water, its projection and an outcrop amount to something like a pedestal, which seems a peculiarly appropriate spot for a moment of first contact. And a moment of first contact this was, not only for the Maori, but for some of the Europeans; Cook had done this kind of thing before, but the Forsters and Hodges were beginners in the art of cross-cultural greeting. An unexpected encounter could not have been more theatrically staged:

> When we were about a mile & a half from the Ship, we were haled from the point of a rock, & when we looked at it we found the voices came from some Natives, one of which stood on the top of a projecting rock. We stood in towards the rock and called to him hallamai Tayo, come here Friend: but he did not stir; now and then he spoke seemingly with violence and threatened with his staff of honour, upon which he leaned. Capt Cook went to the head of the boat, & called him friendly & threw him his hankerchief & I gave him myne likewise. Capt Cook took two sheets of white paper & went on the rock, handed it to the Native, who was then trembling; he took it however & laid it on the rock before him. Then Capt Cook handed both hankerchiefs to him, which he likewise laid down; then Capt Cook shook hands with him, & lastly went up to him & nosed him, which is the mark of friendship among these people. Then Capt Cook pointed at two young people that stood at a distance with lances, that they should lay them down, but the old man misunderstood it & called them; they came both; one of them had on the upperlip a monsterous wen or excrescence; they were both females. The old man had a very fine counternance. The one girl looked not disagreable, & soon began to chatter away in her language, like a magpie. Capt Cook gave the old man a Medal

& I gave one glass bead, the only thing we had about us. A sailor gave a knife & they admired the use of it, & wondered that each of us had one. After half an hour of unintelligable conversation at least as edifying as great many which are usual in politer circles of civilized nations, & which here at least passed with a great deal more sincereity & cordiality on both sides, we took leave of our new friends, & promised to return the next morning.

Johann Reinhold Forster, *Journal*, 7 April 1773

Forster's irony makes it evident that this was a crowded scene: not only were there half a dozen seamen and several Maori present; in a sense so too was 'polite society' and the *philosophe* who deprecate it. An observation on Maori, or rather on the effort to meet Maori, was already a comment upon home. The traveller, still more so the reflective traveller such as Forster, was always both there and here, in Europe as well as the Antipodes.

This is not to say that a singular moment was simply assimilated to a sceptical gesture of European rhetoric of a pretty conventional kind. If the lack of language constituted a barrier to communication, the encounter incorporated moments of embodied understanding, like Cook's *hongi*, or Maori greeting. The mutual discoveries and confusions of this interaction are, however, evacuated from the most notable painting by William Hodges that is connected with this particular spot. Hodges' *View in Dusky Bay* (see p. 68) is the artist's only round work that I know of, and it would be nice to know whether it was produced on commission, for someone who had a space on a wall to fill, or whether Hodges did the picture simply for himself, because it was somehow apt to his experience. We might, at any rate, speculate that the form of the round panel reproduces Hodges' first sighting of the man, through a telescope that was passed around among the gentlemen, as their boat approached the rock.

Yet the content of the picture lacks a basis in this moment. As the telescope abstracted the figure from the surrounding waterscape, the composition abstracts the man from his kin, from the circumstances of a meeting with Europeans, and from a rocky point beneath a camp, a site that is still marked by *hangi* pits (earth ovens), and shallower depressions indicating old huts or shelters. Although the man embraces an enlarged and somewhat adapted version of a Maori *taiaha* or some other kind of club, he is otherwise excised from society and history. He is a patriarch standing in dignified isolation in soft Italianate light; he is a 'noble savage', if ever there was one.

Mark Adams responds to this painting with an opposed circular image that turns the telescope inside out. His 360° panorama is photographed from the very spot where it has been assumed that Hodges' subject stood, though Hodges has substituted a pleasingly overshadowed situation for what is in fact an exposed rock. Adams's photographs restore the intricate particularity of the place – the tangle of rock and stunted vegetation, the expanse of water, the drifts of mist and rain, the intimacy of the islets and the solid remoteness of the surrounding mountains. The isolated figure, which alone is treated in detail, stands between a gesturally delineated foreground and distance, and is contrasted in Adams's image with absolute depth of field: the closest wet rocks and the most distant ridges are equally sharp, or as sharp as the mist and moisture made them. And, while Hodges' painting refers to all time, or no time in particular, the panorama expresses a particular moment, and indeed the passage of time: the clouds and showers that had closed in as one sheet of film was being exposed, receded for the next.

~

This contextualisation, this insistence on the presence and intricacy of the environment, is both a task that these photographs effect, and a metaphor for other contextualising efforts. What Hodges excluded from the round painting, though, he went to some trouble to represent in other works. Whereas, as I noted, the so-called *View in Dusky Bay* suffuses the rugged warrior in Claudean evening light, the *View in Pickersgill Harbour*, which Hodges painted at the time, from Cook's cabin, conveys the bright cloudiness and rapidly shifting weather that any visitor to Tamatea will recognise. But it is the human context, not the variations in the artist's fidelity to nature, that concerns me most.

The women that the Maori man summoned forward on the point, once some kind of amiable footing was established, carried long spears which are mentioned and depicted in a number of Hodges' works, but not much remarked upon in the journals composed at the time. Cook, however, referred to them retrospectively, presuming that they were fighting spears and that Maori women actively participated in warfare 'even the Women are not exempted from carrying Arms as appeard at the first interview I had with the family in *Dusky Bay* when each of the two Women were Armd with a spear not less than 18 feet in length.'[5] It is intriguing that he makes the point in such a matter-of-fact way in passing: although the figure of the Amazon was, of course, known to European culture, Cook nowhere else in the Pacific encountered women who adopted these roles, hence this would have been highly singular if it were true – which it was probably not. The spears appear to conform to a distinctive, fairly light and long type, used particularly for hunting the plump wood pigeons or kereru, which these Maori may have been pursuing.

The question of what the spears were for is not a trivial one. The voyage writers were concerned to make judgements about the character and level of advancement of what they called 'New Zealand' societies, and those judgements, in the late eighteenth century, turned to a significant extent upon the status of women. Women were thought to be denigrated in savage and barbaric societies, and held in higher esteem in more advanced ones. The form of a family was thus not a particular topic, separate from other social and historical questions, but a lens upon government and social development. So far as these issues were concerned, it would be established pretty clearly, in the eyes of the Forsters, that the Maori of Queen Charlotte Sound were vigorous and noble yet somewhat brutal warriors: a martial environment affected the temperament of the men and boys, and led them to use their women cruelly, observers thought. At the northern end of Te Wai Pounamu, such behaviour as was witnessed was consistent with this view. In Dusky Sound, however, the ethnological evidence just did not add up.

The 'Indian family' consisted of the older man painted by Hodges, one older woman, two younger women, and several children. The older woman is distinguished by a wen or excrescence on the upper lip, which is said to render her ugly, and thought to explain the man's apparent indifference to her. These people were to come on board the ship, on 19 April, as George Forster noted:

> In the mean while they had a quarrel among themselves, the man beat the two women who were supposed to be his wives; the young girl in return struck him, and then began to weep. What the cause of this disagreement was, we cannot determine; but if the young woman was really the man's daughter, which we could never clearly understand, it should seem that the filial duties are strangely confounded among them; or which is more probable, that this secluded family acted in every respect, not according to the customs and regulations of a civil society, but from the impulses of nature, which speak aloud against every degree of oppression.
>
> George Forster, *Voyage*, I, p. 160.

It is not clear whether the 'young girl' is one of the supposed 'wives' the man has just beaten; that she strikes him 'in return' suggests so, and she is in fact identified earlier in the text, in the section describing the first encounter with these people, as one of his wives: 'he called to the two women … one of the women, which we afterwards believed to be his daughter, was not wholly so disagreeable …'[6] In Forster senior's journal, upon which George's published narrative was based, one of the wives, or presumed wives, is indeed younger than the other, but it is quite clear from his description of the actual altercation that the 'young girl' was a third woman: 'the old Man beat his two wives, & the young Girl beat her Father & then fell a crying. He sent the wives & Children in the Canoe out a fishing: but he & the Girl went round the Cove', and proceeded to come on board the ship.[7] James Cook's account of these people is generally less detailed, and does not mention the quarrel in which the man both dispensed and received blows. He does, however, make it clear that there were three women and not two, which incidentally is the case in Hodges' *Cascade Cove* painting (p. 80), though Cook also, at one point, reproduces George's conflation of the 'young girl' and the younger of the two wives. The confusion may have arisen because both appear to have been singularly forthcoming and talkative. The interesting point that Cook adds is that the 'girl' is supposed not only to be the daughter of the man, but of the woman whose countenance is disfigured by the wen. There is also, however, an emendation in Cook's manuscript journal that makes George's doubt concerning the relation between the girl and the older man categorical: 'We learnt afterwards that this young Woman was not his Daughter.'[8] This prejudices the very perception of the group as a family, since the woman with the wen is either not the girl's mother, or not the man's wife, unless some polyandrous relationship or illegitimate parenthood is postulated. While the official published narrative does not reveal that the apparent daughter was not a daughter, other revisions of the journal, such as the addition of 'as we supposed' in parentheses after mention of the man's two wives,[9] render identifications less, rather than more, certain.

These complexities are at first exhibited and then suppressed in the prints that were published after Hodges' paintings, in the official edition of Cook's journal, and in subsequent popularisations and plagiarisations. Lerpernière's plate in the official publication may be based on a lost sketch by Hodges, but is otherwise an abstraction and repositioning of the figures in the Cascade Cove painting in the National Maritime Museum in Greenwich. This print claimed to depict precisely what was elusive: *Family in Dusky Bay, New Zealand* (see p. 54). Not only the confusion concerning the number of wives, but also some uncertainty around the character of conjugal relations is suggested here by the fact that two contrasting relations are imaged – between the man and the standing woman, on one side, and between the man and the seated woman with her baby, on the other. The woman holding the spear is like the classic personification of liberty, and is no slave but a companion and fellow warrior. The other is by no means radically bestialised, but is close and conspicuously subordinate to the man, and seemingly carrying a good deal more on her back than her child. These two women personify opposed constructions of barbaric womanhood, the one a denigrated bearer of burdens, who incidentally has frizzy hair that would have been associated with 'negroes' by eighteenth-century viewers, the other so affected by the martial environment that she carries arms herself, and apparently therefore shares the liberty and independence of her husband.

The *Cascade Cove* painting transposes the group to a romantic waterfall they no doubt knew, but never visited in the company of the Europeans. The work is neither explicitly nor implicitly titled 'A Family in Dusky Bay'; the relative isolation and foregrounding of the man surely renders peripheral the question of his relationship to any one or all three of the women. His rugged vigour and musculature might be taken first to echo the undomesticated strength of the rocks and the terrain, while the distinction between the seated girl and the standing adult women might imply, to any viewer concerned to speculate, that the man has two wives and a daughter, as the official narrative suggested. The engraving makes two figures of three by depriving one adult woman of her spear, reducing her to the seated position of the apparent daughter, and giving her custody not only of her child, but of a burden that she lacks in the painting; this is the same conflation of one wife and the daughter or apparent daughter that is made at points in both James Cook's and George Forster's texts.

Later engravings neutralised these complexities. Cook's enormously popular voyages were reprinted in eighty sixpenny parts for a broader audience between 1784 and 1786, which presented itself as 'the most ACCURATE, ELEGANT, and PERFECT EDITION of the WHOLE WORKS and DISCOVERIES of that Celebrated CIRCUMNAVIGATOR'.[10] The preface to this work made much of the 'sinister artifices' of 'mercenary persons' who published similar works of poor quality and at excessive expense, and who thereby obstructed the intention of government by preventing Cook's voyages from being more universally read. Among the faults of compilations of voyages, the printer noted that it had 'of late become a Mode too common to usher periodical Publications into the World with a good Appearance at first; and in the Course of their Execution, to fall off from the original Perfection'. Though the writer proceeded to assure his readers that this would not be true of the 'New, Authentic, and Complete History', a comparison of the fine copperplate engravings issued with the initial parts and those that

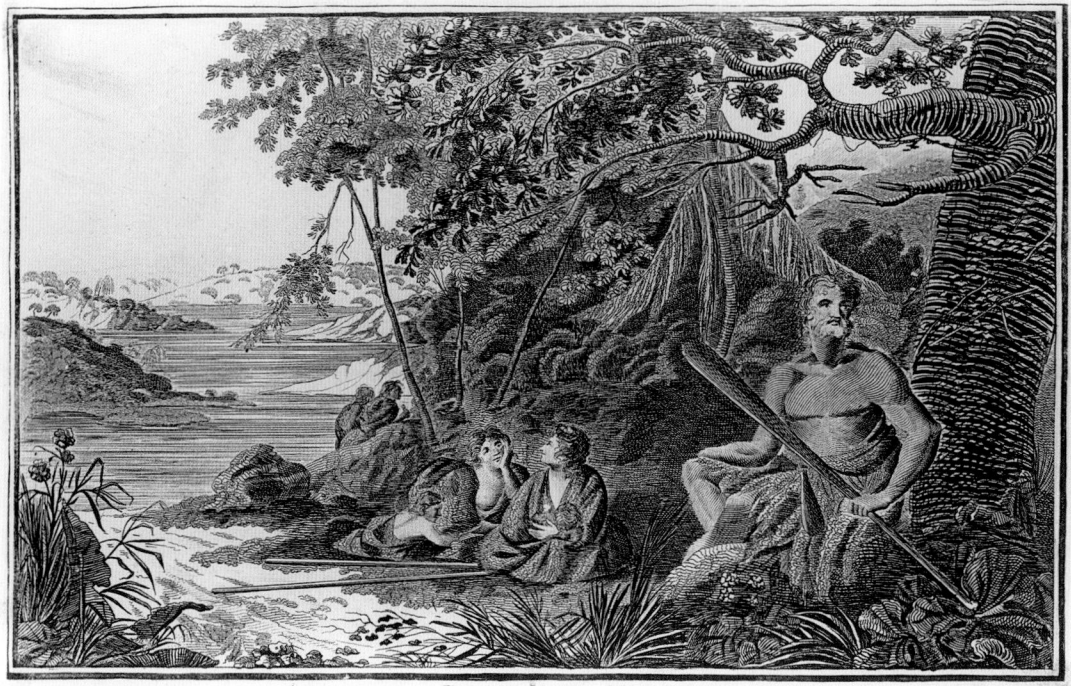

A Family in Dusk Bay [sic], engraving from George William Anderson, *A New, Authentic, and Complete History of Voyages Round the World* (London 1784–86)

appeared subsequently, which are very crudely delineated, makes this charge appear absolutely apt for the very book being advertised. One of the more crudely executed engravings is that of the *Family in Dusk* [sic] *Bay* (above), which completely rearranges the figures, placing the man in the foreground, and emphasising the dependent maternity and femininity of all three women. The women's spears have not been entirely dispensed with, but are prone upon the ground, the connotations of warrior women laid aside.

Later images further dilute the ethnographic particularity of the Lerpernière print. An odd Italian plate (opposite), from an album of assorted travel views, retains the title of the earlier picture, but otherwise possesses the most slender of connections with it. The figures are wholly altered: the man holds a crude club and is a generic barbarian, combining traces of Maori *moko,* (curvilinear facial tattoo) and a feather headdress with native American rather than Oceanic associations. He also bears a curious kind of body-painting or tattooing, featuring snakes that wind their way down his arms, and botanical motifs on his thighs; the woman is emphatically reduced to subservience.

Readers of Domeny de Rienzi's *Océanie,* a three-volume compendium of geographic and ethnographic information on the region, were provided with a further version of the engraving (p. 62). Here, the main warrior with his club is preserved; the sex of the second warrior is changed, and the woman to the right is turned into a savage Venus. The distortions did not stop there: this is no longer 'the family of Dusky Bay', but *Habitants de Mallicollo* – that is, of Malakula in Vanuatu, which is about as far from southern New Zealand as Managua is from Montreal. Yet de Rienzi's book, profusely illustrated with prints that were bowdlerised and plagiarised in this fashion, was swiftly translated into a number of European languages, and became the most widely distributed synthesis of what passed for European knowledge of the Pacific in the mid-nineteenth century. Even today, this is one of the books you will come across most often if you rummage around the 'Océanie' shelves in French antiquarian bookshops. We can be confident, in other words, that the most distorted of these images were those that received widest circulation.

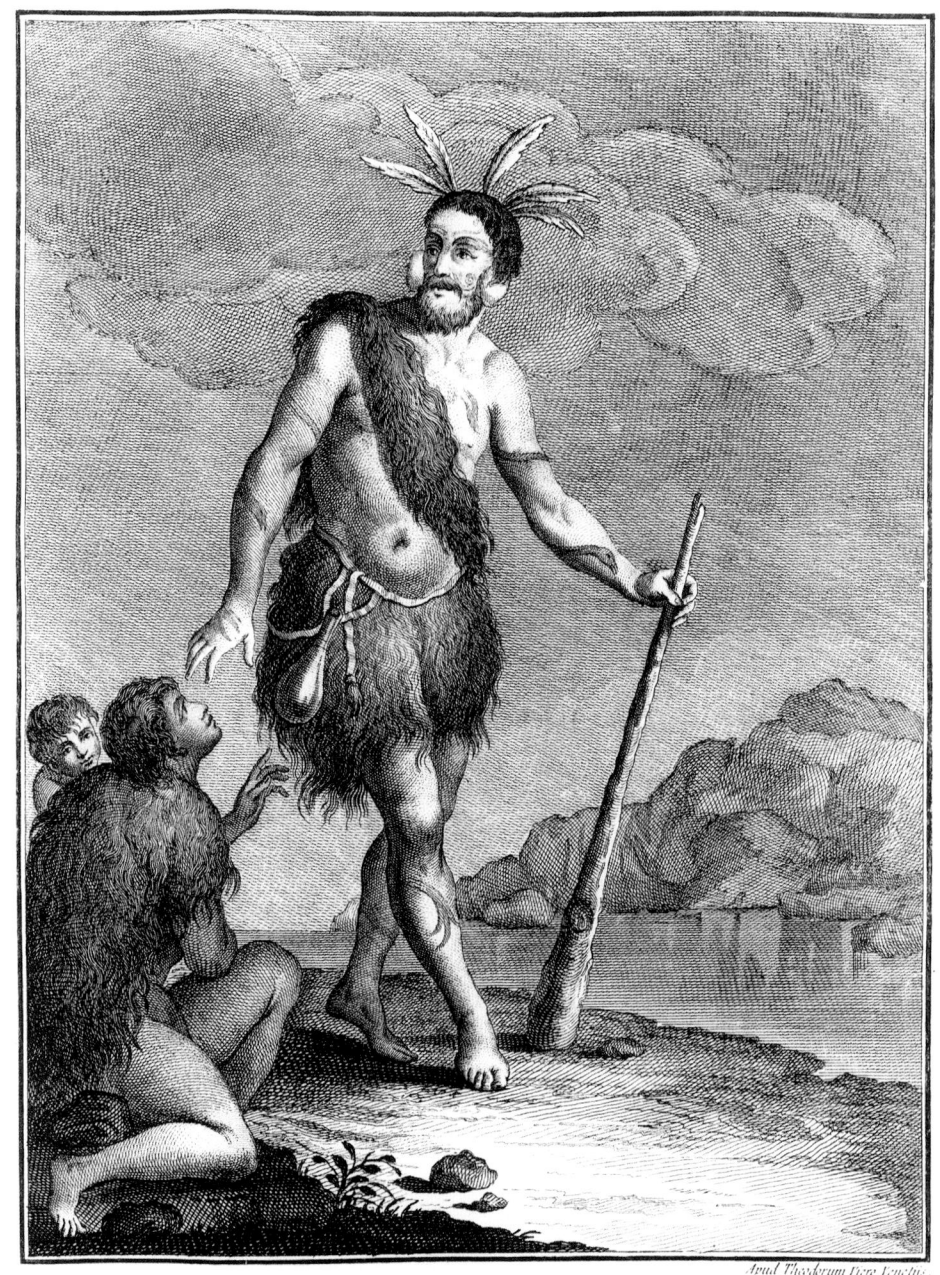

Famiglia della Baja Dusky, Famille dans le Baye Dusky
nella nuova Zelanda. de la nouvelle Zélande.

Apud Theodorum Viero Venetiis

Famiglia della Baja Dusky, nella nuova Zelanda, engraving from Theodora Viero, *Racolti di stampi … di varie nazione* (Venice, c. 1791)

To return to Tamatea itself, and to what was said in the 1770s. As curious as the character of the 'family' was the manner in which the brief encounter was concluded. The Polynesians abruptly broke off their intercourse with the visitors, much to the puzzlement of the latter, who saw the relationship as one characterised by friendliness and a degree of mutual generosity. As George Forster put it, 'we never saw them again, which was the more extraordinary, as they never went away empty handed from us …' But this perplexing conclusion was, like the anomalous 'family', to be explained away in due course.

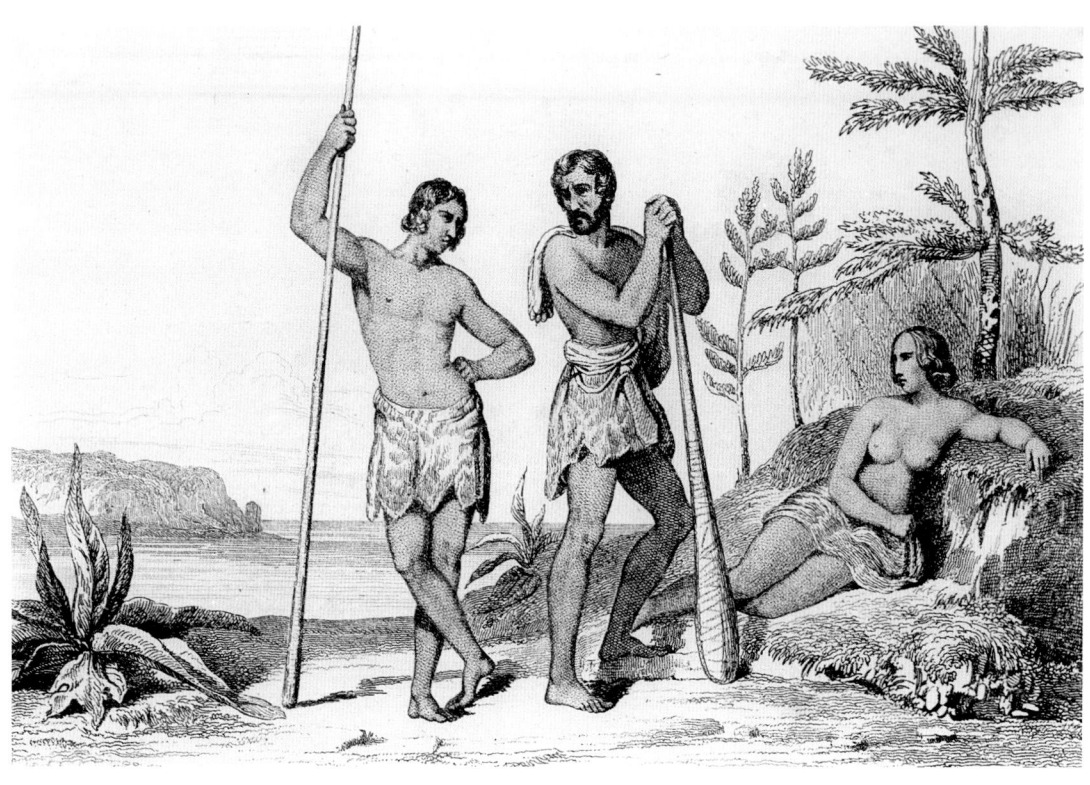

Habitants de Mallicolo – New Hébrides, engraving from Domeny de Rienzi,
Océanie ou la cinquième parti du monde (Paris 1836–37)

9 (a-d)
Northeast Point, Indian Island; site of first contact with the 'Family of Dusky Bay', 19 May 1995

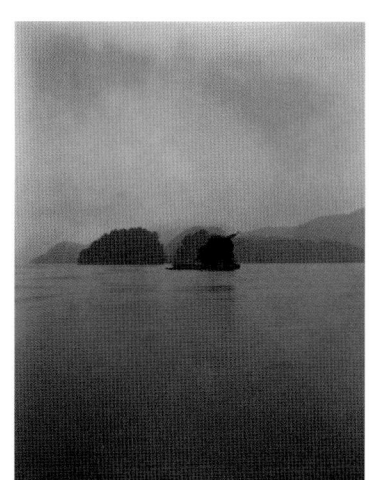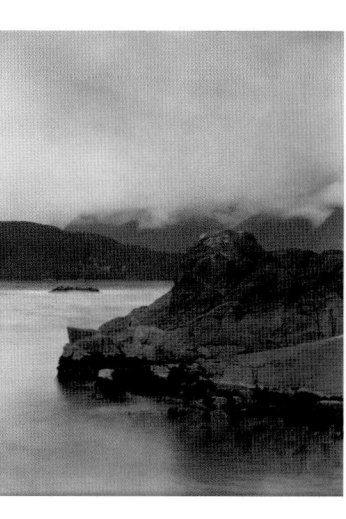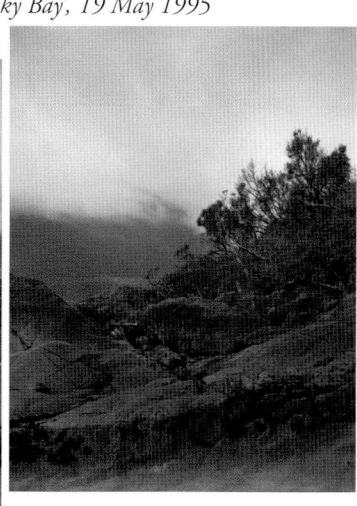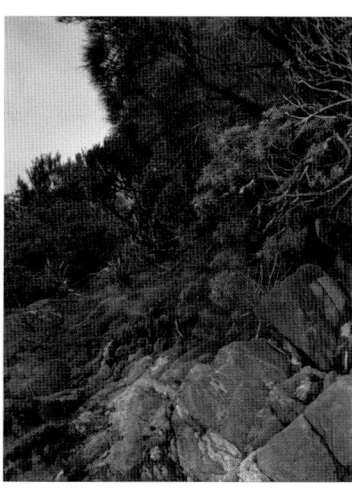

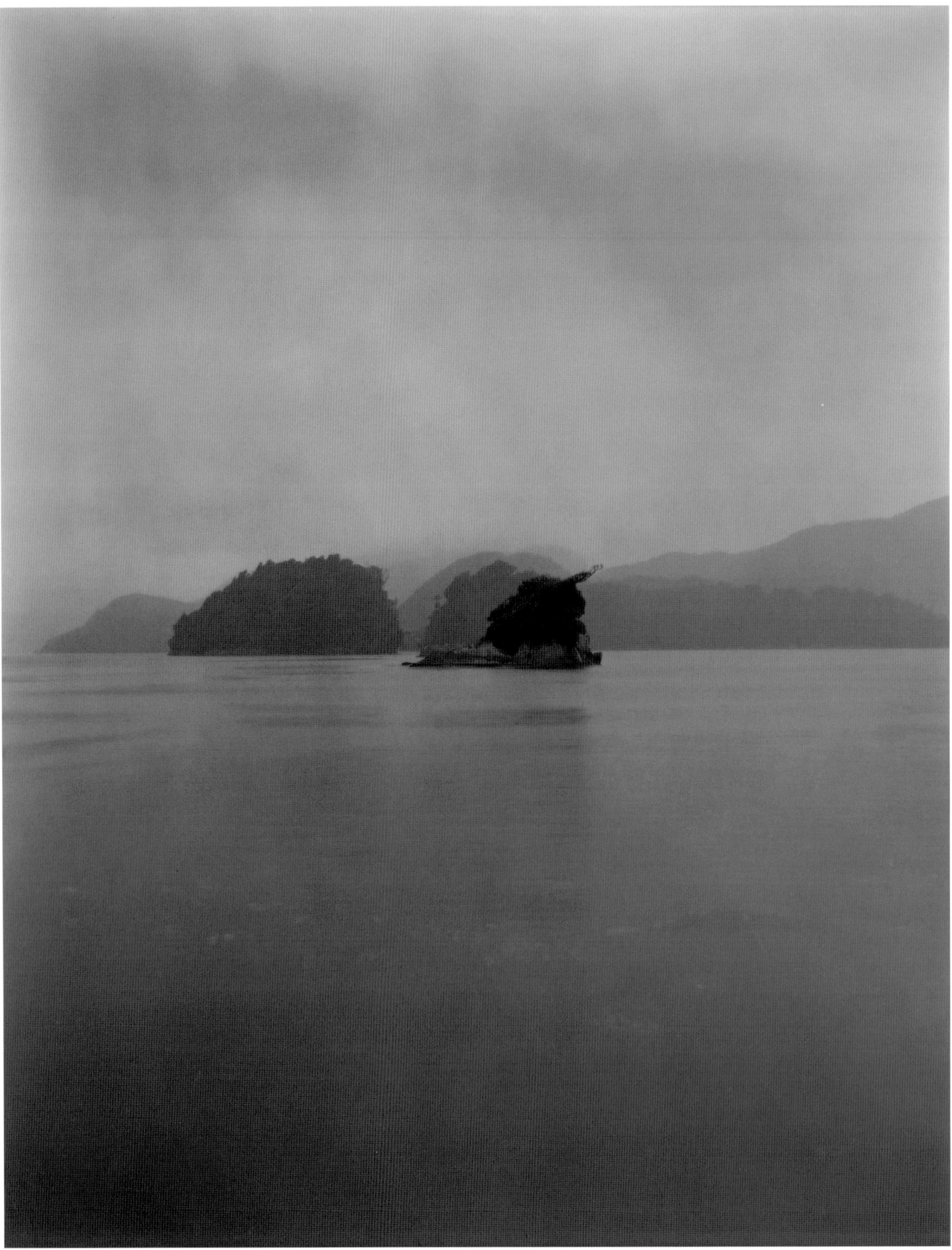

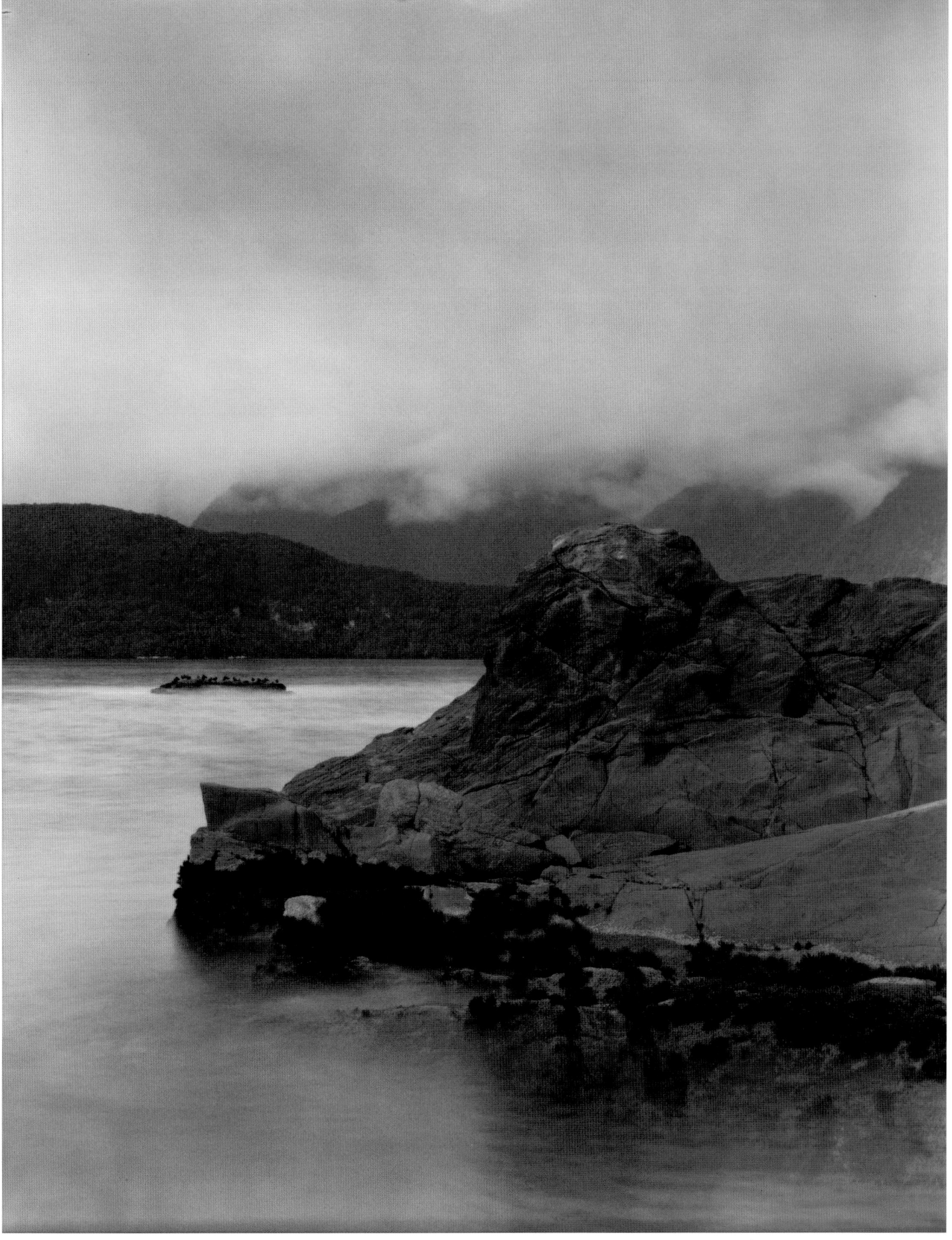

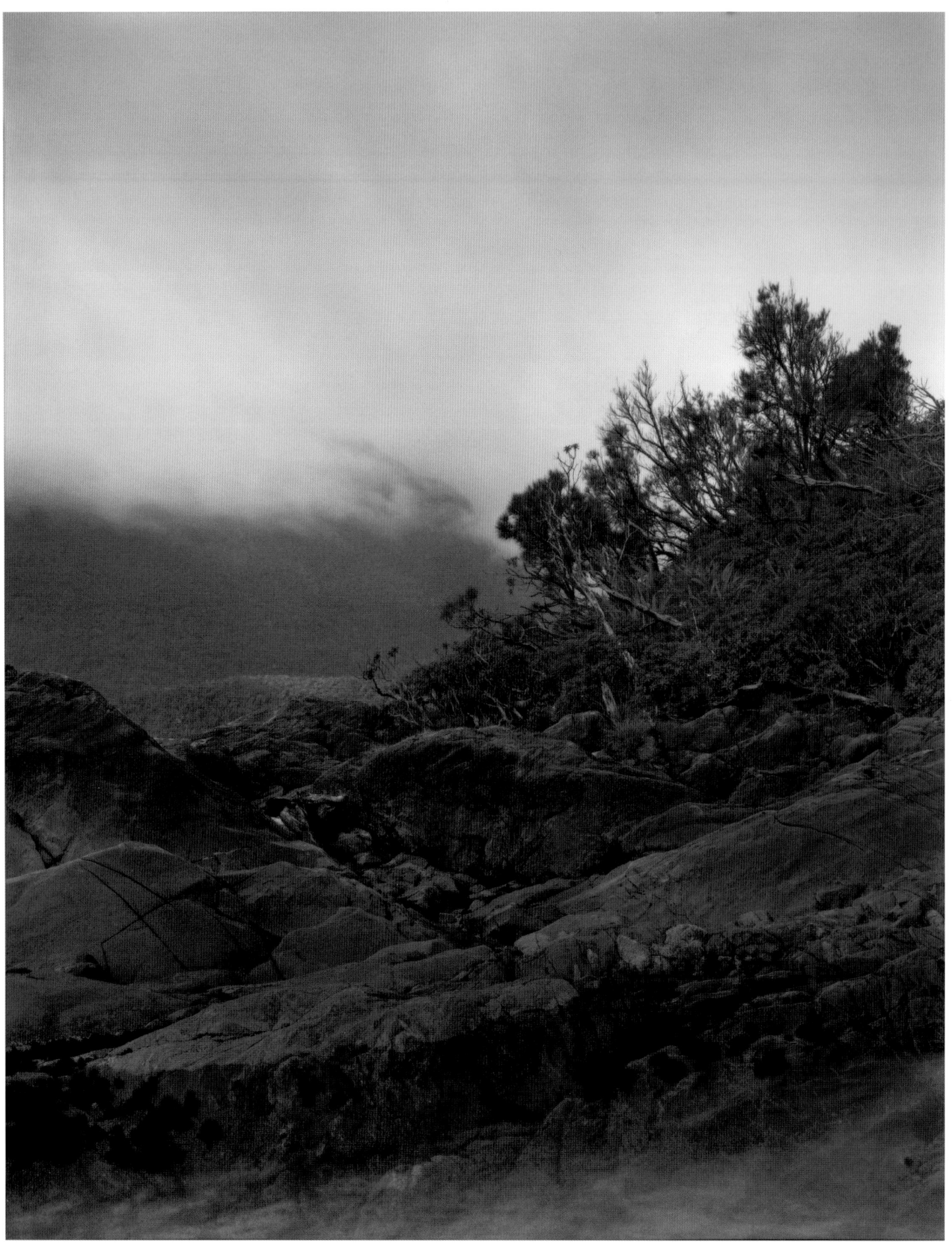

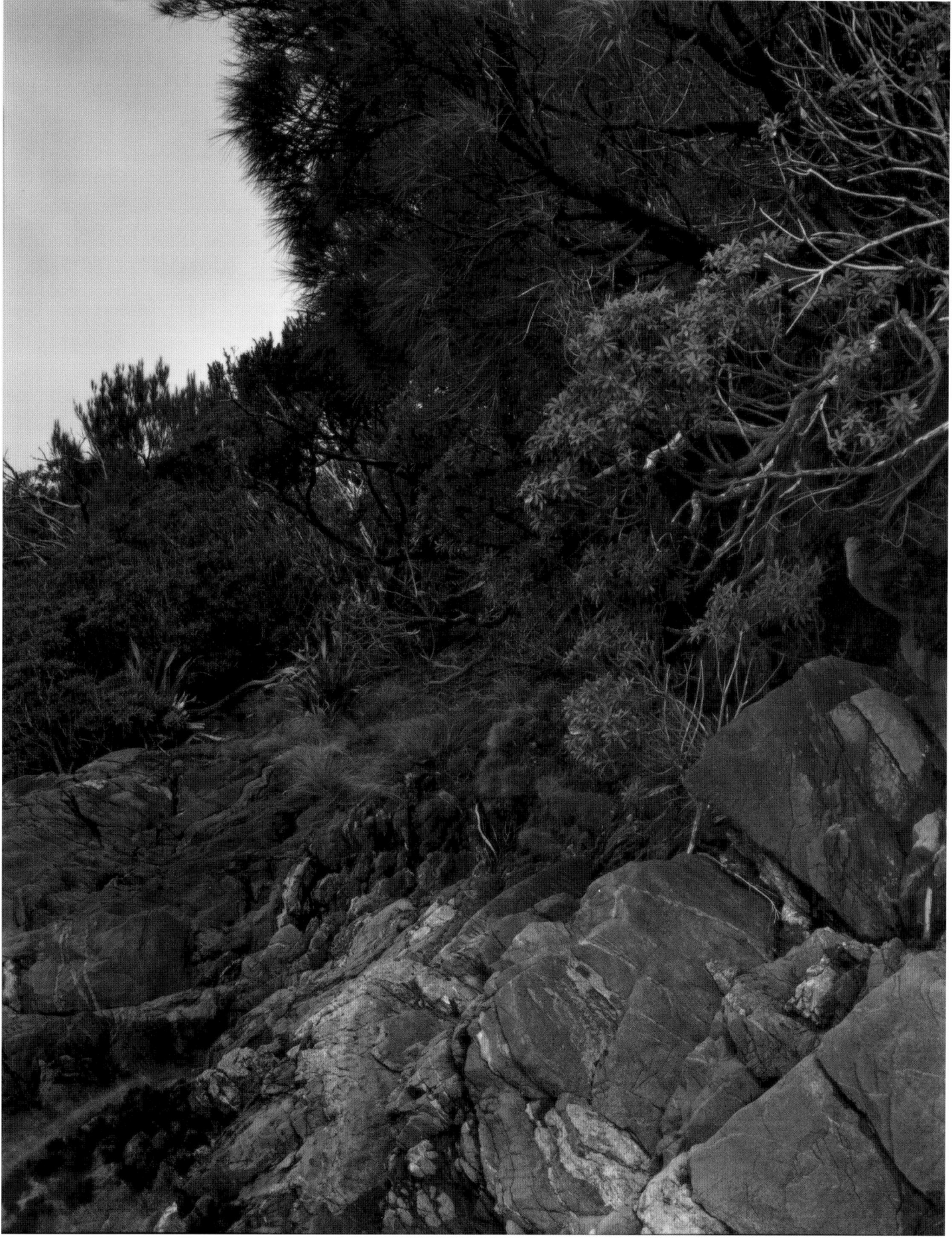

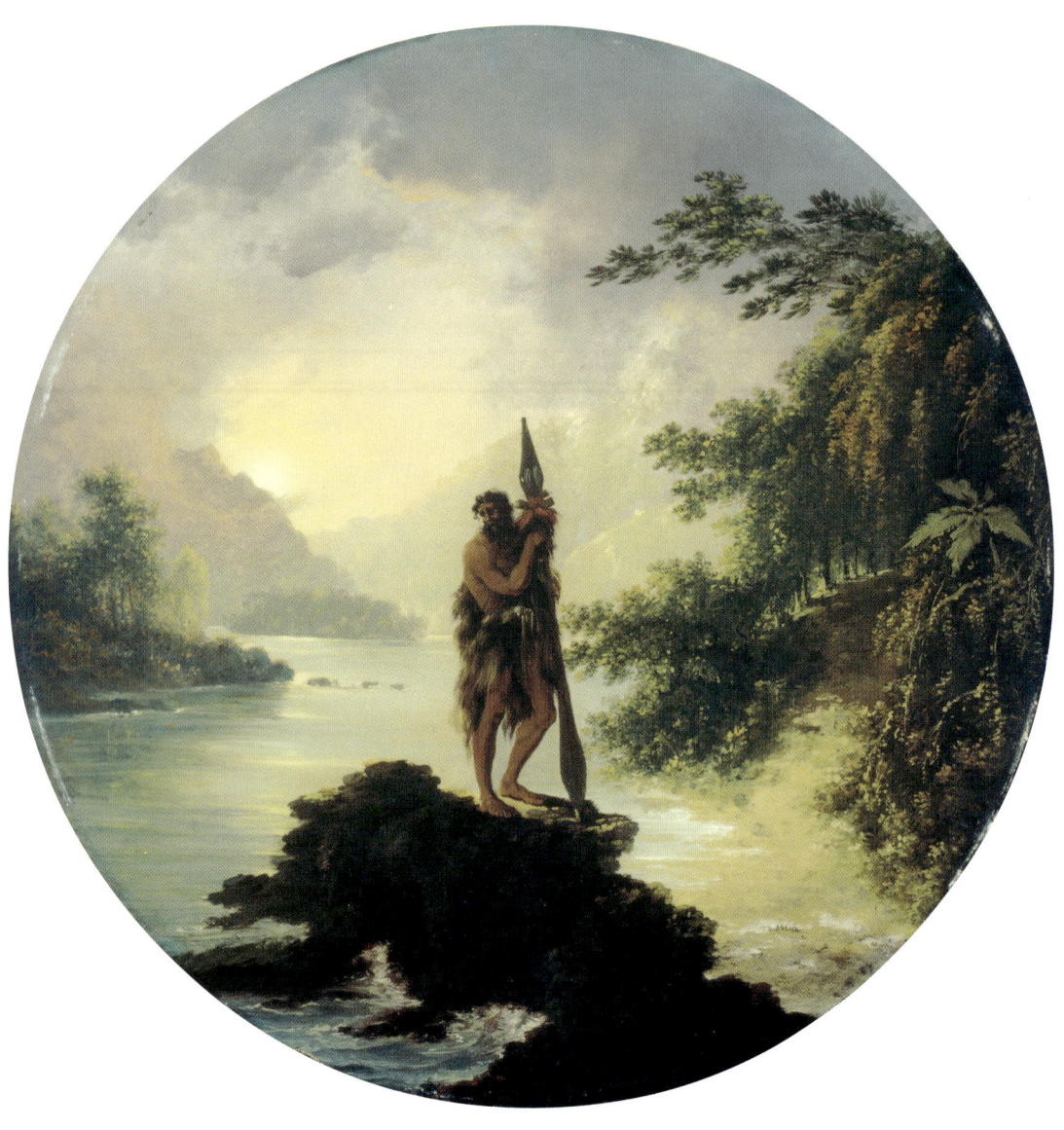

William Hodges, *A View in Dusky Bay, New Zealand, 1775–76,*
oil, 66 cm diameter, Auckland Art Gallery Toi o Tamaki

10 (a-h)
Indian Island, 360° panorama after William Hodges' 'View in Dusky Bay', 2 – 10 August, 1998

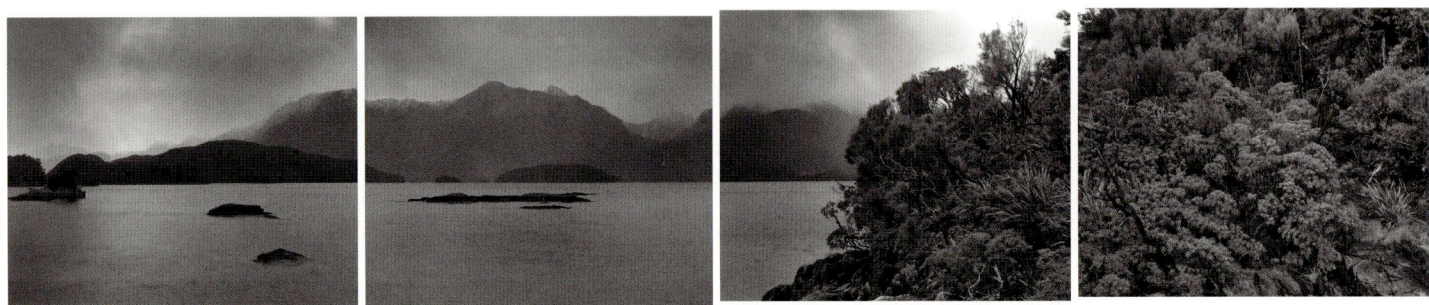

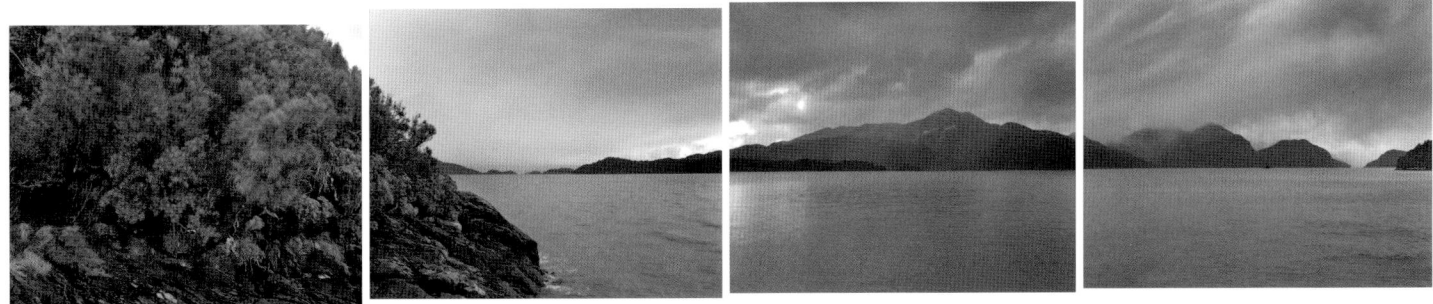

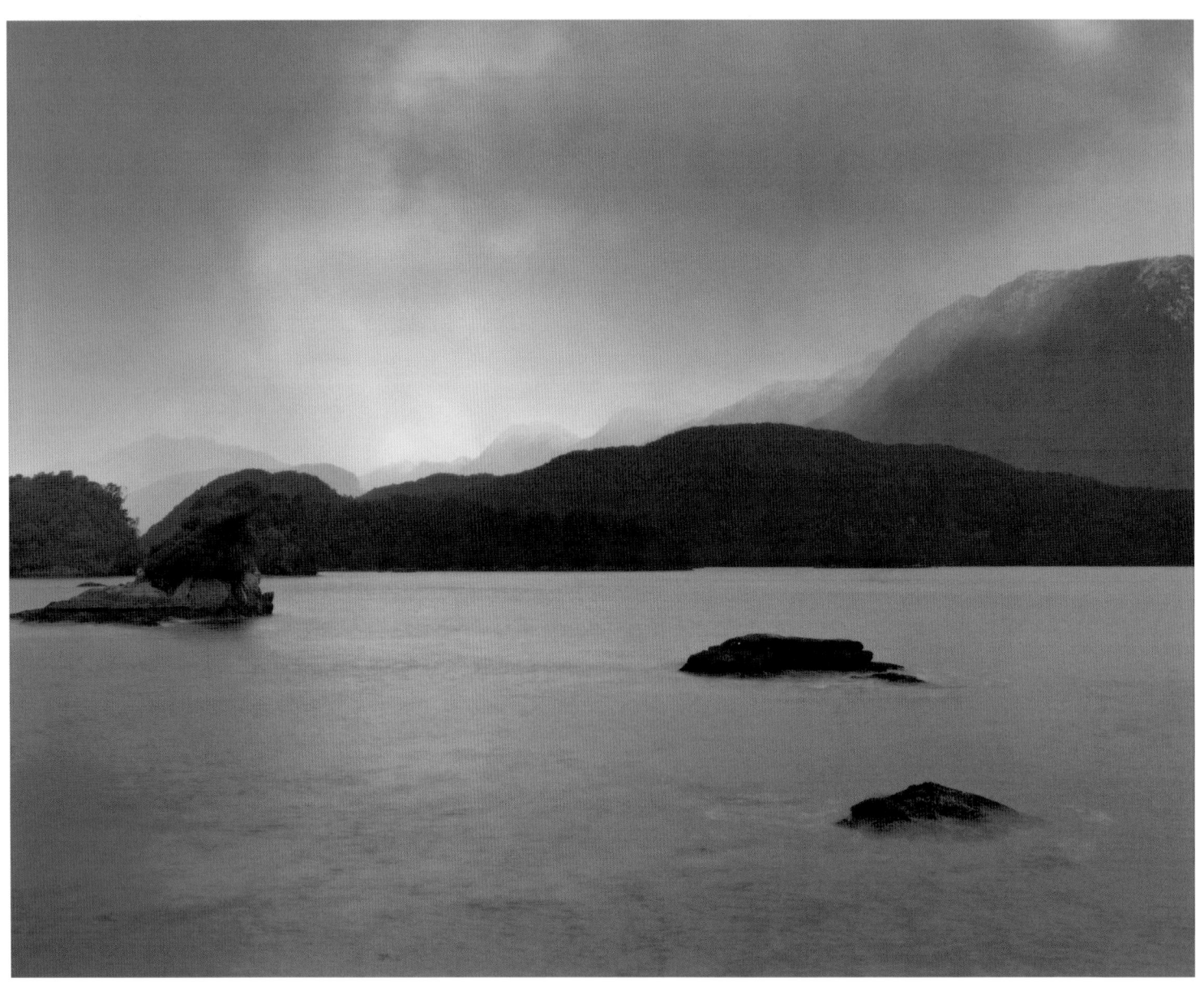

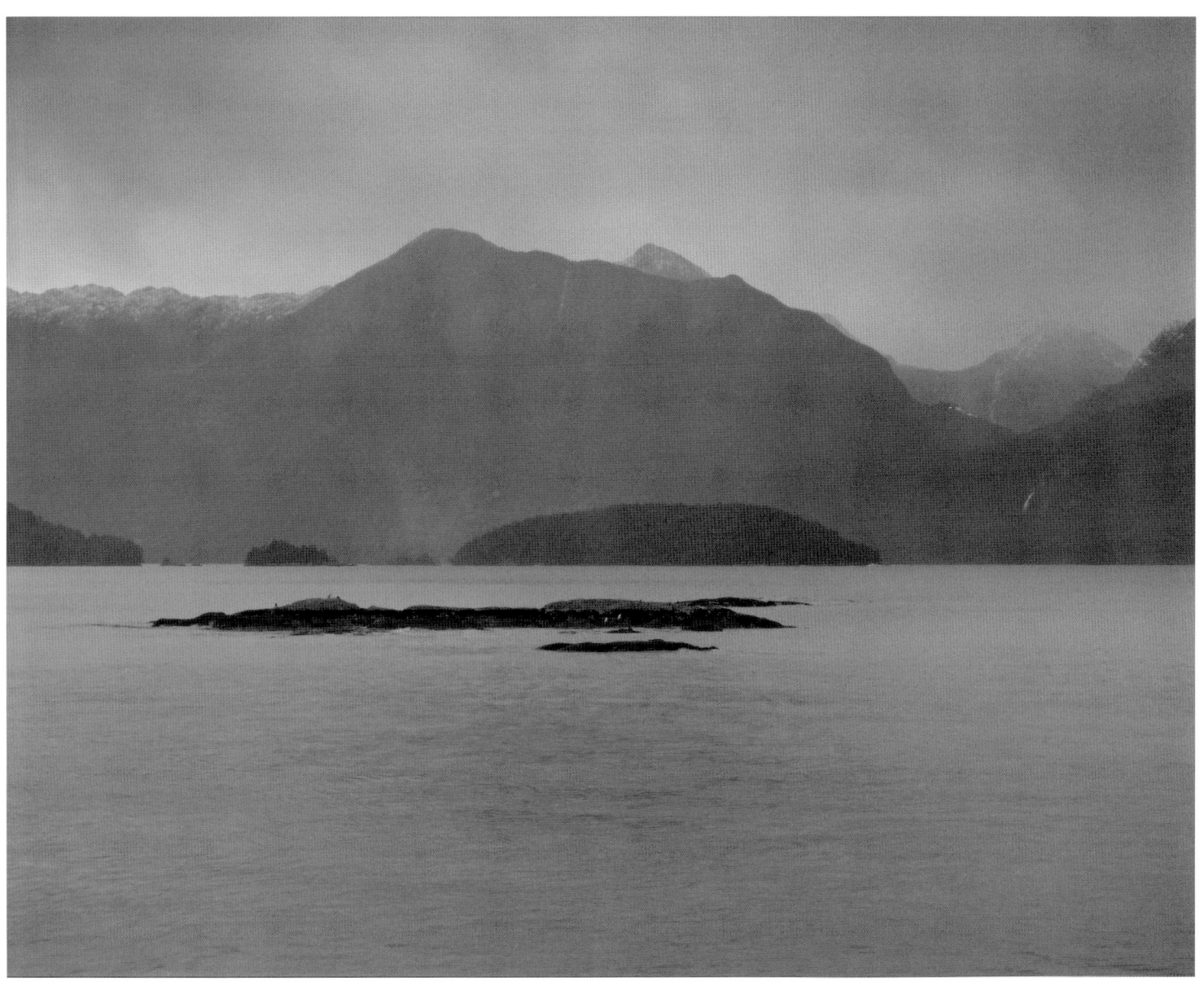

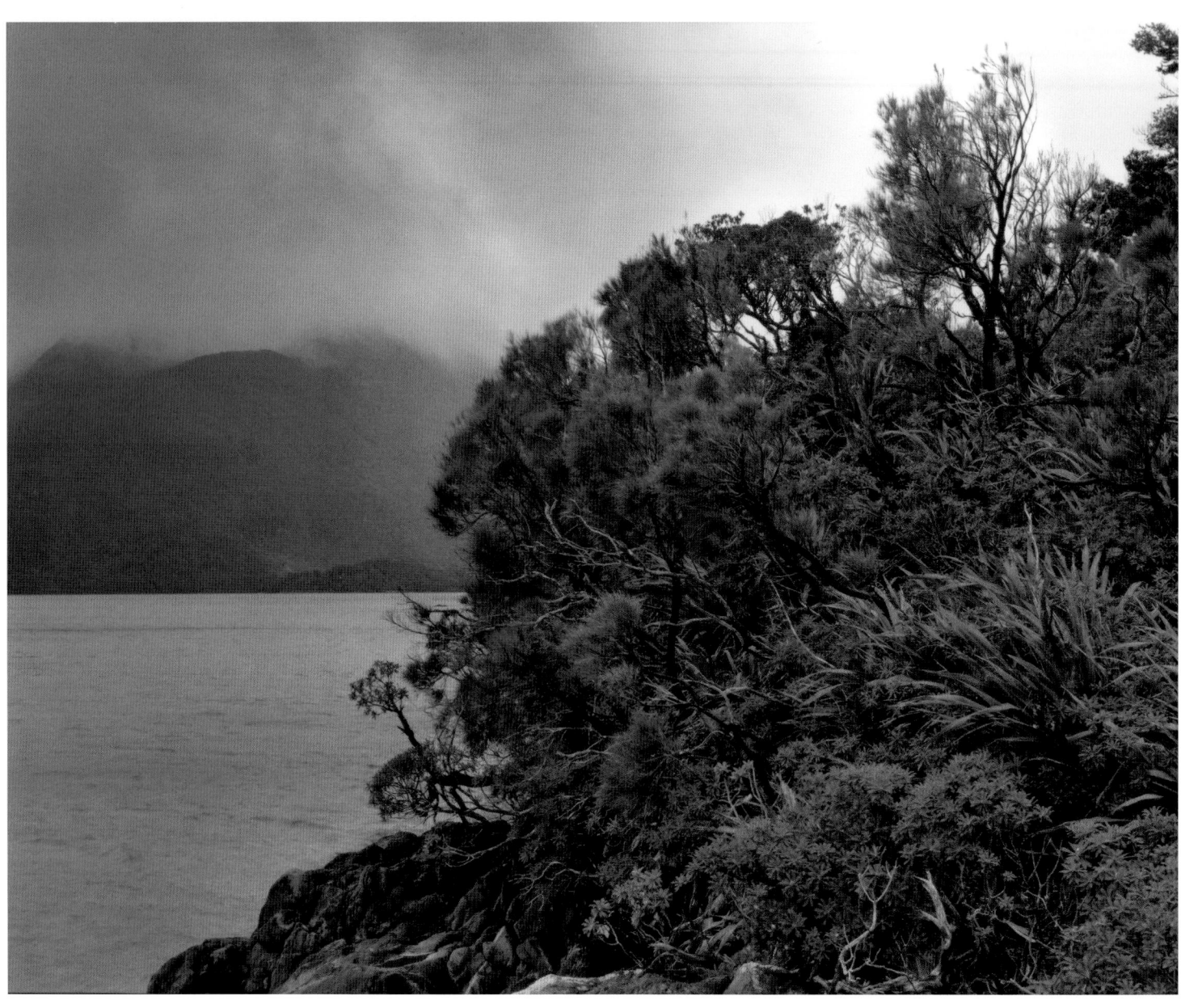

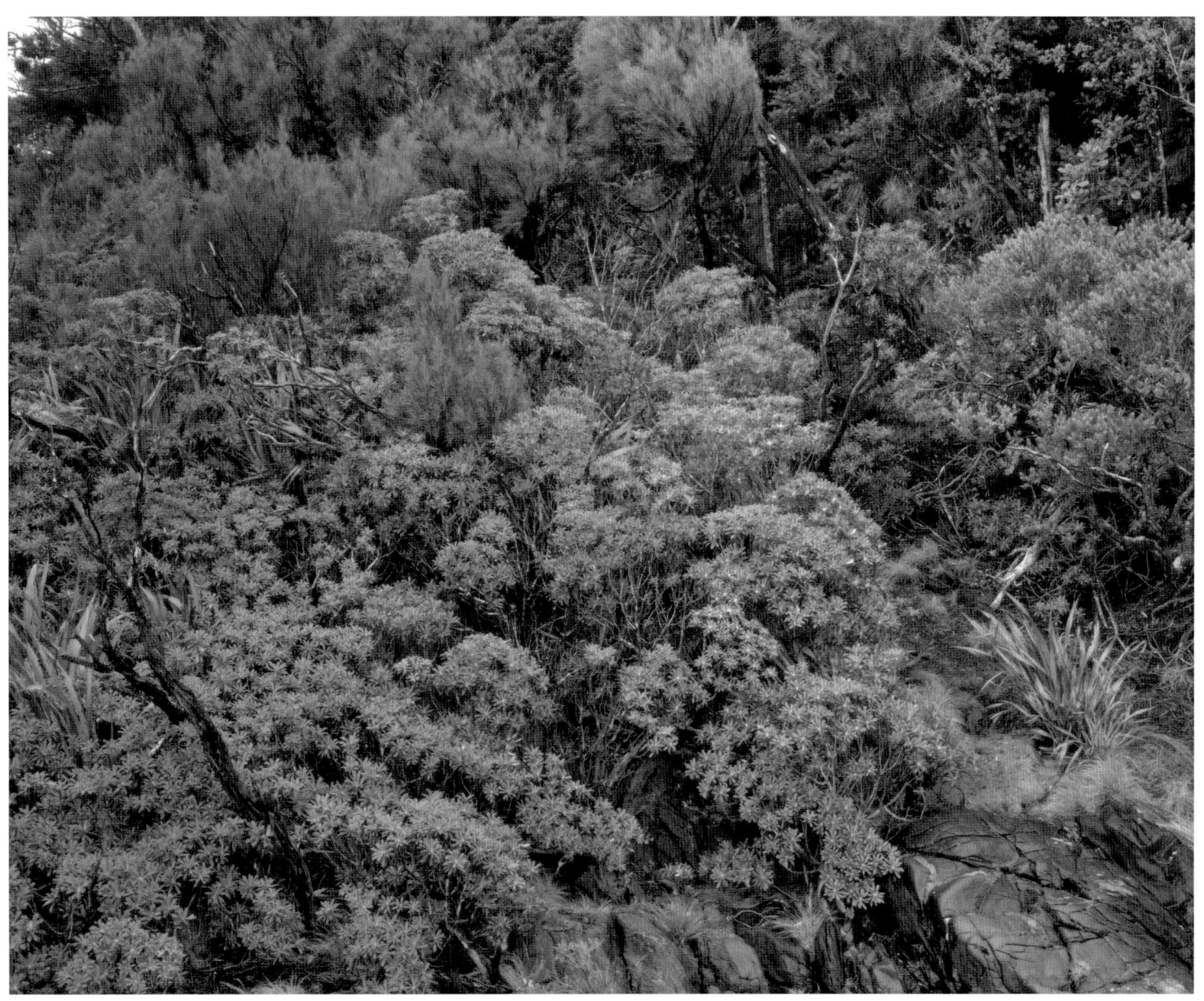

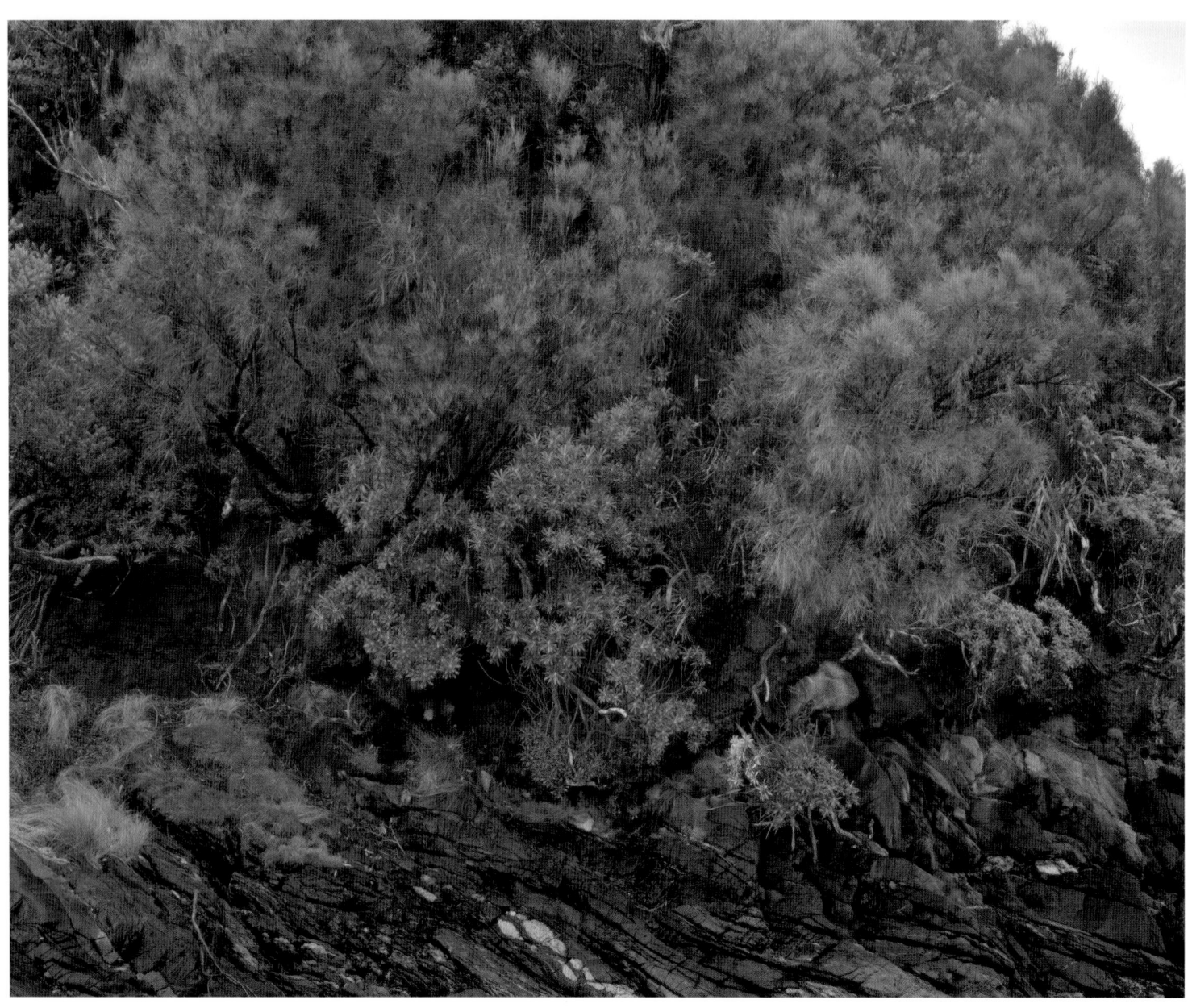

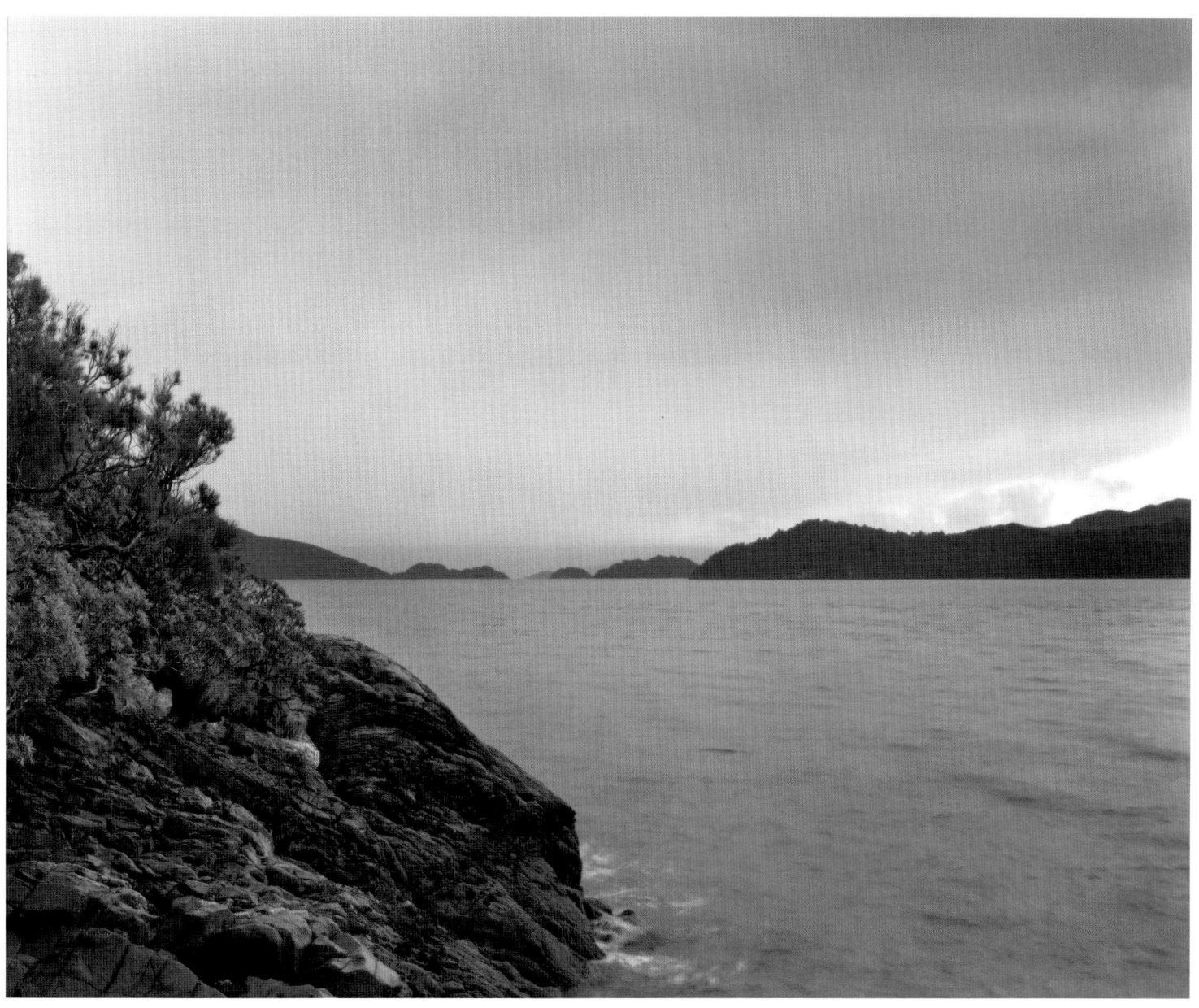

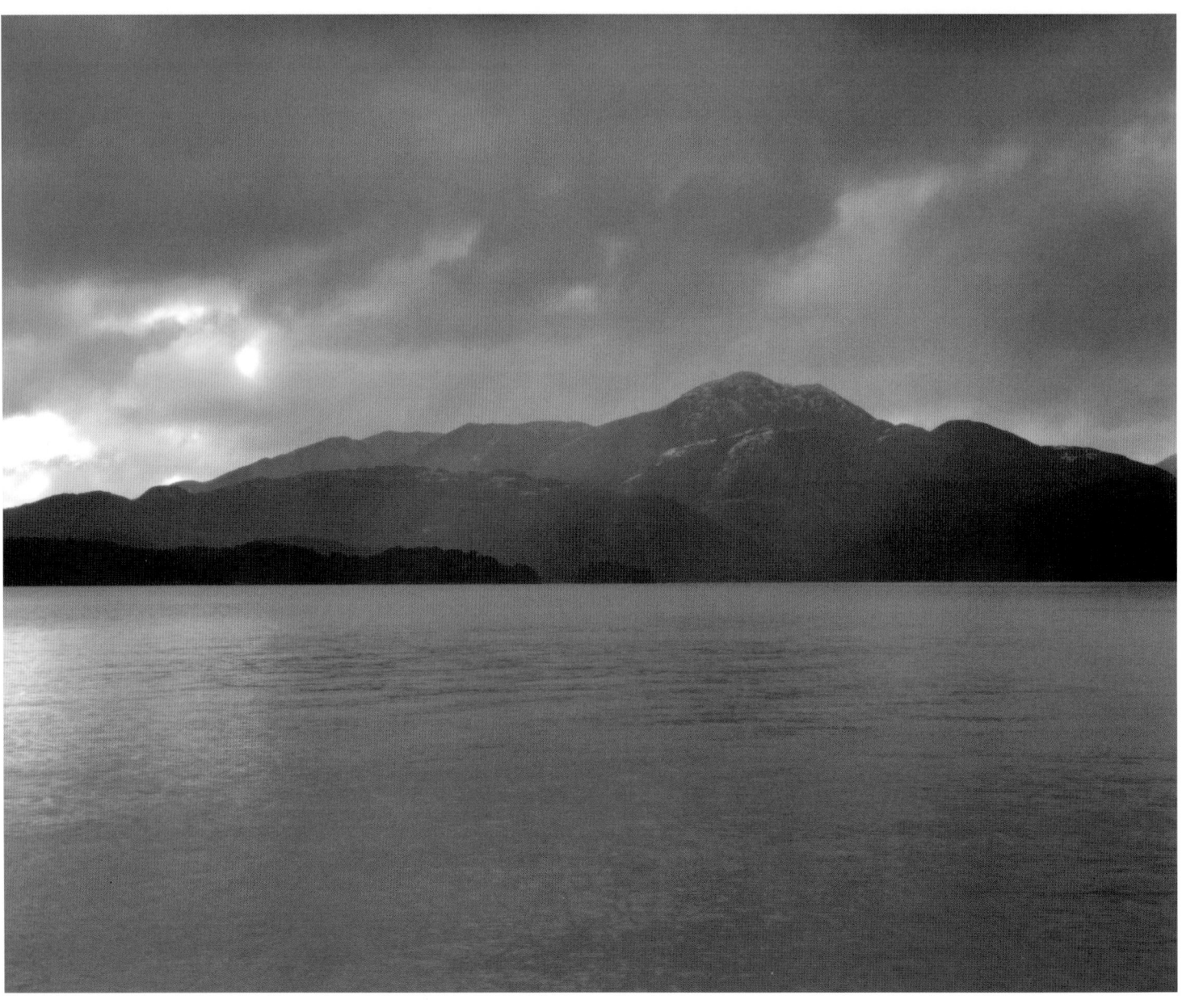

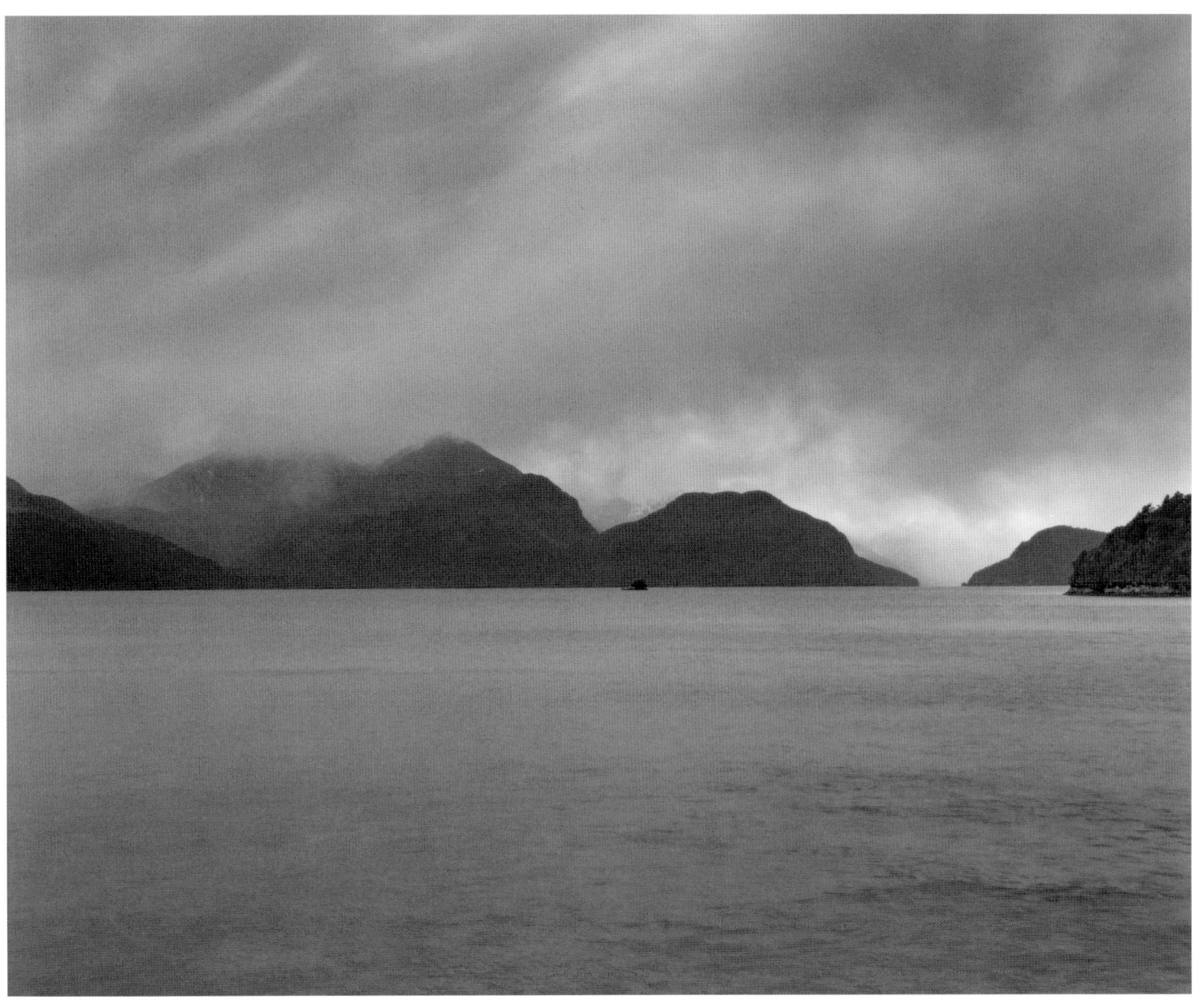

3. The Cascade

On the 11th, the sky being clear and serene promised a fair day ... We directed our course to the cove where we had seen the first canoe of the natives, and particularly to a water-fall, which we had observed from afar a few days ago, and which had induced us to call this inlet Cascade Cove. This water-fall, at the distance of a mile and a half, seems to be but inconsiderable, on account of its great elevation; but after climbing about two hundred yards upwards, we obtained a full prospect of it, and found indeed a view of great beauty and grandeur before us. The first object which strikes the beholder, is a clear column of water, apparently eight or ten yards in circumference, which is projected with great impetuosity from the perpendicular rock, at the height of one hundred yards. Nearly at the fourth part of the whole height, this column meeting a part of the same rock, which now acquires a little inclination, spreads on its broad back into a limpid sheet of about twenty-five yards in width. Here its surface is curled, and dashes upon every little eminence in its rapid descent, till it is all collected in a fine bason about sixty yards in circuit, included on three sides by the natural walls of the rocky chasm, and in front by huge masses of stone irregularly piled above each other. Between them the stream finds its way, and runs foaming with the greatest rapidity along the slope of the hill to the sea. The whole neighbourhood of the cascade, to a distance of an hundred yards around, is filled with the steam or watery vapour formed by the violence of the fall. This mist however was so thick, that it penetrated our clothes in a few minutes, as effectually as a shower of rain would have done. We mounted on the highest stone before the bason, and looking down into it, were struck with the sight of a most beautiful rainbow of a perfectly circular form, which was produced by the meridian rays of the sun refracted in the vapour of the cascade. Beyond this circle the rest of the steam was tinged with the prismatic colours, refracted in an inverted order. The scenery on the left consists of steep, brown rocks, fringed on the summits with over-hanging shrubs and trees; on the right there is a vast heap of large stones, probably hurried down from the impending mountain's brow, by the force of the torrent. From thence rises a sloping bank, about seventy-five yards high, on which a wall of twenty-five yards perpendicular is placed, crowned with verdure and shrubberies. Still farther to the right, the broken rocks are clothed with mosses, ferns, grasses, and various flowers; nay several shrubs, and trees to the height of forty feet, rise on both sides of the stream, and hide its course from the sun. The noise of the cascade is so loud, and so repeatedly reverberated from the echoing rocks, that it drowns almost every other sound; the birds seemed to retire from it to a little distance, where the shrill notes of thrushes, the graver pipe of wattle-birds, and the enchanting melody of various creepers resounded on all sides, and completed the beauty of this wild and romantic spot. On turning round we beheld an extensive bay, strewed as it were with small islands, which are covered with lofty trees; beyond them on one side, the mountains rise majestic on the main land, capt with clouds and perpetual snow; and on the other, the immense ocean bounded our view. The grandeur of this scene was such, that the powers of description fall short of the force and beauty of nature, which could only be truly imitated by the pencil of Mr. Hodges, who went on this voyage with us; and whose performances do great credit and honour to his judgment and execution, as well as to the choice of his employers. Satisfied with the contemplation of this magnificent sight, we directed our attention next to the flowers which enlivened the ground, and the small birds which sung very cheerfully all round us. We had as yet found neither the vegetable nor animal creation so beautiful, or so numerous, in any part of this bay; perhaps, because the strong refraction of the sun-beams from the perpendilar walls of rock, and the shelter from storms, made the climate considerably more mild and genial in this spot than in any other part.

George Forster, Voyage Round the World, *I, p. 146–9*

We visited this place on an unusually fine day in May 1995. It was quite a scramble up a bouldery slope from the shingle beach on the cove; the most difficult part, though, was finding a way down to the pool at the base of the fall. Once there, Forster's description made sense, though the 1773 visit must have been after heavier rain unless he exaggerated the drenching effect of the mist. In 1995 the fall certainly did create vapour, but we were not soaked to the skin; nor did we witness the unusual circular rainbow described in this passage.

Mark Adams comments on the Hodges painting Forster refers to, again through an operation of multiplication. His way of dealing with this place involves not a framed view but a sweep, a partial panorama. His four prints are like steps that first look up to the upper fall, which does not quite form the 'clear column' described by Forster, then into the pool, then at the awesome rock wall that forms a gorge below the cascade, and finally downstream, over rapids toward the open light of the sound.

The visitor who knows Hodges' work will have noted the conventionally sublime ruggedness of the rock and the fall and may find it remarkable that the awesome character of the place is not so much invented, as diminished, by his painting. And one can see why. Hodges, concerned as he presumably was to convey the daunting character of a considerable waterfall and the cliffs that surrounded it, needed a degree of openness that would enable his viewer to grasp these magnificent features from a certain distance, and to appreciate his Maori actors on a distinct rock platform that amounted to a stage. The visitor to the cascade today finds no such open space. The fall plunges into a pool surrounded by high cliffs that lead into a constricted gorge.

It is not that Hodges' painting is fanciful or false and that the panorama shows the truth of the place. In Hodges' day it was accepted that artists would take liberties with particular subject matter in order to reveal a more general truth. Adams's interests are different: he wants to show the very particular character of a place, which is not necessarily 'the truth' about it. It is, in a sense, as fabricated an image as that of Hodges. Because Adams aims to show the larger context of the watercourse, rather than a staged landscape, the panorama looks both upstream and downstream. This is an 'artificial' view, if we are assuming that a 'natural' image is one that corresponds to what the eye sees at a particular moment. Yet all views are artificial. Hodges' painting was built out of the techniques available to an eighteenth-century landscape painter, while Adams's photographs are made with particular equipment, and with particular aims in mind, over two hundred years later.

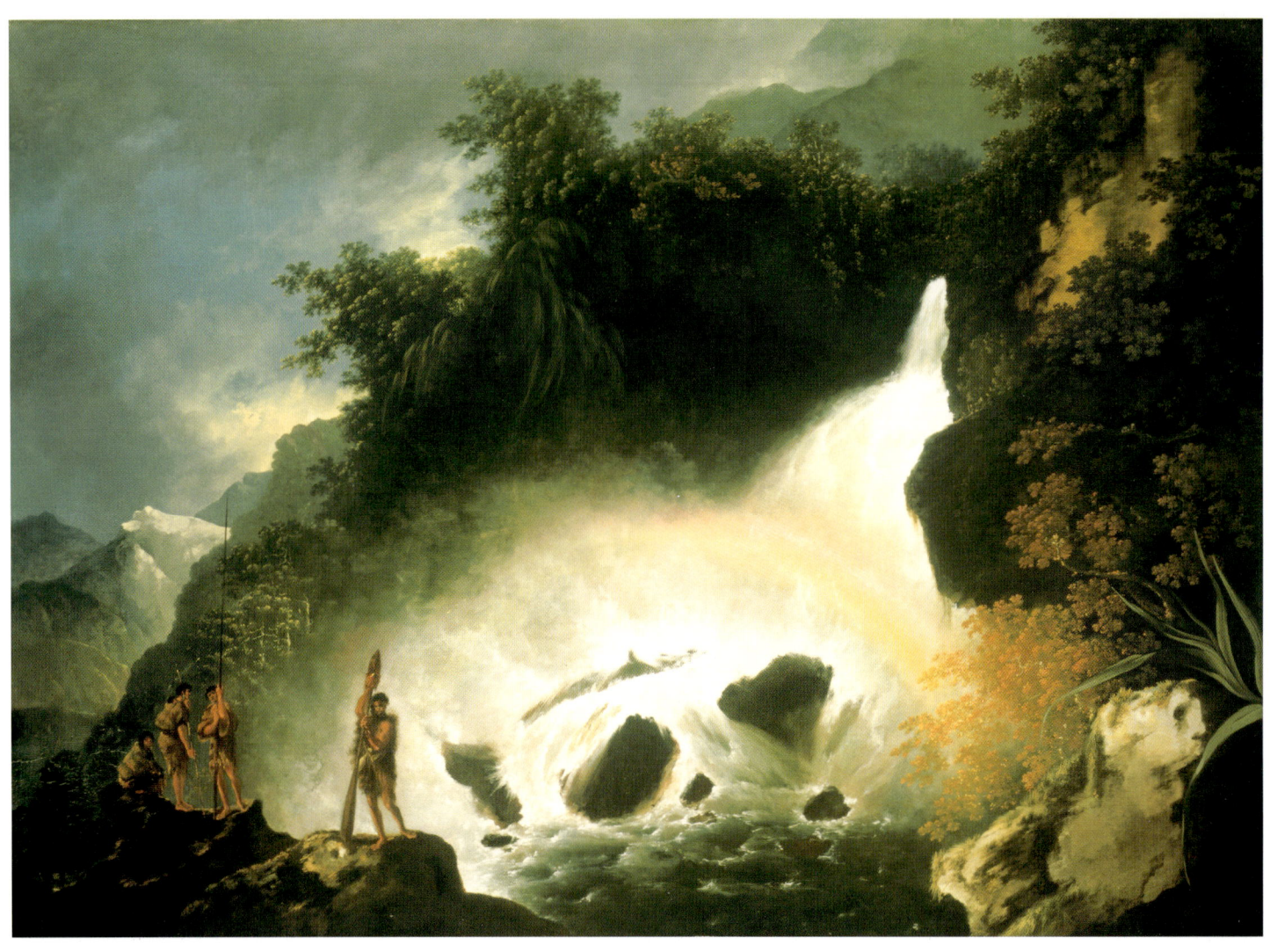

William Hodges, [*Cascade Cove*], *Dusky Bay*, c. 1775–6,
oil, 134.6 x 191.1 cm. National Maritime Museum, London

11 (a-d)
After William Hodges' 'Cascade Cove', 21 May 1995

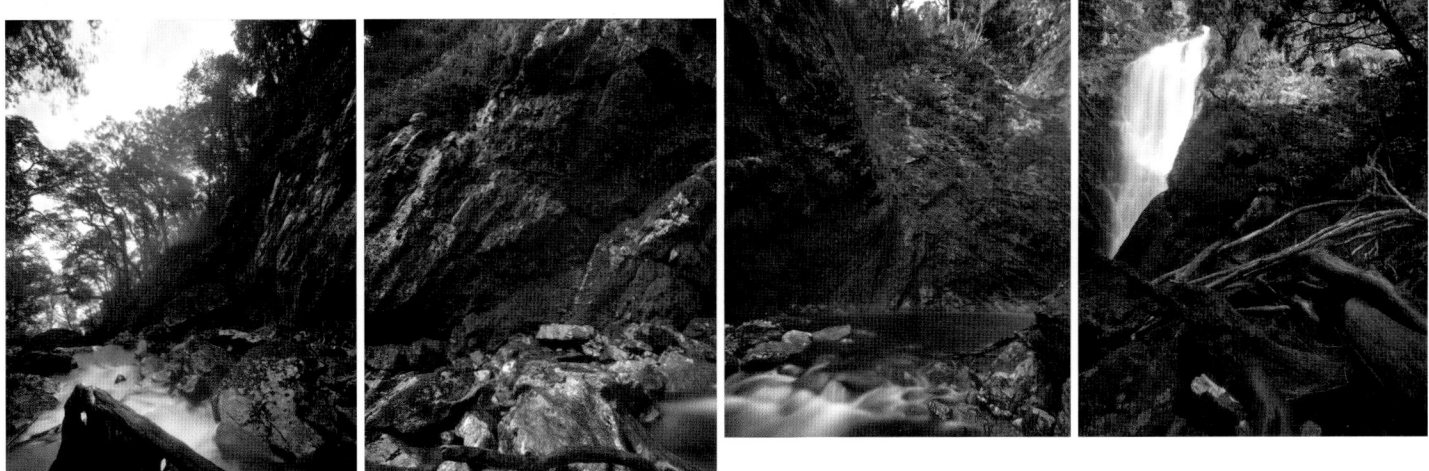

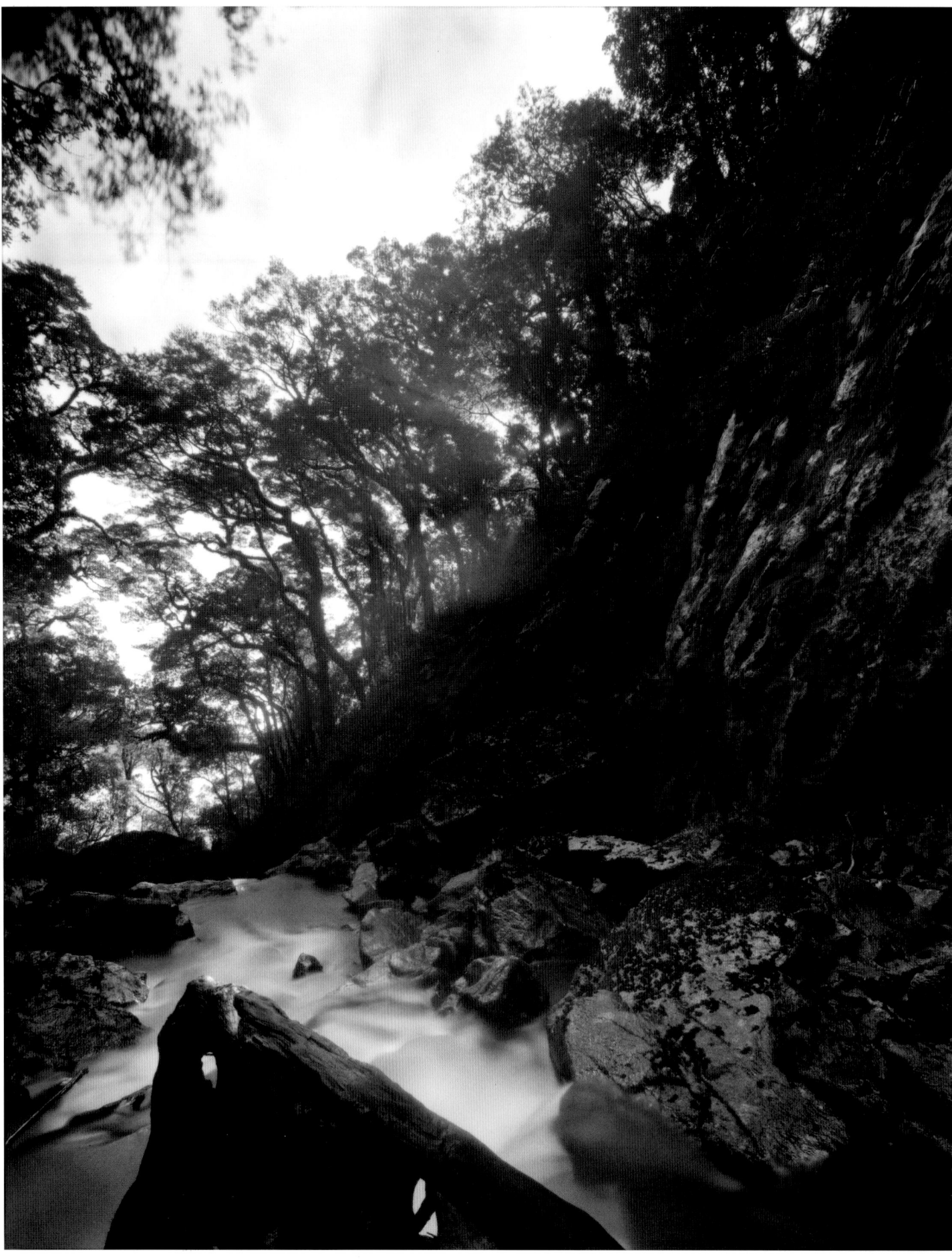

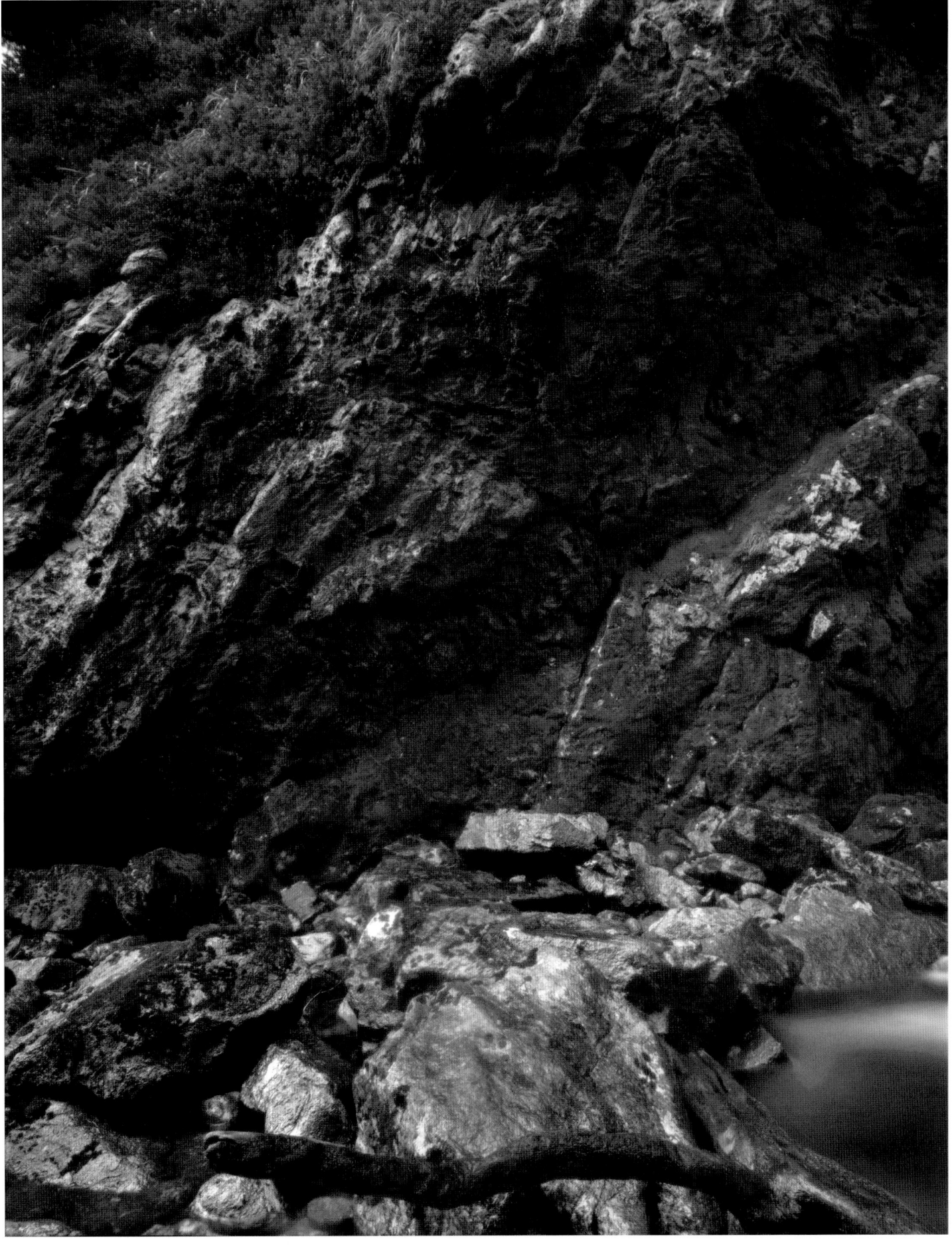

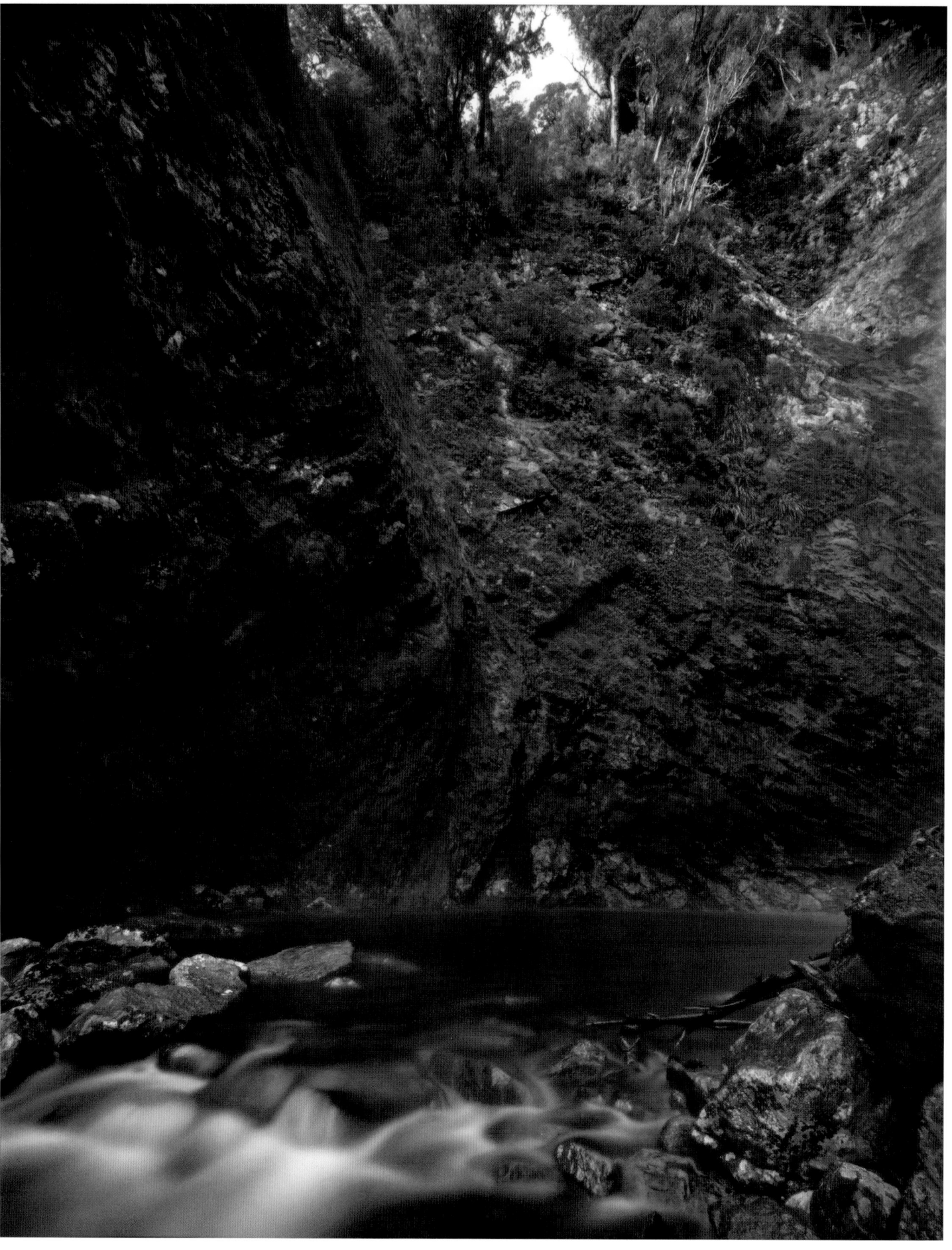

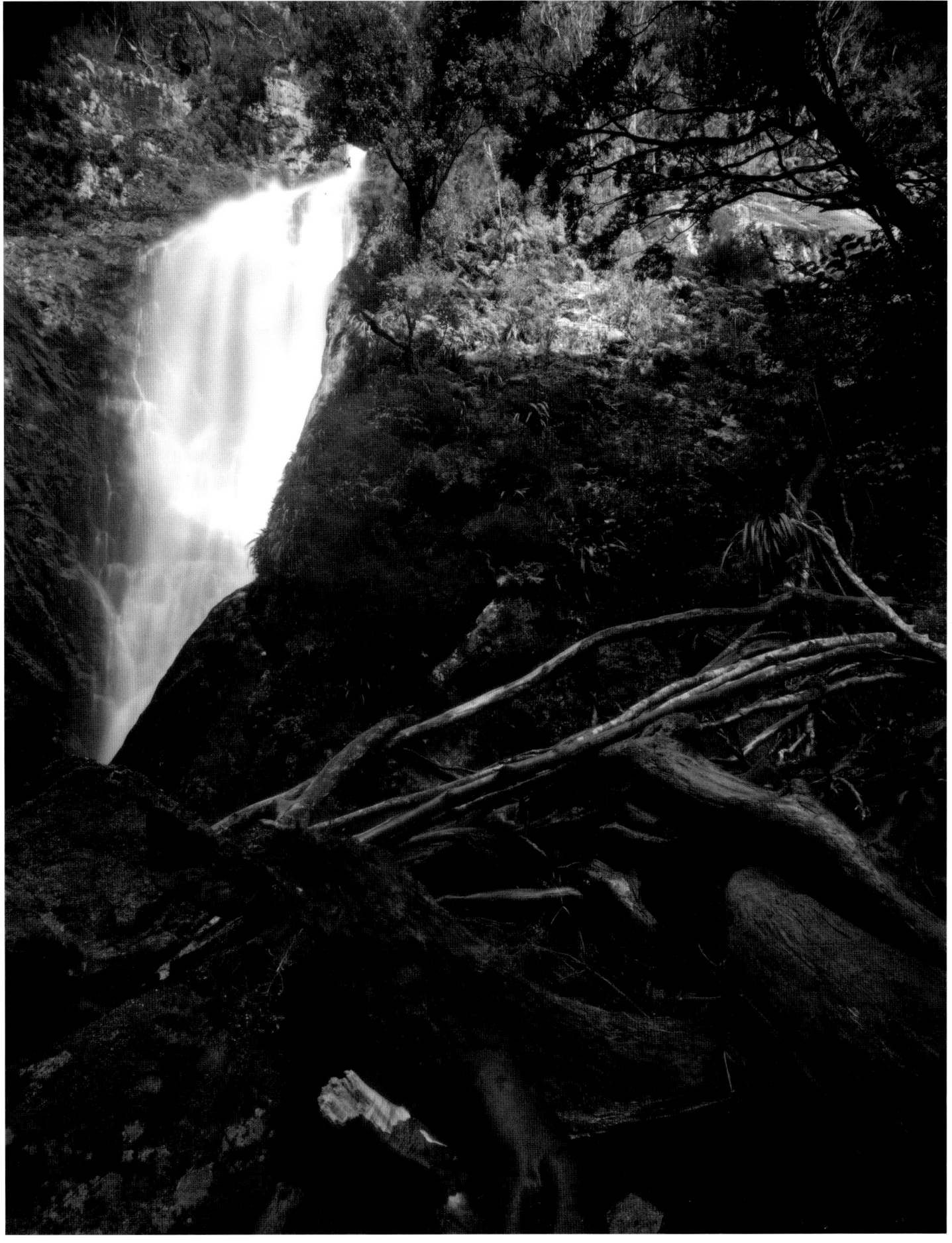

4. The Cave

So far as I know, this is an unnamed, but no doubt once-named, place. It is not a 'scenic' place, not in any usual sense: a broken rock wall hovers over you; there is not much to see in or through a scatter of saplings; there is no view, either of the waters of the sound or the uplands. Yet the loam and the gravel find irregular, intimate channels across the flat ground before the bluff; this is a floodplain in miniature, a place on a human scale. You know that you're walking because the sand and stone collapse and crunch under your feet. It's quiet. You're barely aware of a breeze, but for the gentle oscillation of the ferns.

This is also a space of death, and a sacred place. It's a site from which something has been removed, and something added.

~

In their book *Dusky Bay*, the Beggs were not content to leave the man and his kin, encountered on 'Indian Island' and subsequently back at Pickersgill Harbour, unnamed. They identify him positively as 'Maru', who is mentioned in oral histories collected in the early twentieth century. Although Maru is indeed described as a prominent figure of the period, this claim is so speculative as to be wholly spurious. There was a great deal of movement in the area, considerable uncertainty as to when Maru, and for that matter other named individuals, were living there, and no good reasons for linking these people particularly with those encountered by Cook. Yet this identification, and the story woven around it, has stuck. For some years, Hodges' round *View in Dusky Bay*, in the Auckland Art Gallery, was captioned with the statement that 'This work depicts Maru, the leader of Maori family Cook's men encountered in Dusky Sound. Hodges had no realisation that their visit led to the murder of Maru at the hands of rival Maori.'

The Beggs begin their chapter on the 'family of Dusky Bay' with the announcement that 'The Maoris who were described by the explorers in 1773 were a doomed people.'[11] They proceed to relate that an amateur archaeologist had found human remains in the cave in 1957; the Beggs followed up these investigations and removed more than forty bones, from four individuals. Though most of these bones had been lodged in a high cranny, which is not inconsistent with Polynesian modes of disposing of the dead, they believed that the group had been the victims of a violent assault. An adult male had apparently been killed and eaten (his bones were 'methodically' broken, and two teeth had been fired); the absence of thigh bones was suspicious.

The 'important and exciting discovery' of some oxidised iron at the back of the cave suggested that these people had possessed one of Cook's axes, that they were indeed members of Maru's family, and Maru himself was probably the adult victim. The Beggs propose that another group of hostile Maori were shadowing Maru and his family, who retreated but were nevertheless hunted down and killed, probably for their iron and for Cook's gifts, which had made them 'the richest natives in New Zealand'.

It is indeed possible that the 'family of Dusky Bay' quit the scene because they feared those other Maori, probably Ngai Tahu, who were certainly in the area at the time, and who were more numerous. But it is not clear that these others were their enemies rather than their allies; nor is it clear that those whose bones were found in the cave were at all connected with any group alive at the time of Cook's visit (the iron may have been obtained from one of the many other groups of Europeans who subsequently visited the sound for sealing and other purposes); nor can we really know if or why the one man there, whose bones had apparently been broken, was the victim of a cannibalistic assault. What is most striking, and most fertile, in the Beggs' speculation is not, however, its fanciful character, but its moral burden.

These people were 'doomed'; 'Through Forster's methodical records we can faintly hear the voice of a dying people.'[12] The Beggs' story is a textbook exemplification of a fatal impact narrative, that postulates that Indigenous peoples vanish in the aftermath of European arrival, yet neatly exempts Europeans from any responsibility for their tragic passing. The 'family of Dusky Bay' were fated, it seems, simply because they had accepted Cook's gifts, which could only engender agonistic jealousy and violence on the part of other Maori; the very generosity of the Europeans, their deployment of gifts to foster friendly exchange, is perversely transformed into a death sentence that is swiftly carried out. The people died not as a result of colonialism, of struggles over land and sovereignty, nor even as the result of disease or guns introduced by early visitors, but simply as the by-product of the most ephemeral of contacts that nevertheless somehow propel a martial society to self-destruction. Maori had fought and killed each other before, and there is evidence for no more than one man's killing here; yet this is seized on as something unprecedented, something that must have a significance more awful than that of any previous act of Maori revenge; it is a fateful moment that marks the end of the tribe, the end of the Maori population of this part of southern New Zealand. The Beggs go further, relating the story of an old Ngatimamoe woman who allegedly lived alone on Five Fingers Peninsula, and who was killed and consumed by a marauding Ngai Tahu in approximately the 1820s. Noting that the daughter would have been about seventy at this time, the Beggs ask whether it would be 'too fanciful to think of her as the last surviving member of Maru's family?'[13] There is a simple answer to this question, which is: yes.

For these historians, however, the woman's death closes the chapter: 'the secrets of her life and her family were locked away in the silent cliffs and chasms of her homeland'.[14] This ending of a genealogy neatly also forecloses all the puzzles concerning the constitution of the Dusky Sound family itself. A set of relationships among a pretty small group of people had perplexed Cook, the Forsters, Hodges, and several engravers. The woman 'who we afterwards discovered was not his daughter', whose independent spirit confounded European expectations of Maori behaviour, is redescribed as a daughter, in order that she might play a fairly hackneyed part, that of being the last of her family and race.

~

Around the cave, the air moves gently; hence the blurring of the palm fronds in the long exposures of a dim afternoon. This may be less a breeze than a breath; despite the depopulation of Tamatea, we might entertain the idea that the site remains a Maori place, a place with a living history.

But it is palpably also a site that has had violence done to it. What has taken place here is less like scientific excavation than grave-robbing; the deposit has been gutted. Ash, food, and bone that attested to occasional meals here, and to the warmth of a fire on an afternoon as dim and chilly as this, have been dug out, creating a curious void among stones that were once plainly embedded in the burnt vestiges of human activity. Though there are still traces of smoke on the rocks, what the site now contains is not dirt and archaeological evidence, but the evidence that a pseudo-archaeology has done its dirty work.

The material that connected this place with history has been taken away, but something has also been left behind: a gratuitous history that stands between us and the past, that obscures the real confusions that Cook and Forster, for all their faults, were at pains to exhibit. This combination of subtraction and addition seems, too often, to mark the operations of history-making upon the past. Yet the ferns and bracken breathe; all cannot be lost.

12 (a,b,c)
Cascade Cove, Tauwhare, rock shelter and midden, 14 May 1995

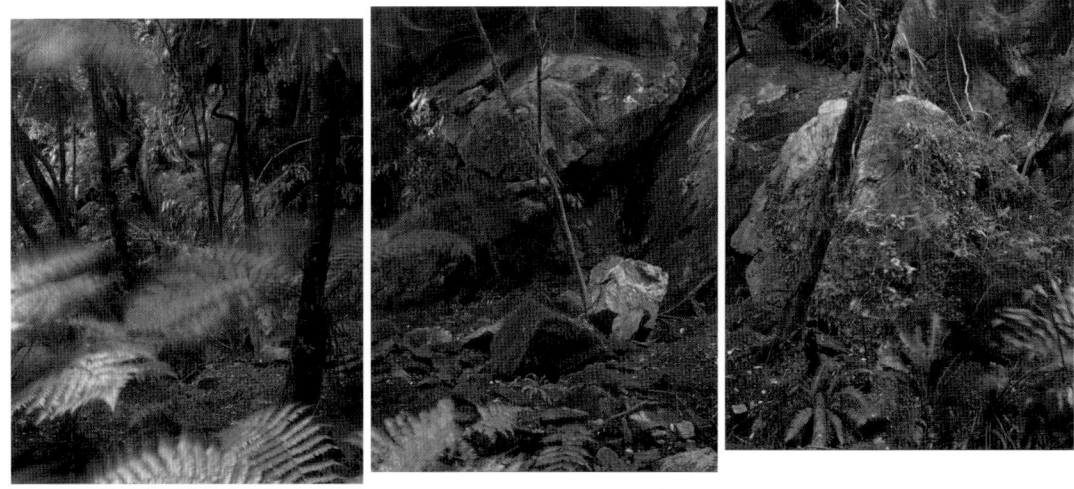

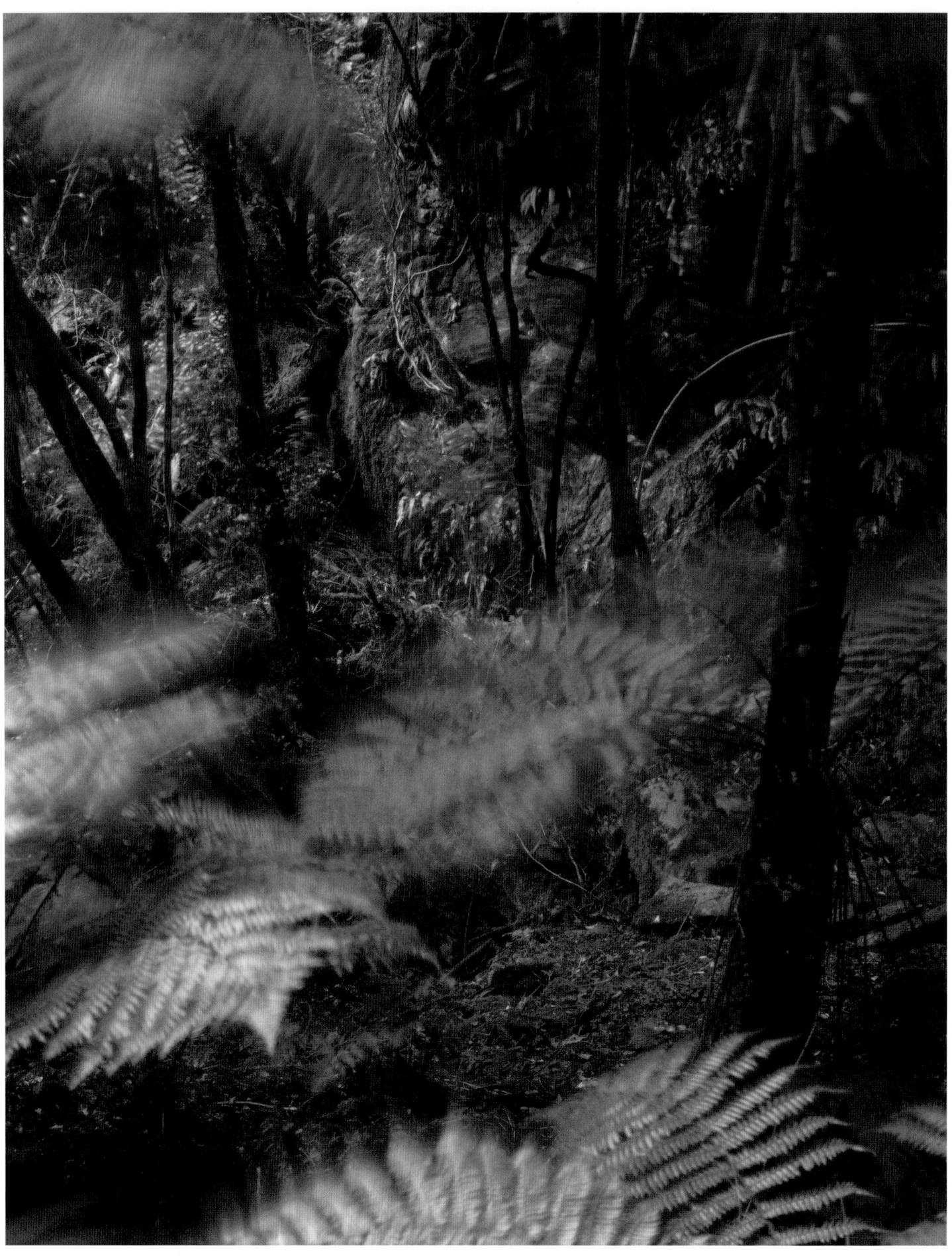

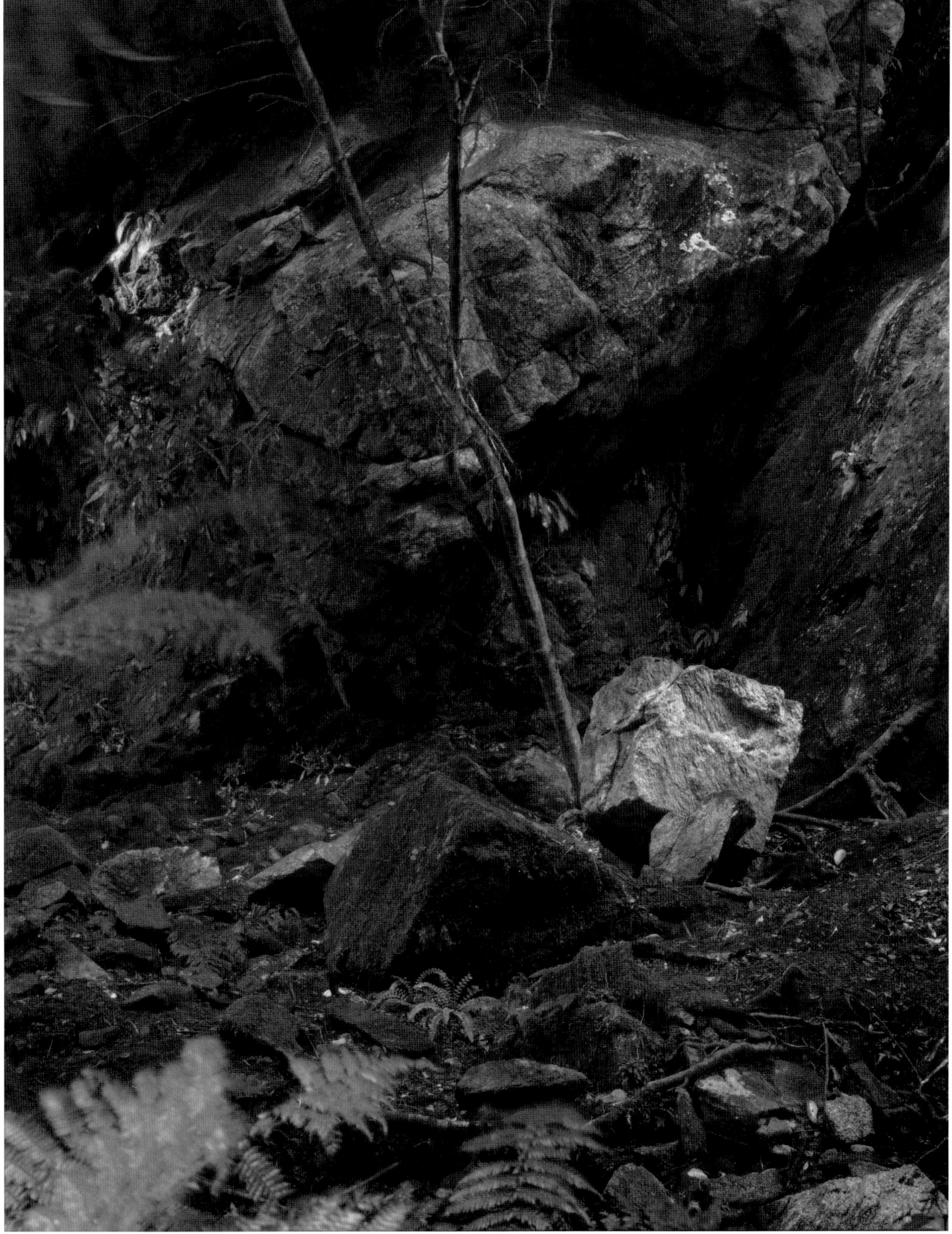

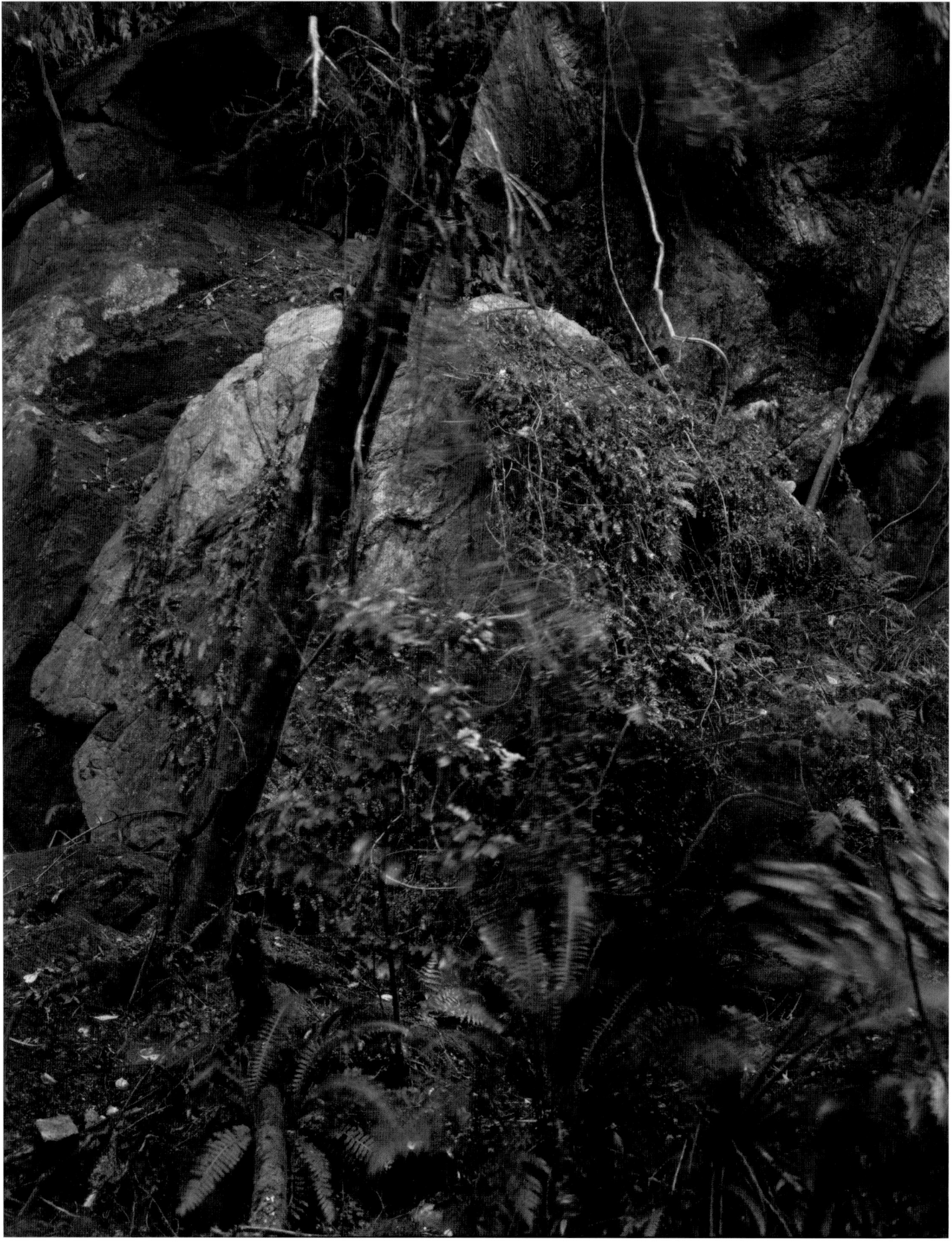

13 (a,b)
Cascade Cove, Tauwhare, rock shelter and excavated midden,
24 May 1995

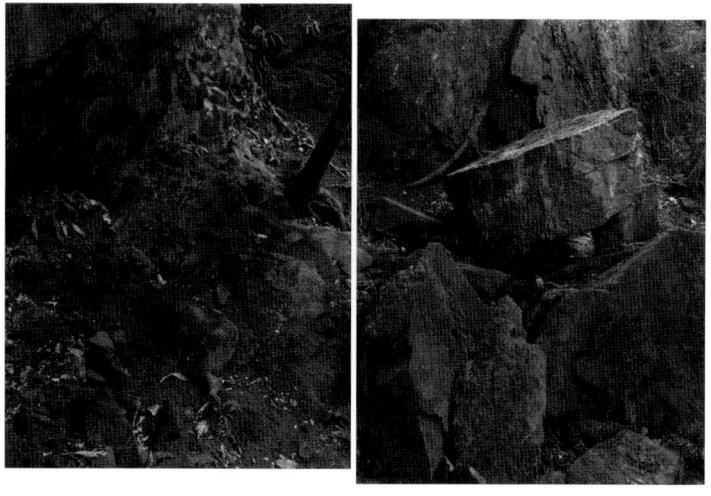

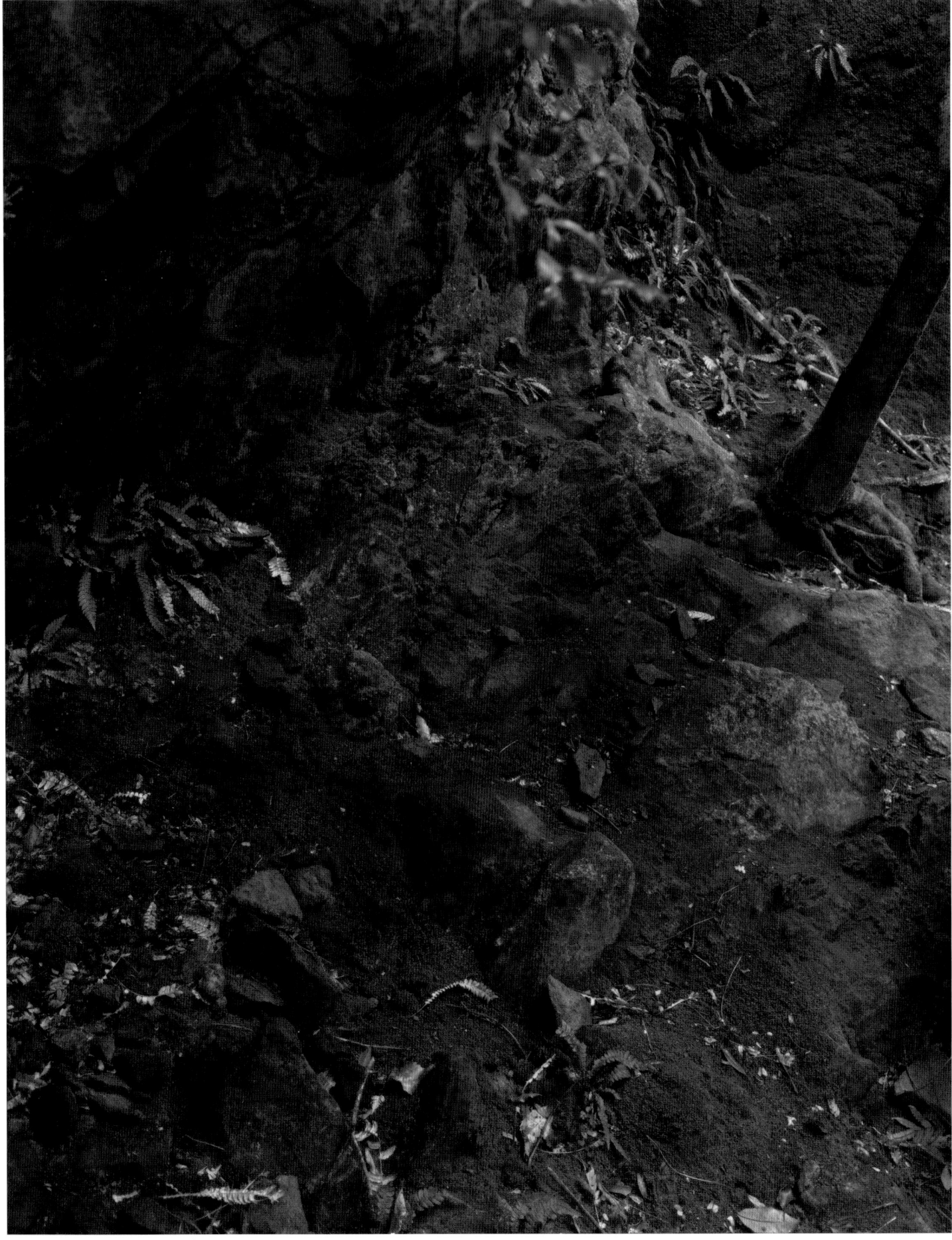

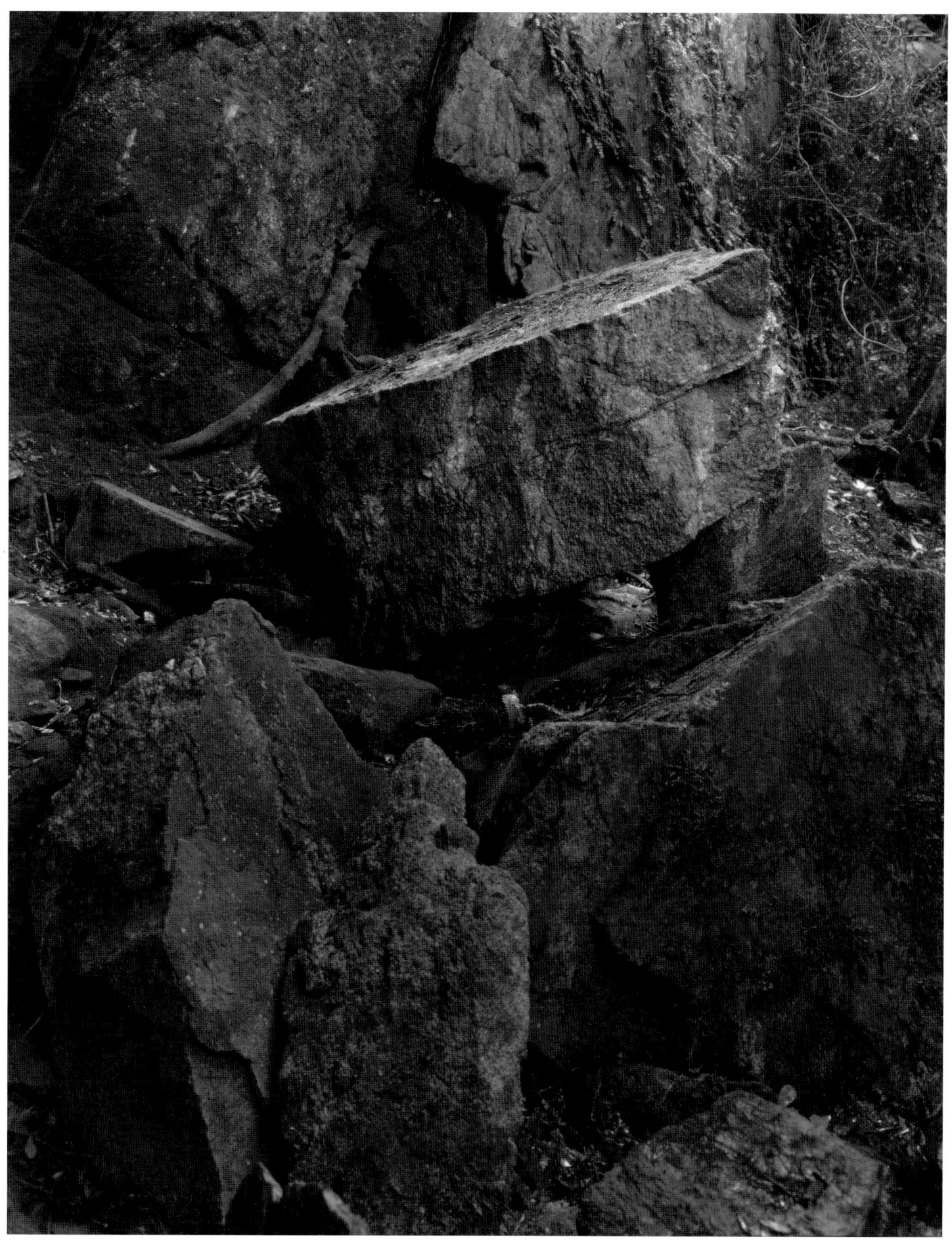

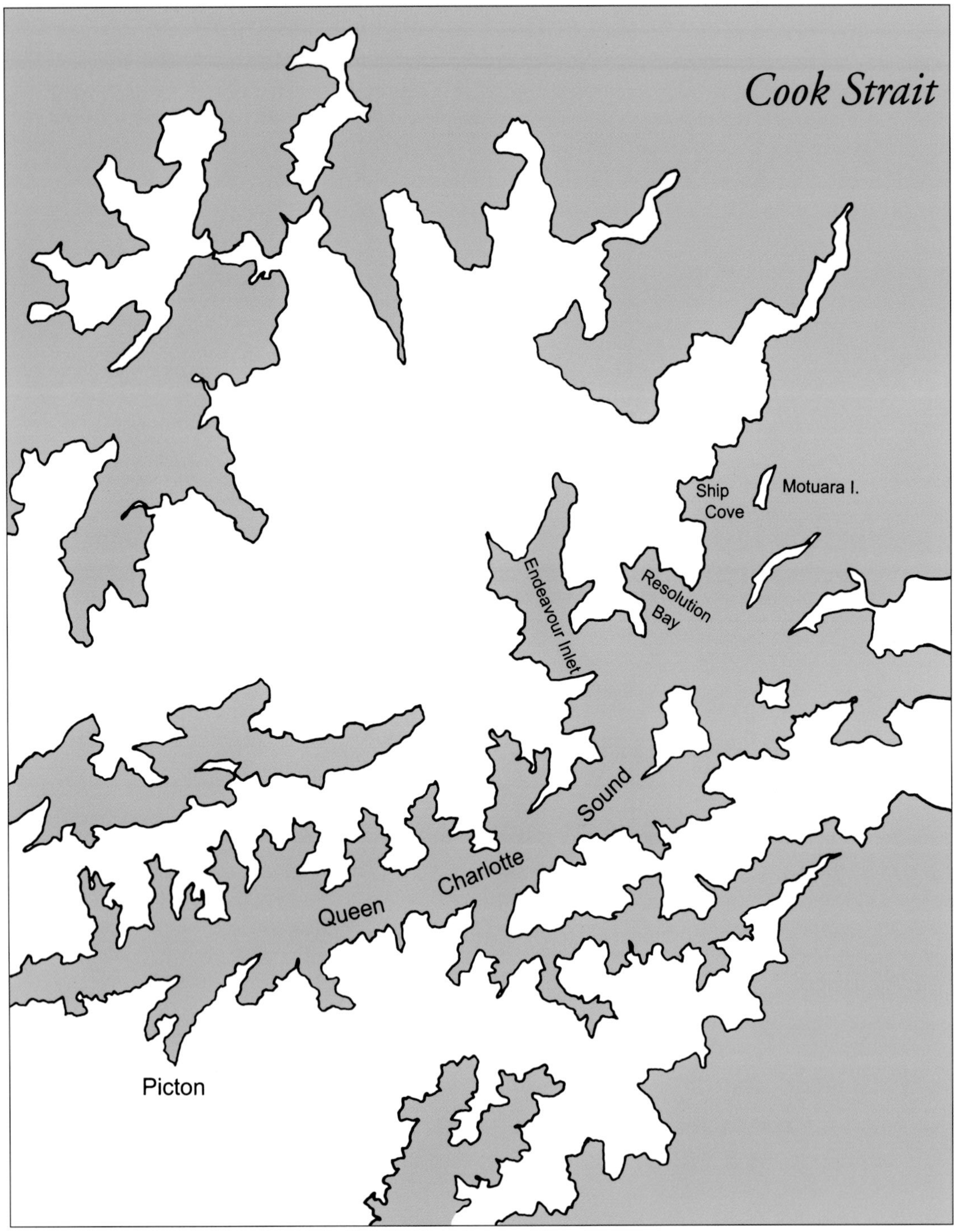

Cook Strait

Ship
Cove

Motuara I.

Resolution
Bay

Endeavour Inlet

Sound

Charlotte

Queen

Picton

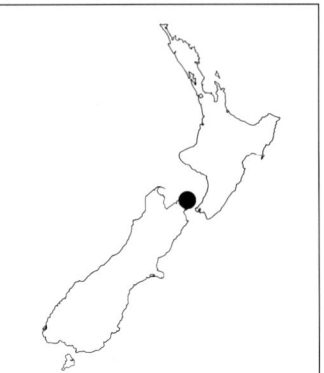

Queen Charlotte Sound, showing Ship Cove.

5. Ship Cove and Grass Cove

The weather can change dramatically in Queen Charlotte Sound; I remember waterspouts and abrupt gusts of wind and rain, but I think most of all of the sunshine and an expansive blue sky. The environment has been preserved here, but the place is not what it was: in 1995 it is now all sun and recreation. Around the Picton ferry terminus, all kinds of tours are advertised; there are pubs and postcards, and the fish – local groper – and chips are good. The newsagent's window gives equal space to true romances and *The New Zealand Pig Shooter*, the graphic covers of which are better imagined than described.

Cook's sites are not here but north, toward the mouth of the sound, in Cook Strait. About a dozen people are crammed with a lot of gear into a water taxi; some are hikers, others are heading for their holiday shacks. The launch is no speedboat, but nevertheless moves briskly enough across the flat sound. Two or three blokes, not residents but regulars, break open their beer, tell us about the fishing, and about how to deal with the catch: 'The groper, you know the groper, wants to be done on the skillet.'

There are houses and guest houses in the bays, but not many. Beyond the scattered cottages are the scrubby hills and forested gullies. The islets and islands of the sound are barren and generally undeveloped. The tourist and backpacker lodges all have names like Endeavour Lodge and Resolution Cabins. These historical references are hard to associate with the business of being there. The sunlight, the salty splash, the blue water, the beer are sensual, outdoor, antipodean; this is the pure presence of hedonistic activity. This hedonism has a history; recreations have histories, I know; but when you or I do things like fishing for fun, history is something that we have no use for.

⌒

Yet there is a kind of extravagant wildness in the history of contacts between Europeans and Maori in this area. However accustomed mariners and travellers were to extreme and dangerous situations, there were moments of sudden violence here, which left them speechless, which left them able only to itemise things without describing them, which robbed trained observers of their capacity to evoke scenes and situations. But there was much beside violence that was remarkable in the disorderly traffic of services and commodities. During Cook's first visit to this area, in the *Endeavour* over late 1769 and early 1770, Joseph Banks reported claims about native sexualities:

> One of our gentlemen came home to day abusing the natives most heartily whom he said he had found to be given to the detestable Vice of Sodomy. He, he said, had been with a family of Indians and paid a price for leave to make his addresses to any one young woman they should pitch up for him; one was chose as he thought who willingly retird with him but on examination proved to be a boy; that on his returning and complaining of this another was sent who turnd out to be a boy likewise; that on his second complaint he could get no redress but was laught at by the Indians.
>
> Joseph Banks, *Journal*, I, p. 461

Almost the whole history of travel writing consists of people doing this – that is, responding to a peculiar circumstance, or some aspect of their own muddled interaction with a people, by drawing a conclusion about local custom or standard temperament. And this was already, in the late eighteenth century, a notorious feature of the genre. Those travellers who offered the baldest of authoritative generalisations on the basis of the most patently singular situations were conventionally censured by other writers, no doubt concerned to distinguish their own methods and integrity. 'One of his fellow-travellers reports this story of him, that at an inn on their route, the landlady was a coarse red-haired woman, and a great scold. – Dr. Smollett immediately set down in his pocket-book, "All the women in this town are red-haired, and insufferable shrews."'[15] If, however, in the anonymous gentleman's anthropology, the Maori were forever a race of sodomites, Banks was not fully convinced:

> Far be it from me to attempt saying that that Vice is not practisd here, this however I must say that in my humble opinion this story proves no more than that our gentleman was fairly trickd out of his cloth, which none of the young ladies chose to accept of on his terms, and the master of the family did not chuse to part with.
>
> Joseph Banks, *Journal*, I, p. 461

The notion of 'fair trickery' is a nice one, and one apt to much exchange across the beach – not least because it suggests an opposed modality, that of 'unfair honesty'. Between one term and the other, traffic in this liminal zone proceeded.

⁓

Ship Cove is, of course, Cook's name. It is one of those empirical names like Cloudy Bay or Doubtful Sound that were applied judiciously to places, not just by any Cook, but most of all by the pragmatic Cook, presented and vindicated by the authoritative editor of Cook's journals, J.C. Beaglehole, also the author of the longest and most authoritative biography of Cook. Other Cooks were imperial servants, and named islands after royalty and naval men like the corrupt and profligate Earl of Sandwich. A different Cook again could acknowledge that places were already named. He, for example, inscribed 'Te Wai Pounamu' along the length of what we now call the South Island of New Zealand. Among the irregularities around the north-eastern end of that island is Totaranui, the body of water that is also called Queen Charlotte Sound; Meretoto, or Ship Cove, is situated on that sound's western shore. This is the place that Cook visited five times over the course of his three voyages.

⁓

This is, in a way, surprising. Certainly, provisions were to be had in New Zealand, but the Dusky Sound encounter was exceptional for its pacific character. Elsewhere, 'insolence' was frequently encountered; the Europeans were pelted with stones on more occasions than I imagine they cared to recall, and in several cases reciprocity took a negative turn, and Maori were unjustly killed. As Banks wrote, after four Maori were shot in Poverty Bay in October 1769, 'Thus ended the most disagreable day My life has yet seen, black be the mark for it and heaven send that such may never return to embitter future reflection.'[16] In his private journal, Banks did not consider whether the inevitability of cross-cultural misunderstanding, and hence such violence as took place in Poverty Bay, impinged upon the morality of voyaging and indeed upon the question of whether voyages should be conducted at all. John Hawkesworth, however, did reflect on precisely this problem in the introduction to his official publication of Cook's first voyage. If his book was contentious for many reasons, one of the underlying problems must have been that it so explicitly acknowledged the injustice of firing upon islanders, while proceeding to legitimise voyaging through sophistry that may or may not have fully convinced the author himself, let alone his readers.

> I cannot however dismiss my Readers to the following narratives, without expressing the regret with which I have recorded the destruction of poor naked savages, by our fire-arms, in the course of these expeditions, when they endeavoured to repress the invaders of their country; a regret which I am confident my Readers will participate with me; this however appears to be an evil which, if discoveries of new countries are attempted, cannot be avoided: resistance will always be made, and, if those who resist are not overpowered, the attempt must be relinquished. It may perhaps be said, that the expence of life upon these occasions is more than is necessary to convince the natives, that further contest is hopeless, and perhaps this may sometimes have been true: but it must be considered, that if such expeditions are undertaken, the execution of them must be intrusted to persons not exempt from human frailty; to men who are liable to provocation by sudden injury, to unpremeditated violence by sudden danger, to error by the defect of judgment or the strength of passion, and always disposed to transfer laws, by which they are bound themselves, to others who are not subject to their obligation; so that every excess thus produced is also an inevitable evil.
>
> If it should be said, that supposing these mischiefs to be inevitable in attempting discoveries, discoveries ought not to be attempted; it must be considered, that upon the only principles on which this opinion can be supported, the risk of life, for the advantages of the same kind with those proposed in discovering new countries, is in every other instance unlawful. If it is not lawful to put the life of an Indian in hazard, by an attempt to examine the country in which he lives, with a view to increase commerce or knowledge; it is not lawful to risk the life of our own people in carrying on commerce with countries already known. If it be said that the risk of life in our own people is voluntary, and that the Indian is brought into danger without his consent, the consequence will still follow; for it is universally agreed, at least upon the principles of Christianity, that men have no more right over their own lives than over the lives of others, and suicide being deemed the worst species of murder, a man must be proportionably criminal in exposing his own life, for any purpose that would justify his exposing the life of another. If the gratification of artificial wants, or the increase of knowledge, are justifiable causes for the risk of life, the landing by force on a newly discovered country, in order to examine its produce, may be justified; if not, every trade and profession that exposes life for advantages of the same kind is unlawful; and by what trade or profession is not life exposed?
>
> John Hawkesworth, *An Account of the Voyages Undertaken ... for Making Discoveries in the Southern Hemisphere*, 1773, I, p. xix–xxi

If Cook and his crews were in uncharted waters in a strictly navigational sense, they were also surely at sea among such unresolved questions as these; and nowhere were the issues as confronting as in New Zealand, and in Totaranui in particular. Cook himself was later to write, in June 1773, 'we debauch their Morals already too prone to vice and we interduce among them wants and perhaps diseases which they never before knew and which serves only to disturb that happy tranquillity they and their fore Fathers had injoy'd. If any one denies the truth of this assertion let him tell me what the Natives of the whole extent of America have gained by the commerce they have had with Europeans.'[17]

~

Meretoto and Totaranui were, for the British, spaces of revelation, and particularly the spectacular demonstration that cannibalism was not an obscure fiction but a real practice. Confirmation that Maori did in fact consume the bodies of slain enemies came in stages, with circumstantial evidence and oral corroboration on the first voyage and eyewitnessing on the second.

> The family were employd when we came ashore in dressing their provisions, which were a dog who was at that time buried in their oven and near it were many provision baskets. Looking carelessly upon one of these we by accident observed 2 bones, pretty clean pickd, which as apeard upon examination were undoubtedly human bones. Tho we had from the first of our arrival upon the coast constantly heard the Indians acknowledge the custom of eating their enemies we had never before had a proof of it, but this amounted almost to demonstration : the bones were clearly human, upon them were evident marks of their having been dressd on the fire, the meat was not intirely pickd off from them and on the grisly ends which were gnawd were evident marks of teeth, and these were accidentaly found in a provision basket. On asking the people what bones are these? they answerd, The bones of a man. – And have you eat the flesh? – Yes. – Have you none of it left? – No. – Why did not you eat the woman who we saw today in the water? – She was our relation. – Who then is it that you do eat? – Those who are killd in war. – And who was the man whose bones these are? – 5 days ago a boat of our enemies came into this bay and of them we killd 7, of whoom the owner of these bones was one. – The horrour that apeard in the countenances of the seaman on hearing this discourse which was immediately translated for the good of the company is better conceivd than describd. For ourselves and myself in particular we were before too well convincd of the existence of such a custom to be surprizd, tho we were pleasd at having so strong a proof of a custom which human nature holds in too great abhorrence to give easy credit to.
>
> Joseph Banks, *Journal*, I, p. 455

> Some of the officers went on shore to amuse themselves among the Natives where they saw the head and bowels of a youth who had lately been killed, the heart was stuck upon a forked stick and fixed to the head of their largest Canoe, the gentleman brought the head on board with them, I was on shore at this time but soon after returned on board when I was informed of the above circumstances and found the quarter deck crowded with the Natives. I now saw the mangled head or rather the remains of it for the under jaw, lip &c[a] were wanting, the scul was broke on the left side just above the temple, the face had all the appearence of a youth about fourteen or fifteen, a peice of the flesh had been broiled and eat by one of the Natives in the presince of most of the officers. The sight of the head and the relation of the circumstances just mentioned struck me with horor and filled my mind with indignation against these Canibals, but when I considered that any resentment

I could shew would avail but little and being desireous of being an eye witness to a fact which many people had their doubts about, I concealed my indignation and ordered a piece of the flesh to be broiled and brought on the quarter deck where one of these Canibals eat it with a seeming good relish before the whole ships Company which had such effect on some of them as to cause them to vomit. [Oediddee] was [so] struck with horor at the sight that [he] wept and scolded by turns, before this happened he was very intimate with these people but now he neither would come near them or suffer them to touch him, told them to their faces that they were vile men and that he was no longer their friend, he used the same language to one of the officers who cut of the flesh and refused to except, or even touch the knife with which it was cut, such was this Islanders aversion to this vile custom.

Cook, *Journals*, II, p. 292–3

These incidents can be seen as origin-points for some of the most shocking and dangerous dynamics of cross-cultural history. On the one hand, Banks's matter-of-fact interest in the head inaugurated the pseudo-scientific traffic in human remains in Australasia and the Pacific that has since been regarded by Indigenous peoples, among others, as perhaps the worst of the outrages inflicted by the colonial powers upon the cultures of the region. On the other, the theatricality of the performance of cannibalism, the degree to which Maori seem to have grasped the Europeans' preoccupation with, and horror of, the practice, and responded with staged savagery – all this marks the extent to which the terms and values of culture might swiftly change, from the moment of their mutual entanglement on the beach. Practices stereotyped and anathematised by Europeans might be stereotyped in a new way and staged by Maori themselves. The British who became the victims of the Grass Cove massacre were 'asking for it', and not only because, as Cook understood, the injudicious behaviour of the boat's crew from the *Adventure* provoked the events. In a discursive sense, too, their very fear, anger, and contempt of cannibals, their constant enquiry, their horror at the performance that they had commissioned – all this drew attention to cannibalism, and even elicited and invited it:

Saturday December 18th 1773. This morning, I was orderd in the Launch (she being well man'd & armd) to go in quest of the Cutter. My instructions were first to look well into West Bay & then proceed to Grass Cove (the place where Mr Rowe was order'd) & if I heard nothing of the Boat there to go further up the Sound & and come down along the West Shore. As Mr Rowe had left the ship an hour earlier than the time proposed, & in a great hurry, I was strongly perswaded his Curiosity had carried him into East Bay, none in our Ship having ever been there before, or else Some accident has happen'd to the Boat; either gone adrift through the Boatkeepers Negligence, or been stove among the Rocks—this was almost every body's opinion, & on this Suposition the Carpenters Mate was sent with me with some sheets of Tin. I had not the least suspicion of their having receivd any injury from the Natives, our boats having frequently been higher up & worse provided. About 10 we left the Ship—having a light breeze in our favour we soon got round Long Island & within Long Point. I rounded every Cove on the Larboard Hand as we went along, looking well all round with a Spy Glass which I took for that purpose—at + past 1 We Stoppd at a beach on the left hand side going up East Bay, to boil some Victuals, as we brought nothing with us but raw meat—while we were cooking I saw an Indian on the Opposite Shore running along a beach up towards the head of the Bay. Our Victuals being drest, we got it in the boat & put off—& in a short time got to the head of this Reach where we saw an Indian Settlement—as we drew near Some of the Indians came down on the Rocks & waved for us to begone, but seeing we disregarded them, they alterd their Notes—here we found 6 large Canoes hauld up on the Beach—most of them double ones—a great many people but not so many as one might expect from the Number of houses & Size of the Canoes. leaving the Boats Crew to guard the Boat, I stept on shore with the Marines (the Corporal & 5 men) & searchd a good many of their houses, but found nothing to give me any Suspicion—3 or 4 well beaten paths led further into the Woods, where were many more houses—but the people continuing very friendly I thought it unnecessary to continue our search—coming down to the Boat, one of the Indians had brought a bundle of Hepatoos (long spears) down to the beach—but seeing I lookd very earnestly at him, he put them on the ground & walkd about with seeming unconcern. Some of the people appearing to be frightend I gave a Looking Glass to one & a large Nail to another—from this place the Bay ran as nearly as I could guess NNW a good mile where it Ended in a long sandy beach—I lookd all round with the glass but saw no boat, Canoe of Sign of Inhabitants—I therefore contended myself with firing some Guns which I did in every Cove as I went along. I now kept close to the East Shore & came to another Settlement where the Indians invited us ashore. I enquired of them about the Boat, to which they pretended ignorance—they appeard very friendly here & sold us some fish—within an hour after we left this place, in a small beach adjoining to Grass Cove we saw a very large double canoe just hauld up, with 2 men & a Dog—the men on seeing us left their Canoe & ran up into the woods—this gave me reason to Suspect I should here get some tidings of our Cutter—we went shore & Searchd the Canoe where we found one of the Rullock ports of the Cutter & some shoes one of which was known to belong to Mr Woodhouse, one of our Midshipmen, who went with Mr Rowe—one of the people at the same time brought me a piece of meat, which he took to be some of the Salt Meat belonging to the Cutter's crew—on examining this & smelling to it I found it was fresh meat—Mr Fannin, (the Master) who was with me, supos'd it was Dog's flesh & I was of the same opinion, for I still doubted their being Cannibals: but we were Soon convinced by most horrid & undeniable proofs—a great many baskets (about 20) laying on the beach tied up, we cut them open, some were full of roasted flesh & some fern root which serves then for bread—on further search we found more shoes & a hand which we immediately knew to have belong'd to Thos Hill one of Forecastlemen, it being markd T.H. which he had got done at Otaheite with a tattow instrument—I went with some of the people a little way up the woods, but saw nothing else—coming down again was a round spot cover'd with fresh earth, about 4 feet diameter, where Something had been buried: having no spade we began to dig with a Cutlass—in the mean time I launchd the Canoe with a intention to destroy her—but seeing a great smoke ascending over the nearest hill, I got all the people in the boat & made what haste I could to be with them before Sunsett—on opening the next bay, which was Grass Cove, we saw 4 Canoes—a Single, & 3 double ones—a great many People on the beach—a large fire was on the top of the High Land beyond the woods, from whence all the way down the Hill the place was throngd like a Fair—those who were near the Shore had retreated to a small hill within a Ships length of the Water side, where they stood talking to us—as we came in I order'd a Musquetoon to be fired through one of the Canoes, as we suspected they might be full of men laying down in the bottom, but nobody was in them—the Savages on the little hill still kept hollowing & making Signs for us to come ashore—however as soon as we had got close in we all fired—the first Volley did not seem to affect them much—but on the 2^d they began to scramble away as fast as they could, some of them howling—we continued firing as long as we could see the least glimpse of a man through the bushes—amongst the Indians were 2 very stout men who never offer'd to move till they found themselves forsaken by their companions & then they walkd away with great composure & deliberation—their pride not Suffering them to run—one of them however stumbled, & just made Shift to crawl off on all fours—the other got clear without any apparent hurt—I then landed with the Marines & left Mr Fannin to guard the boat—on the beach were 2 bundles of Cellery which had been gather'd for loading the Cutter—a plain proof the attack was made here—a broken piece of an Oar was stuck upright in the Ground to which they had tied Canoes—I then searchd all along at the back of the beach to see if the Cutter was there—we found no boat—but instead of her—Such a shocking scene of Carnage & Barbarity as can never mentiond or thought of, but with horror.—whilst we remained almost stupified on this spot Mr Fannin call'd to us that he heard the Savages gathering together in the Valley, on which I returned to the Boat & hauld alongside the Canoes, 3 of which we demolished—whilst this was transacting, the fire on the top of the High Land disappeard & the Indians had gatherd together in the wood, where we heard them at very high words, doubtless quarelling whether or no they should come to attack us & try to save their Canoes—it now grew dark. I therefore just stept our & lookd once more along the back of the beach to see if the Cutter had been hauld up in the bushes—but seeing nothing of her returned & put off—our whole force would have been but barely sufficient to have gone up the Hill, & to have ventured with half (for one half must have been left to guard the Boat) would have been madness—As we open'd the upper part of the Sound we saw a very large fire about 3 or 4 miles higher up—this fire formd a complete Oval, reaching from the top of a hill down to the water Side—the middle space being inclosed all around by the fire, like a hedge—I consulted with Mr Fannin & we were both of Opinion that we could expect to reap no other advantage than the poor Satisfaction of killing some of the Savages—at leaving Grass Cove we had fired a general Volley towards where we heard the Indians talking—but by going in & out of the boat the Arms had got wet & some 4 of the pieces mist fire—what was still worse it began to rain—our ammunition was more than half expended & we left 6 Large Canoes behind us in one place—I therefore did not think it worth while to proceed where nothing could be hoped for but revenge.

Coming between 2 round Islands that lay to the Southward of East Bay we imagined we heard somebody calling—we lay on our Oars & listened but heard no more of it—we hollowd several times but to little purpose the poor Souls were far enough out of hearing—& indeed I think it some comfort to reflect that in all probablility every man of them must have been killd on the Spot. We got on board between 11 & 12—

The people lost in the Cutter were Mr Rowe, Mr Woodhouse, Francis Murphy Quartermaster, Wm Facey. Thos Hill. Edwd Jones, Michael Bell, Jno Cavanagh Thos Milton & James Swilley the Capt^ns Man—4 of them belong to the Forecastle & 2 to the After guard—being 10 in all—most of these were of our very best Seamen—the Stoutest & most healthy people in the Ship—We brought on board 2 Hands—one belonging to Mr Rowe, known by a hurt he had received in it the other to Thomas Hill as beforementioned, & the head of the Capt^ns Servant—these with more of the remains were tied in a Hammock & thrown overboard with ballast & Shot sufficient to sink it—we found none of their Arms or Cloaths except part of a pair of Trowsers, a Frock & 6 shoes—no 2 of them being fellows-

I am not inclined to think this was any premeditated plan of these Savages, as the morning Mr Rowe left the Ship he met 2 Canoes who came down & staid all the forenoon in Ship Cove. It might probably happen from Some quarrel, or the fairness of the Opportunity tempted them; our people being so very incautious & thinking themselves to Secure—another thing which encouraged the Zealanders was, they were sensible a Gun was not infallible. that they sometimes mist & that when

It was misty and rainy in turn. On 12 or 13 February 1777, John Webber, the official artist on Cook's third voyage, began a sketch of a group of Maori sitting about their huts just at the back of the beach at Ship Cove (p. 112). Cook appears in Webber's sketch. He has just walked up the beach from the boat and is greeting a Maori man. This is a history painting of a modest sort, something that did not but might have ended up as an engraving in the official publication from the third voyage, Cook and King's *Voyage Around the World*. The meeting is not an incident but a beginning: a sociable relationship is inaugurated between benevolent Europeans and Maori who may be unrefined, but are not savage, not in this representation. The sketch has affinities with another work, executed only a fortnight earlier, *An Interview between Captain Cook and the Natives*; in this case those encountered are a group of Aboriginal Tasmanians. Cook advances to offer a man a string of beads; the paired figures are surrounded by a crowd of witnesses.

These encounters occurred some seven months into the voyage, but only Tenerife, the Cape of Good Hope, and Kergeulen Island, the last inhabited only by penguins, were visited before Tasmania. Hence, at the end of January, and in the middle of February 1777, Webber was only beginning to depict non-European people, and explore the ways in which the voyage could be translated into art. What Webber was doing in these two works was beginning a series of compositions that were plainly moral, that insisted on the significance of the meetings between Europeans and Indigenous people, meetings that are still regarded – in conflicting ways – as foundational, by the descendants on both sides.

The Cook voyages not only made history, they made it consciously. Or rather, the artists and writers did so. But this was not always a straightforward matter of imposing the conventions of a genre. It was an effort that might falter. As, it seems, it did in this case: Webber's series was no sooner begun than abandoned. True, there are a few works from later in the voyage – some Tongan scenes for instance – that depict amiable intercourse between the British and the Polynesians. But there are no more contrived and dignified meetings; there are not even sketches for history paintings, except those connected with a different transaction altogether, when Cook's life was taken. There was to be nothing comparable to the corpus of engravings of Hodges' images of landings in Tonga, Vanuatu and elsewhere – these 'Landings' that dramatised and ennobled moments of initial contact for the person who browsed through the opulently illustrated narrative of Cook's second voyage.

More than a decade later, Webber produced another view of contact at Ship Cove. In his judgement, the composition warranted a finished oil, which was probably exhibited at the

Royal Academy; it was certainly published, both as an etching in 1790 and as an aquatint in 1808, after the artist's death (p. 107). It is striking that it images no meeting at all. Maori are on the beach, and in their canoes; Europeans too are on the beach, and in a boat in the background; they stand by their tents in what is temporarily a shared space. The patriarchal sociability of the Maori warriors and the squatting woman in the foreground possesses its own intelligibility, as does the relationship between the sailors' camp, the boat, and the ship. But these two planes do not connect (or scarcely seem to; beside the tent an officer bends over, speaking to a man whose chest is uncovered, who may be either a sailor or a Maori). What is manifest is a moment of co-presence without exchange. It is moreover striking in comparison with the Tasmanian view, and with the conventions of historical art, that the picture presents actions but no witnesses to them; there is no group that acknowledges the significance of any relationship or circumstance. There is no history, and perhaps no meaning, here.

Of course, I have no idea what Webber's thoughts were during or after the voyage. But it seems to me that he lurched from an optimistic expectation of benign commerce to a sense that European and Indigenous populations were mutually indifferent to each other, and that the warlike society of the Maori would be trenchantly sustained, without amelioration or improvement. While a few participants in these voyages inaugurated the business of regretting a fatal impact, there is no sense here of impact for either better or worse. What is lamented is the lack of influence or amelioration.

What might have changed Webber's mind was the spectre of the Grass Cove massacre. The crew of a boat from the *Adventure* had been killed and partly consumed, leaving their shipmates paralysed with horror – 'almost stupified' as James Burney put it – and incidentally providing further proof on a philosophical point: that the New Zealanders were cannibals. This occurred after the two vessels on the second voyage had been separated; hence Cook was unaware of the details and used the 1777 visit to reconstruct events. A series of conversations confirmed in his mind what he had already inferred. There had been a good deal of provocation on the sailors' side, to such an extent that it would have been inappropriate to inflict any punishment upon the Maori of Totaranui, even upon the man considered to be the chief perpetrator, who sat in Cook's cabin and rehearsed the events.

Whatever morality or logic these events possessed was not something John Webber could make much out of. Yet if this work – painted after not only the massacre but also after Cook's death – is made precisely out of the absence of such intelligibility, it is notable that unintelligibility could be a public fact, an oil painting fact, a condition published in prints rather than an incidental circumstance to be forgotten in a portfolio of field sketches.

~

There is no lack of law in Ship Cove in November 1995. The grass is mown. There are picnic tables, barbecues that uncannily resemble Sidney Nolan's famous image of Ned Kelly, and cannons which have no connection with Cook at all. Camping is not permitted. There is a new sign and an old monument. On one of the days we were there, a Maori woman, her

Pakeha husband, and their kids were among those who wandered around the absurd five-metre cement edifice erected in the 1920s. They seemed not much interested. On another occasion, a group of sea scouts performed some practical exercises and esoteric, vaguely tribal drills. I recalled that Baden-Powell had to some extent modelled scouting on Indigenous southern African bush 'lore'. I doubt that that mimicry was present in the minds of this group; whether they cast their minds back to the *tangata whenua* of Totaranui, I cannot say.

A well-signposted walking track connects the cove with Resolution Bay, Endeavour Inlet, and a number of other places. Charter boats and, as I mentioned, water taxis operate in the sound, for visitors, the few residents, and those who own holiday cottages or operate the small guesthouses that extend only as far as Resolution Bay. Beyond this, the sound is just bush, though it is hardly wilderness.

Although the Dusky Sound that we had seen was something different to the place visited by Cook, though the state and nation had marked and defined sites there, and though a handful of tourists tramped around those sites, I felt – we felt – an indefinable sense of proximity to the incidents of contact in Tamatea. We carried no fourteen-foot spears, but the plump wood pigeons were there.

Ship Cove was different. In spite of the monuments and information sheets, and the faded and water-damaged reproductions of Hodges' paintings behind glass under little shelters, it was almost impossible to imagine the dense and disorderly meetings that had taken place here, the promiscuous violence and violent promiscuity. There were also supposedly happy, if brief, liaisons; there were scuffles and incidents of petty theft; there was a good deal of fair trickery. The Forsters lamented the collusion of brutal sailors and Maori men in the coercive prostitution of Maori women, as well they might, for there can be little doubt that the disease consequent upon sexual traffic had tragic longer term ramifications. If reading the sorry longer history of colonial dispossession into these first contacts is unavoidable, disease indeed did play the part of a vanguard. Whereas, in Tamatea, a fanciful history says that the Maori were doomed by a few gifts, in Totaranui exchange really was poisoned, and really did enflame local intra-Maori hostilities.

Amidst all this, Cook tried, as he did elsewhere, to set a good example. He kept away from women, and planted cabbages and potatoes. This was not just gardening, but an endeavour to improve the country, in the interest of visiting mariners and inhabitants alike. As such, it was a doubly nostalgic civilising gesture, for the kind of progress that was founded in and signified by agriculture, land, and secure property had already been eclipsed, back in Britain, by voracious trade and urban luxury. Yet a cyclical theory of history would have been short-circuited in Ship Cove: there was nothing urban here; no opulent effeminacy, but excessive commerce already forestalled the gowth of any virtuous peasant or honest landed community. As Maori women (perhaps women slaves) were trading sex, it seems to benefit their male relatives (or captors) rather than themselves, Maori men were making war against their neighbours, in order to acquire *taonga* – weapons, ornaments, and heads – to satisfy the obsessions among Cook's common sailors and scientific gentlemen alike for curiosities.

This strange wildness is belied by the silence around the picnic tables. The gross monument speaks not of the events of the 1770s, but of the loyal citizens and the state that subscribed to it, erected it, and maintained it. It elicits a devotional attitude toward history in principle, and blocks our view of the past circumstances that elude moralising narrative now as much as then.

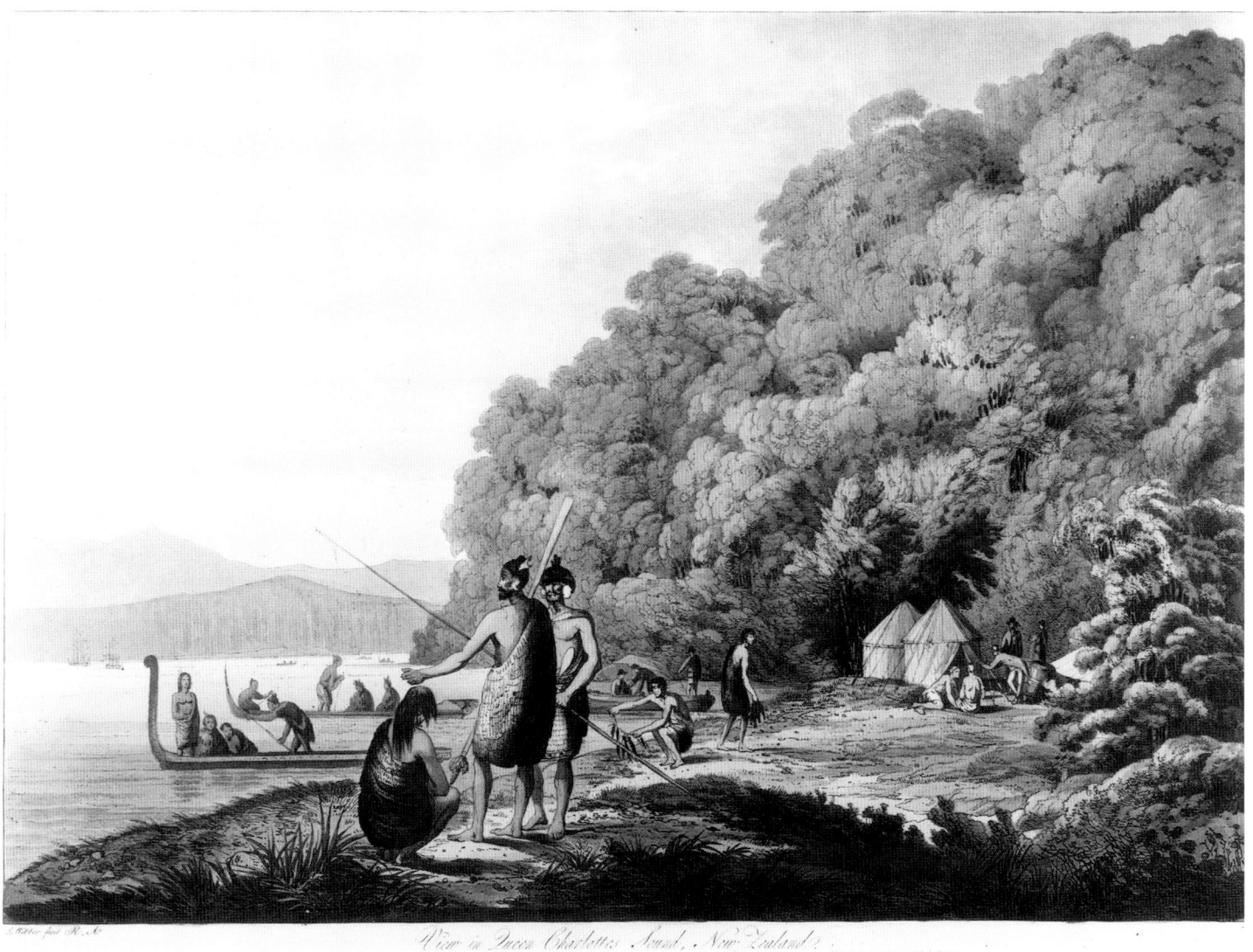

A View in Queen Charlotte Sound, New Zealand, coloured aquatint, from John Webber,
Views in the South Seas, from Drawings by the Late John Webber, Draughtsman on Board the Resolution,
published by Bodell & Co. (Cheapside 1808), plate 1. National Library of Australia, Canberra

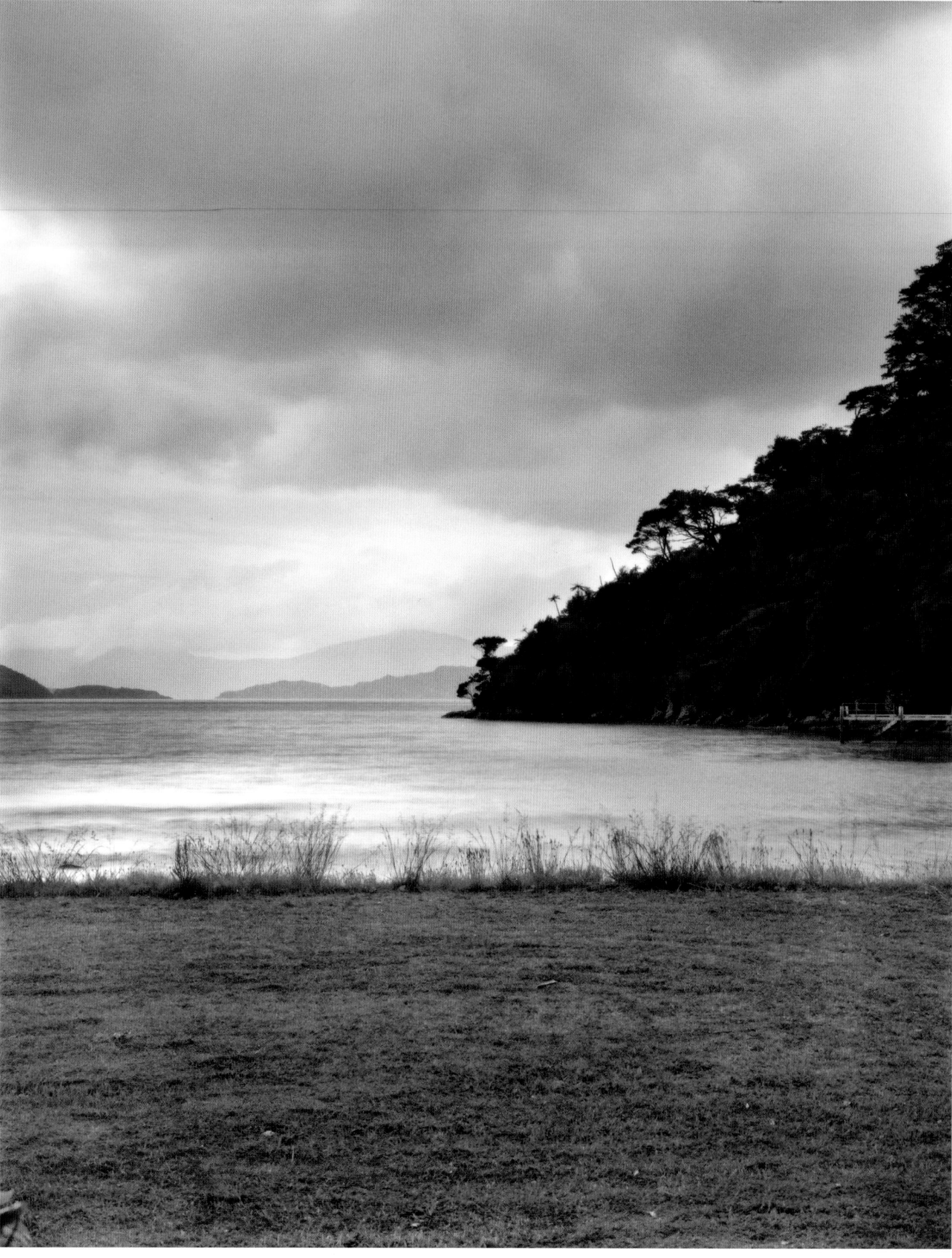

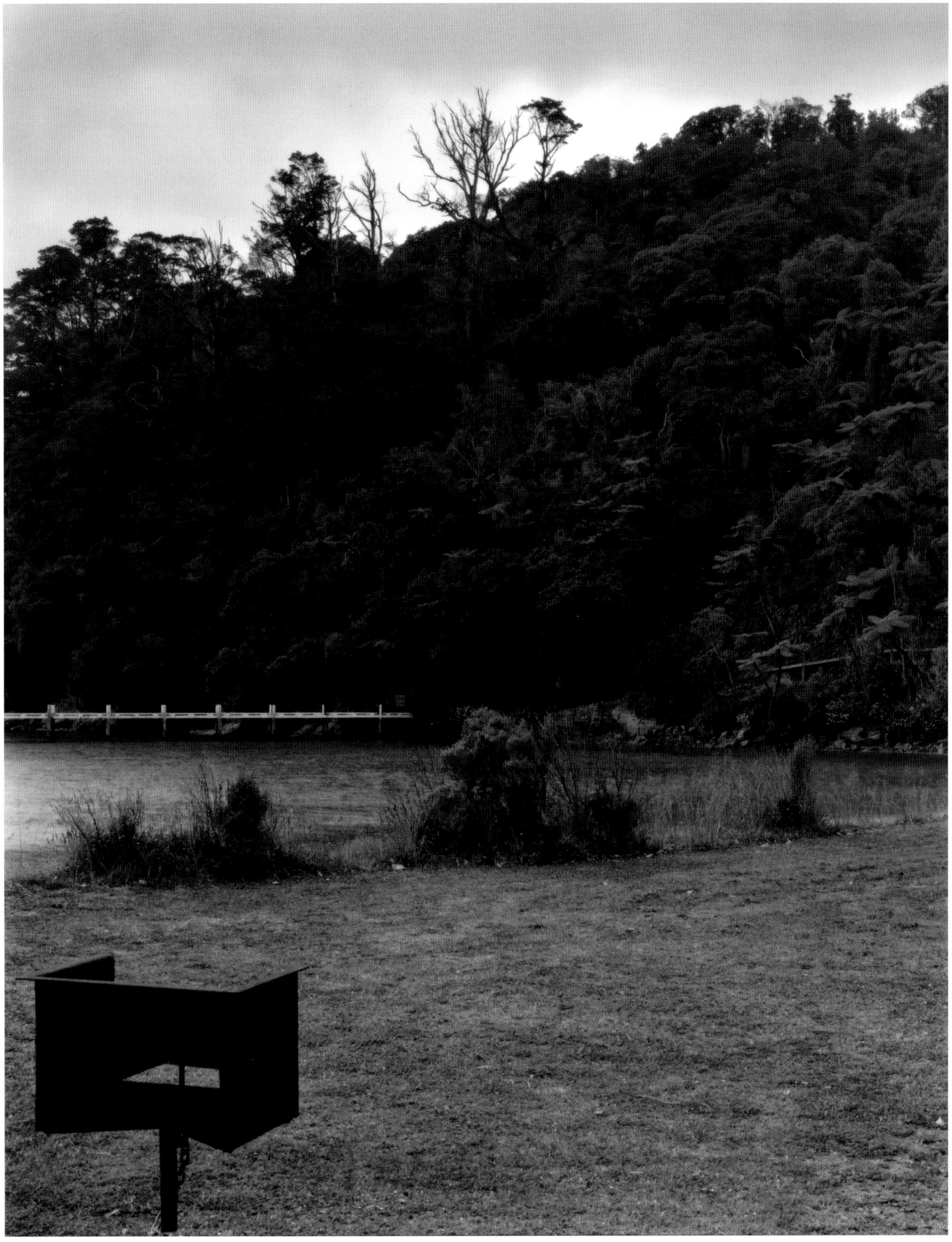

14 (a,b,c)
View at Meretoto/Ship Cove after John Webber, 11 December 1995

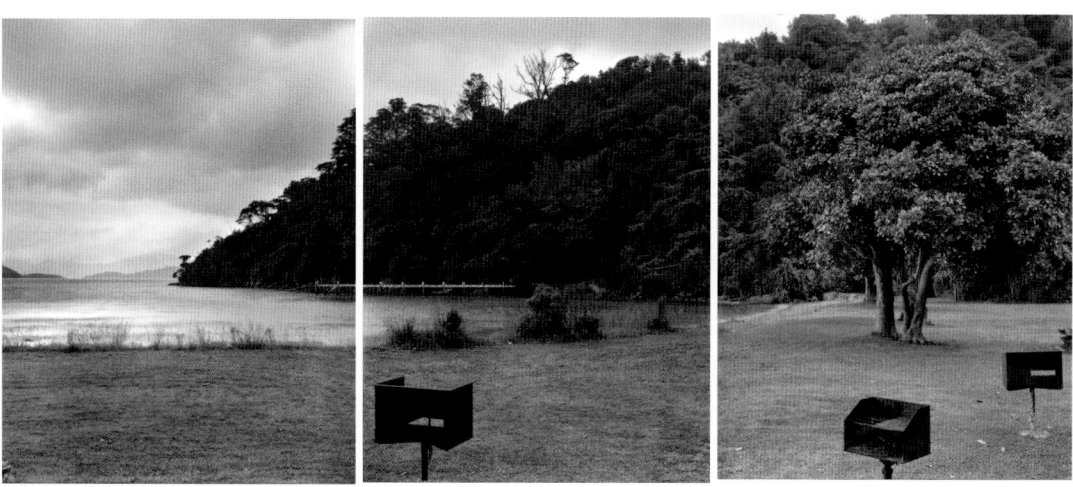

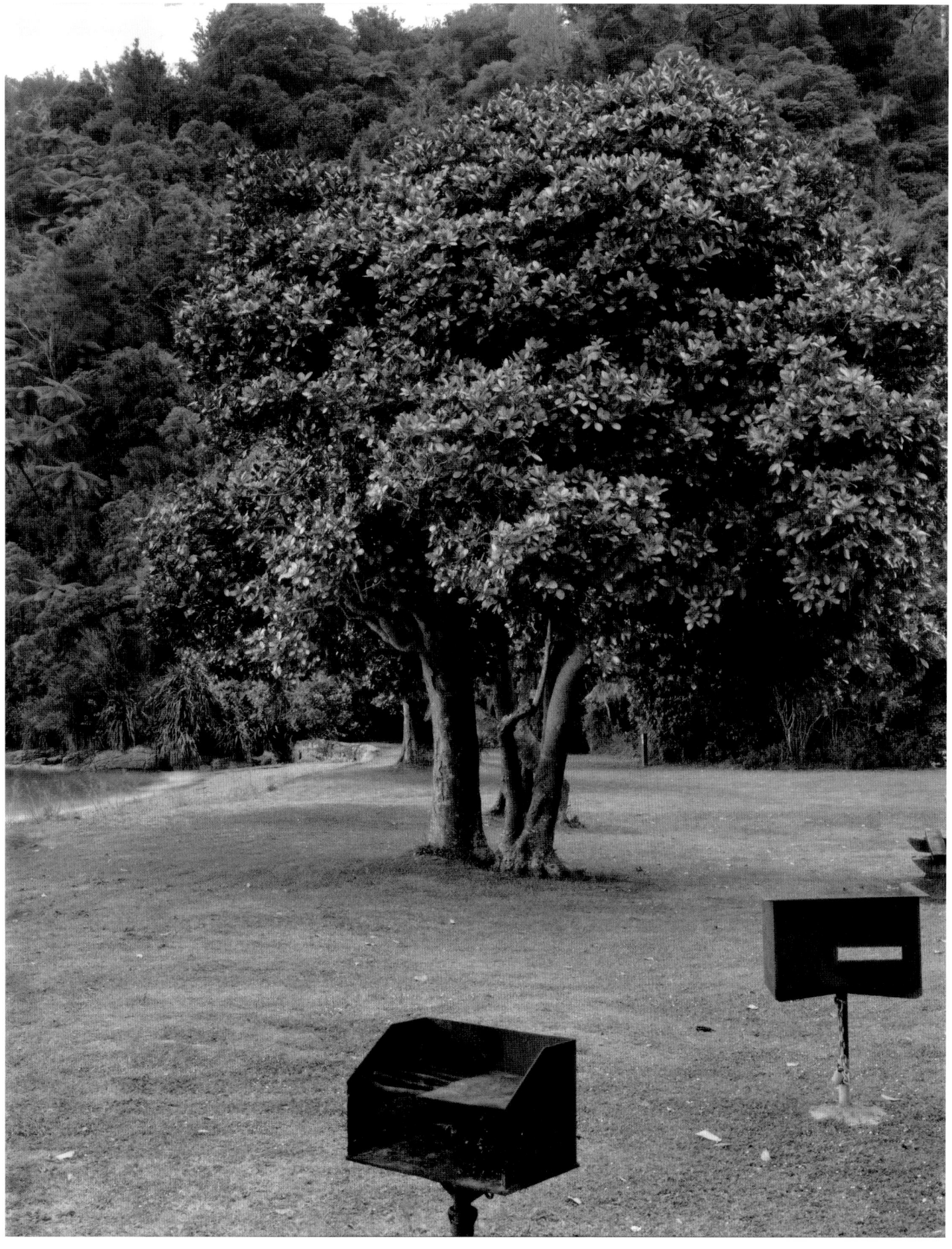

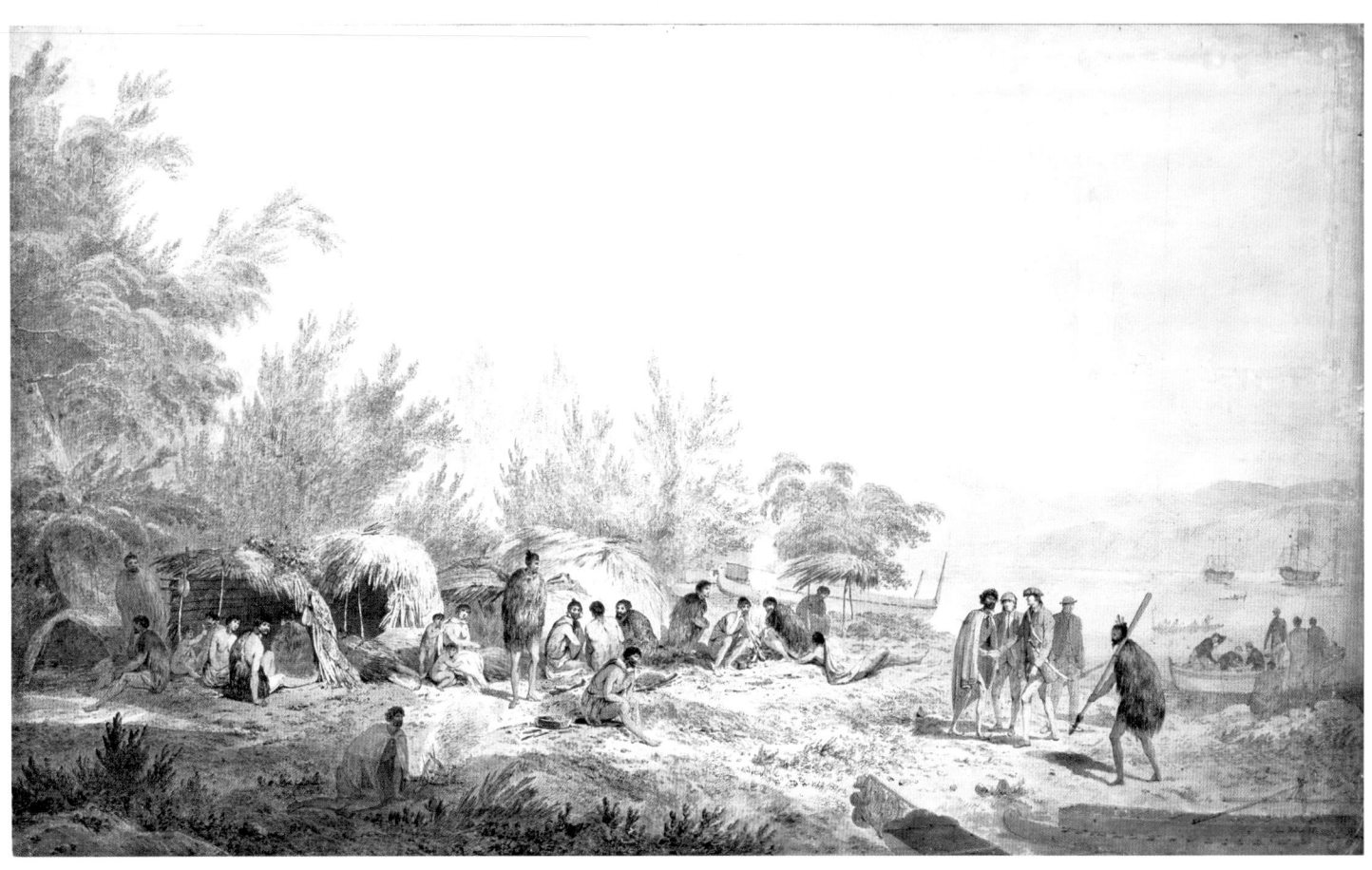

John Webber, [*Captain Cook in Ship Cove*], 1777, pen,wash and watercolour,
60.7 x 98.5 cm. National Maritime Museum, London

15(a,b)
View at Meretoto/Ship Cove after John Webber, 11 December 1995

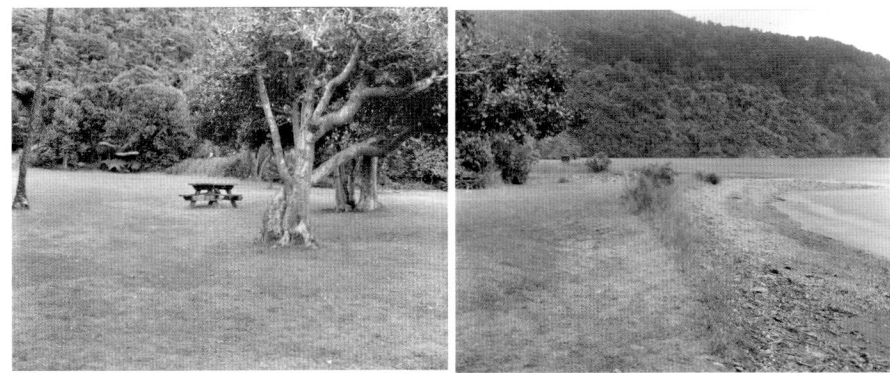

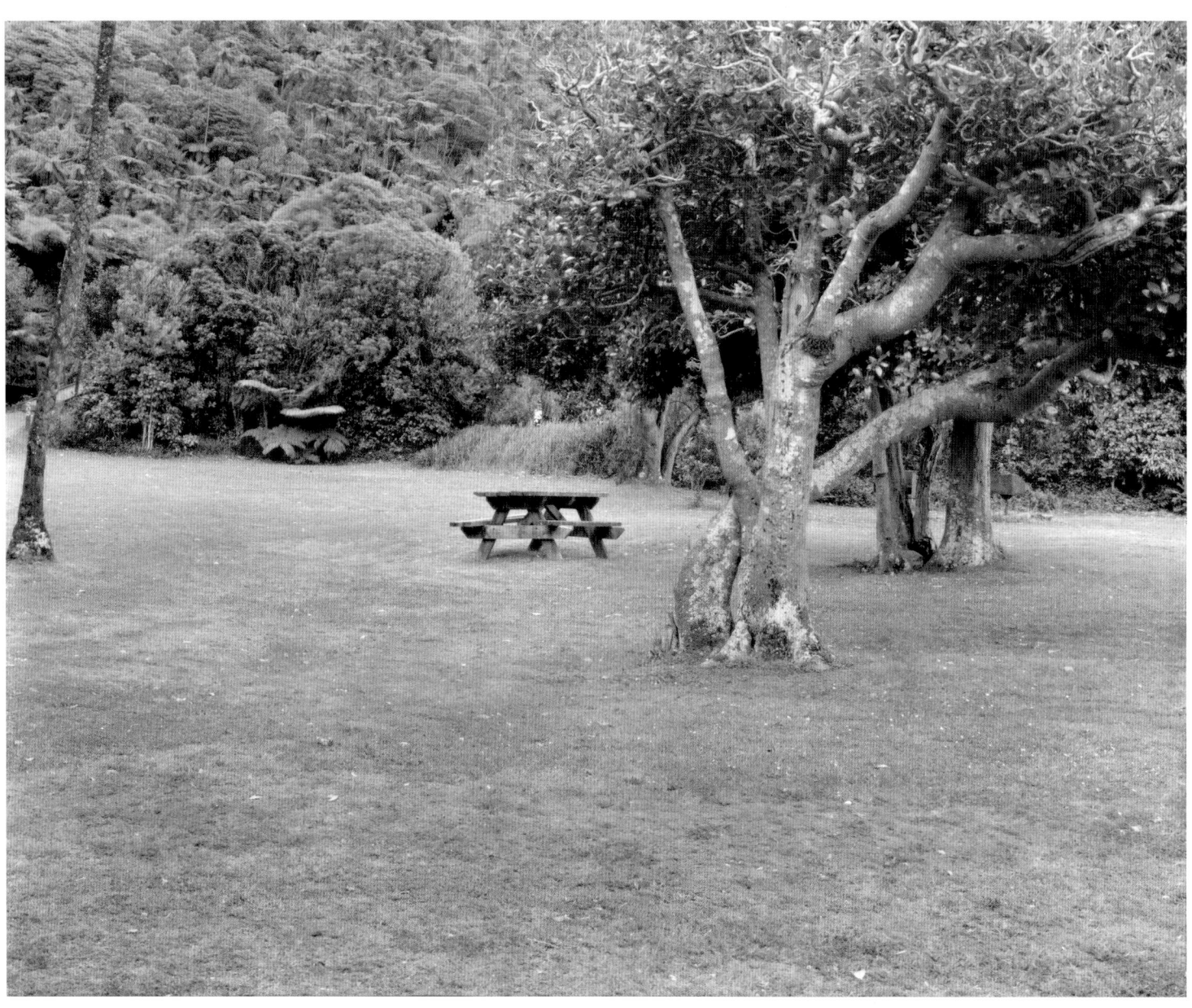

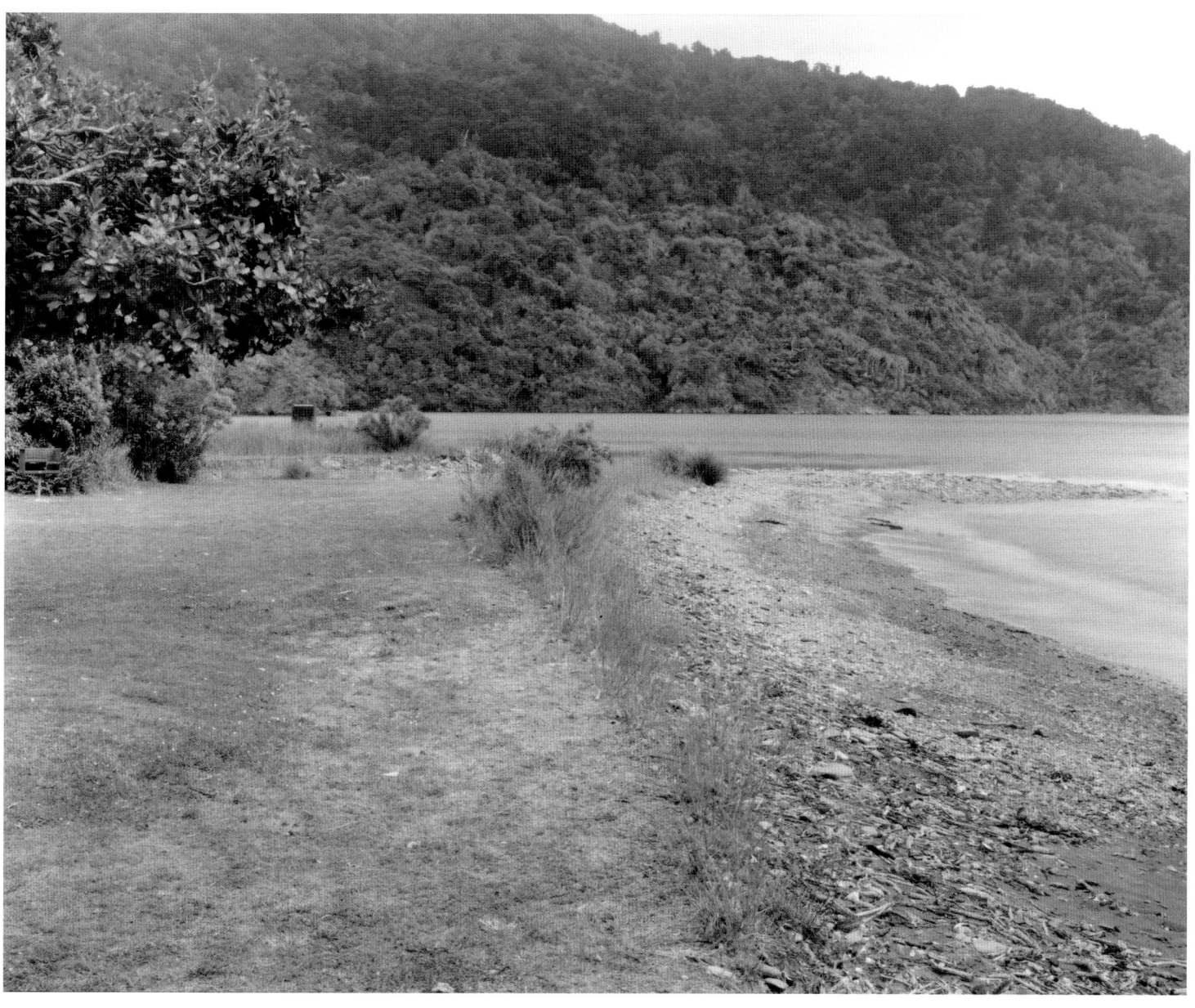

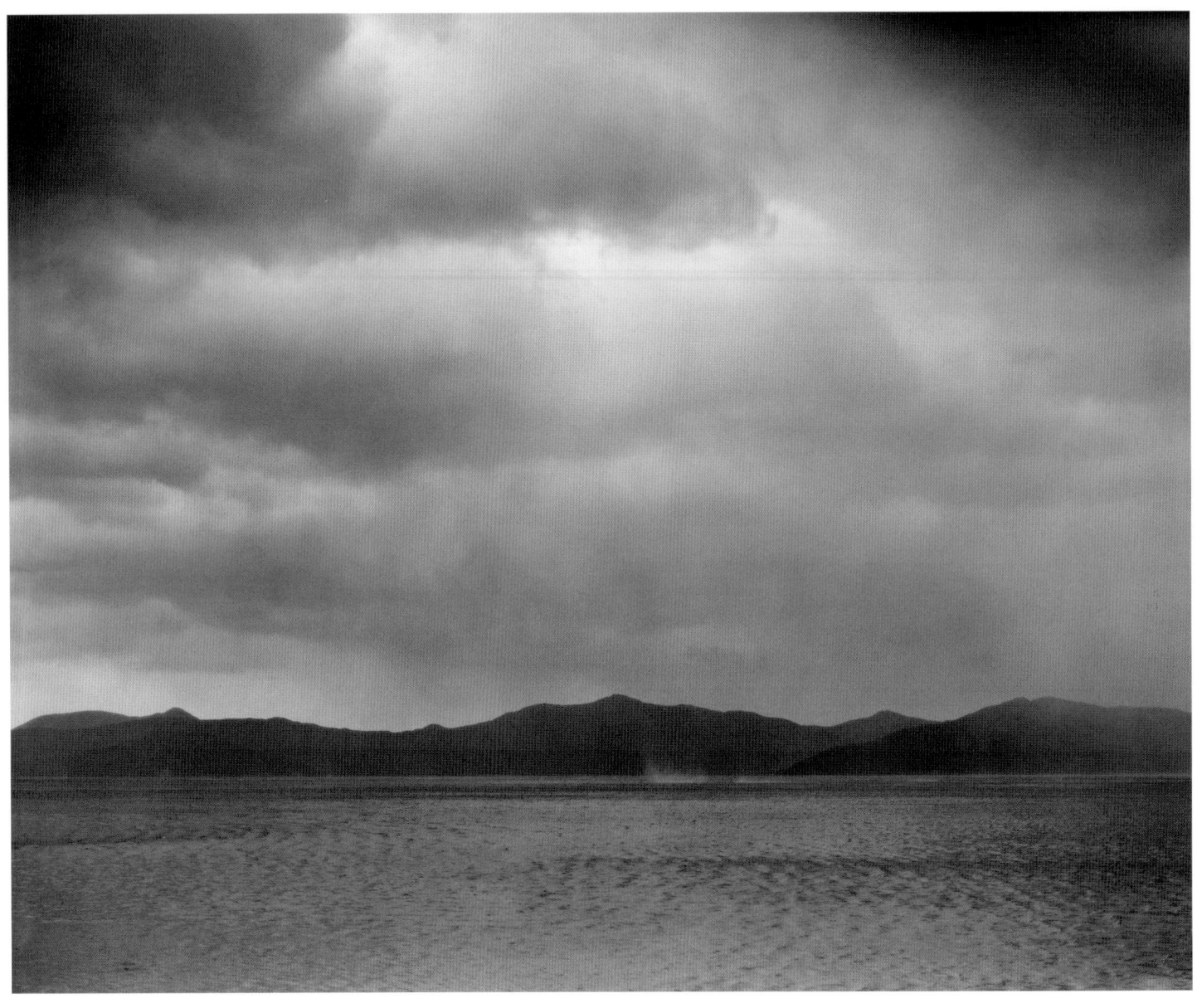

16 View toward Grass Cove from Resolution Bay, 13 December 1995

17 (a,b)
View at Grass Cove, 24 September 1997

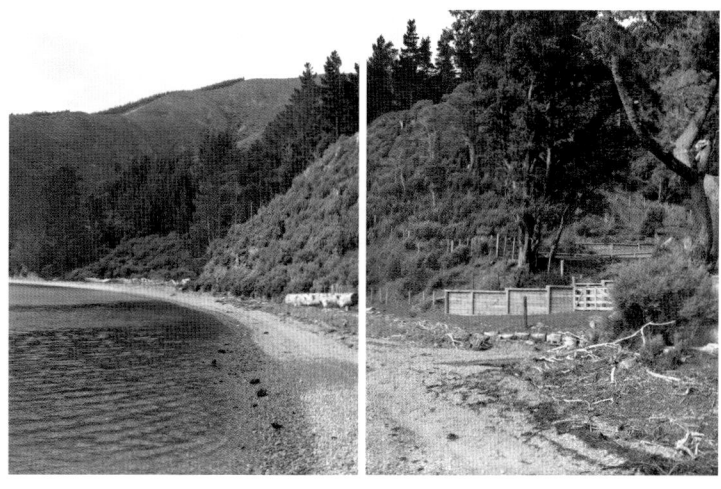

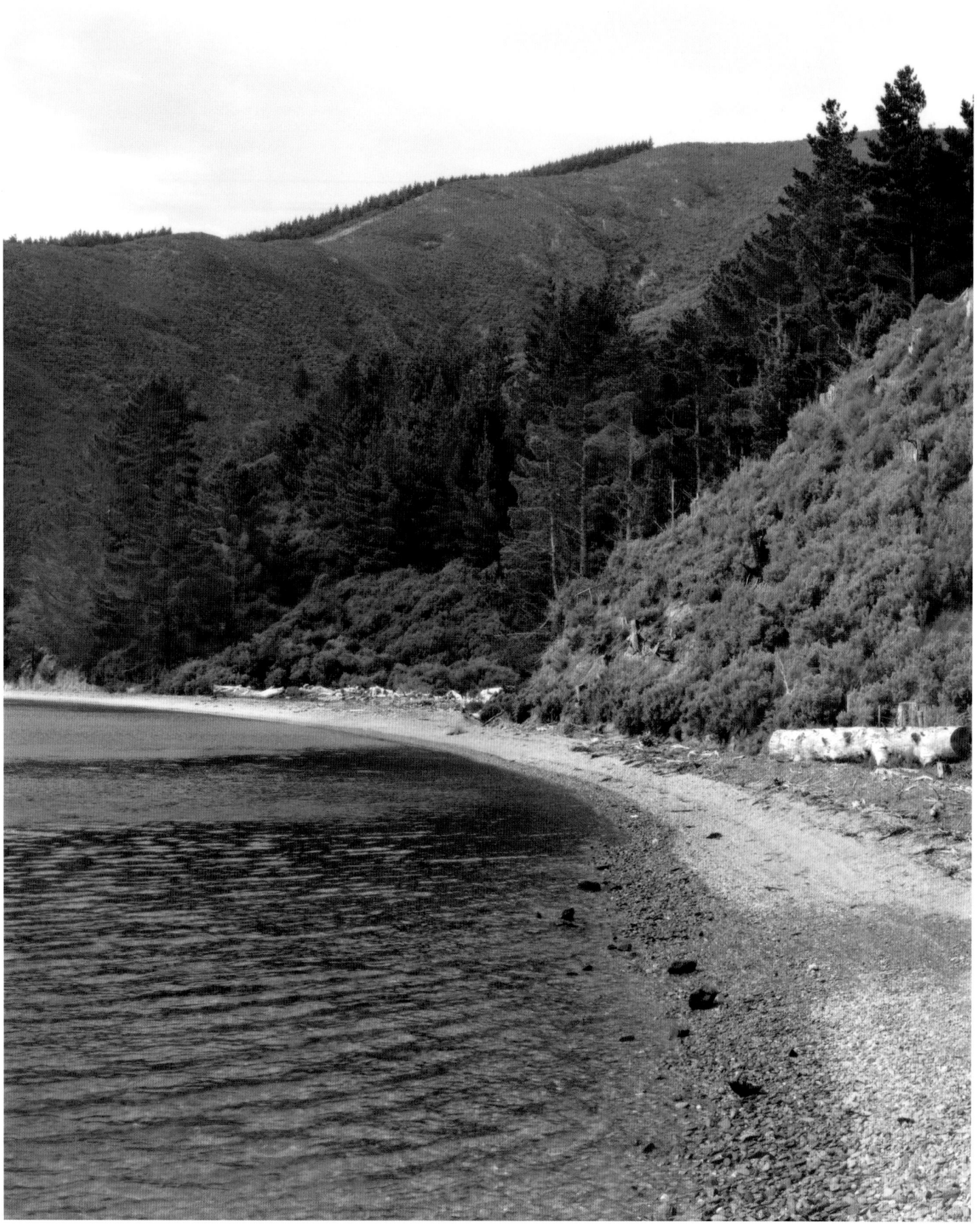

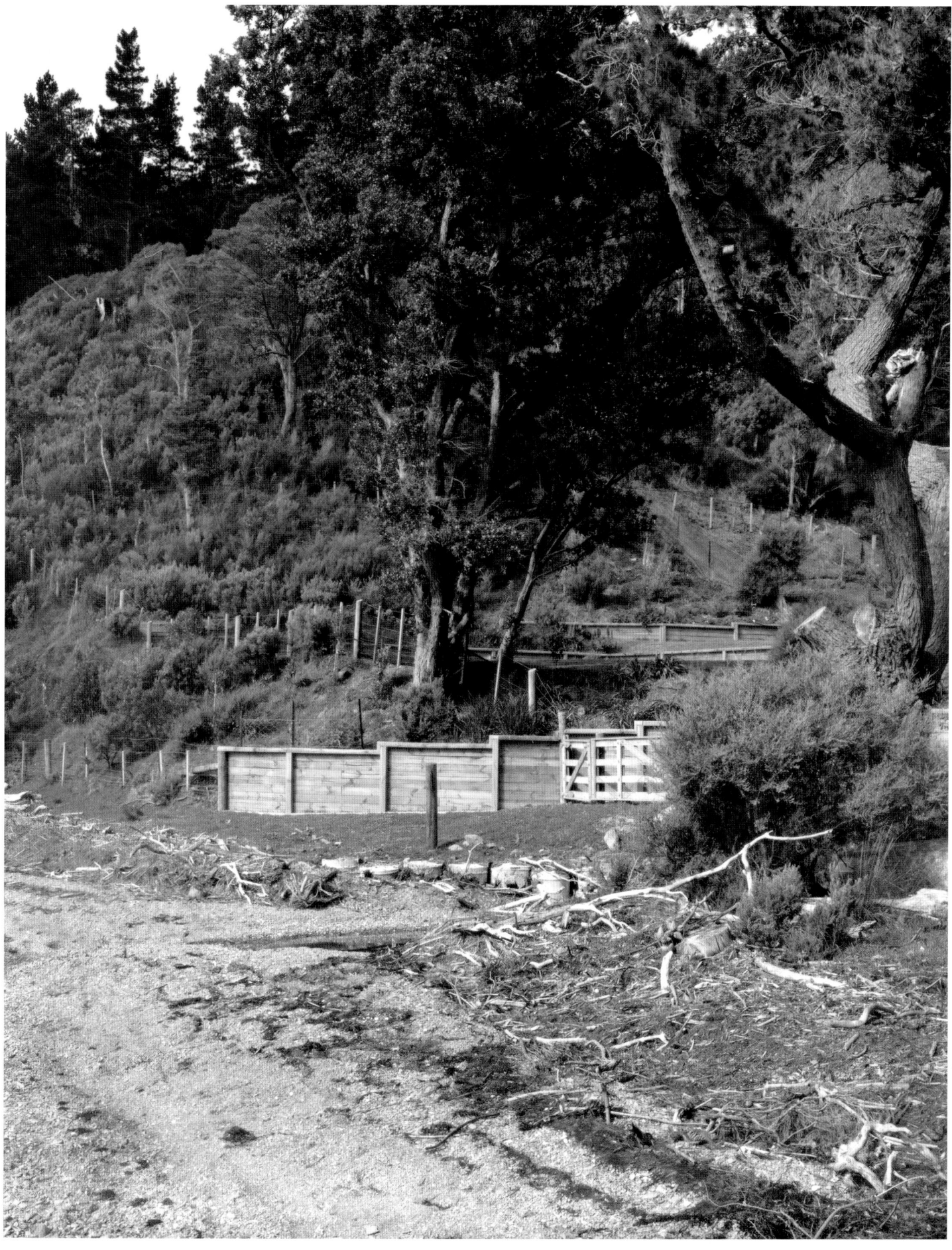

18 (a,b)
View into Meretoto/Ship Cove and Cannibal Cove from Motuara Island,
12 December 1995

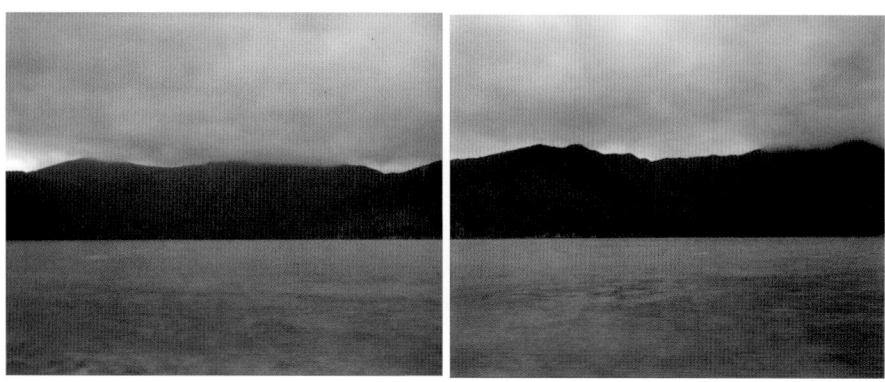

19 (a,b)
Meretoto/Ship Cove, the Cook Monument, 10 December 1995

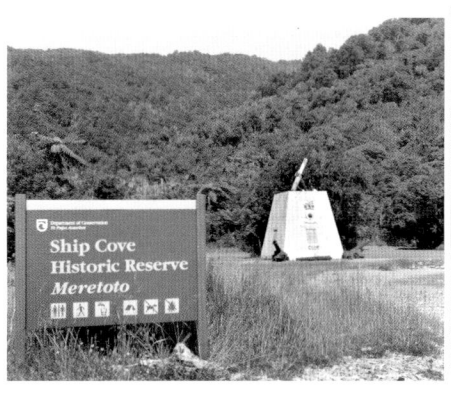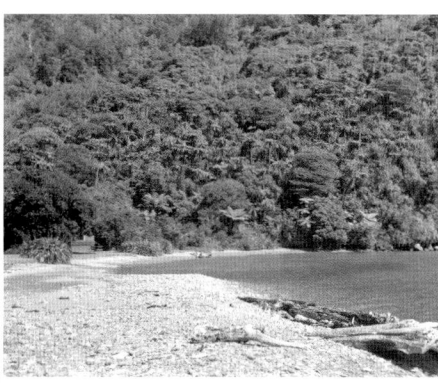

20 (a, b)
Meretoto/Ship Cove, the Cook Monument, evening, 15 December 1995

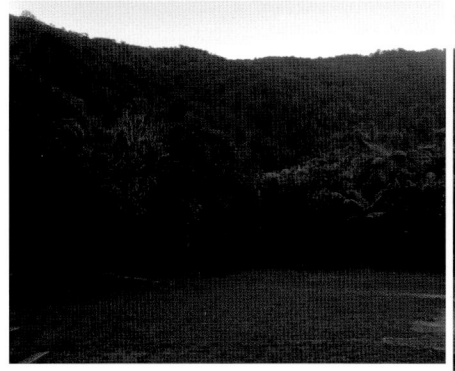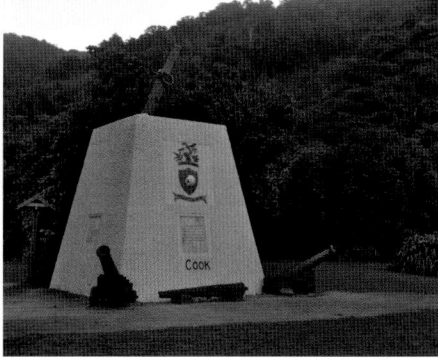

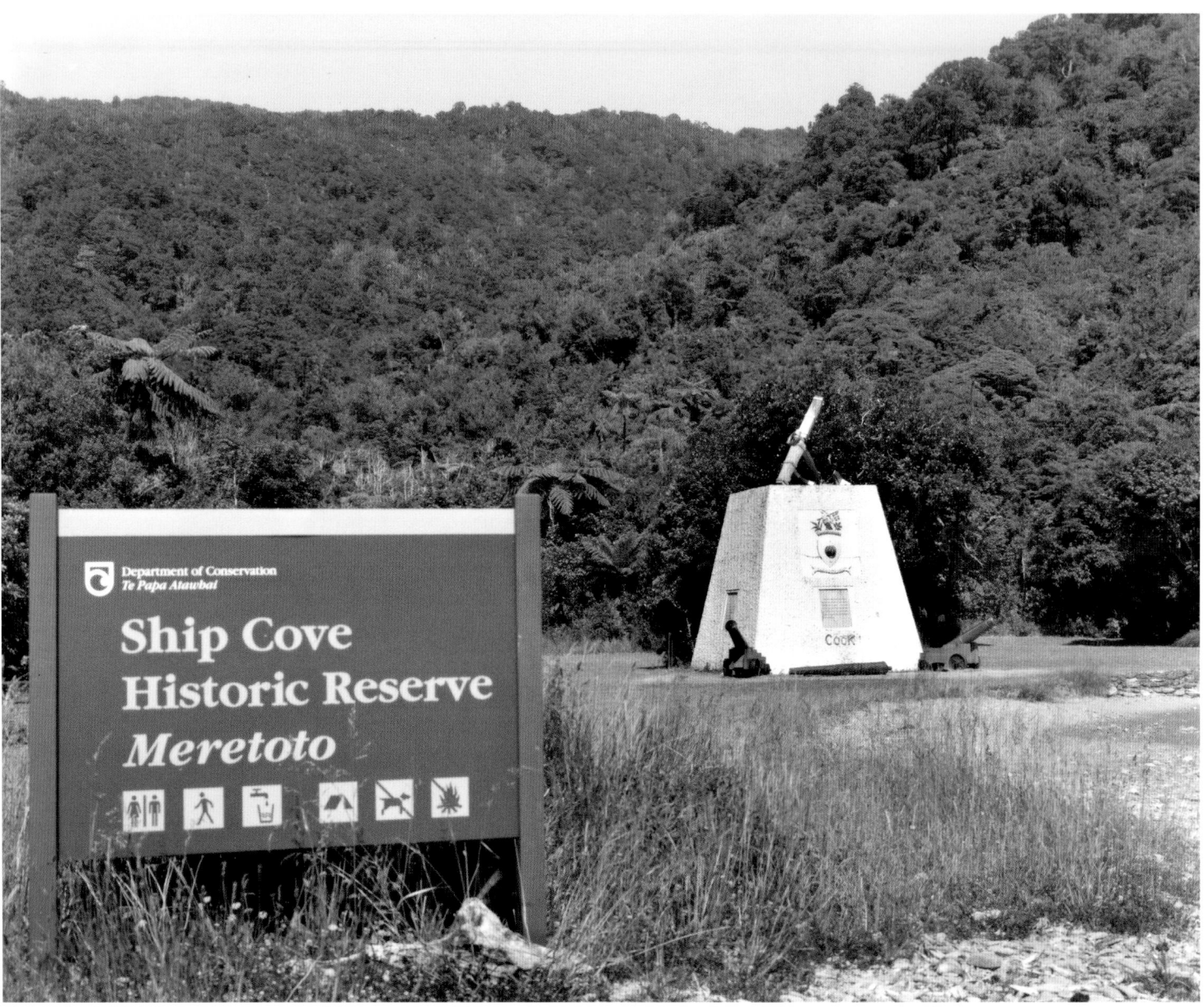

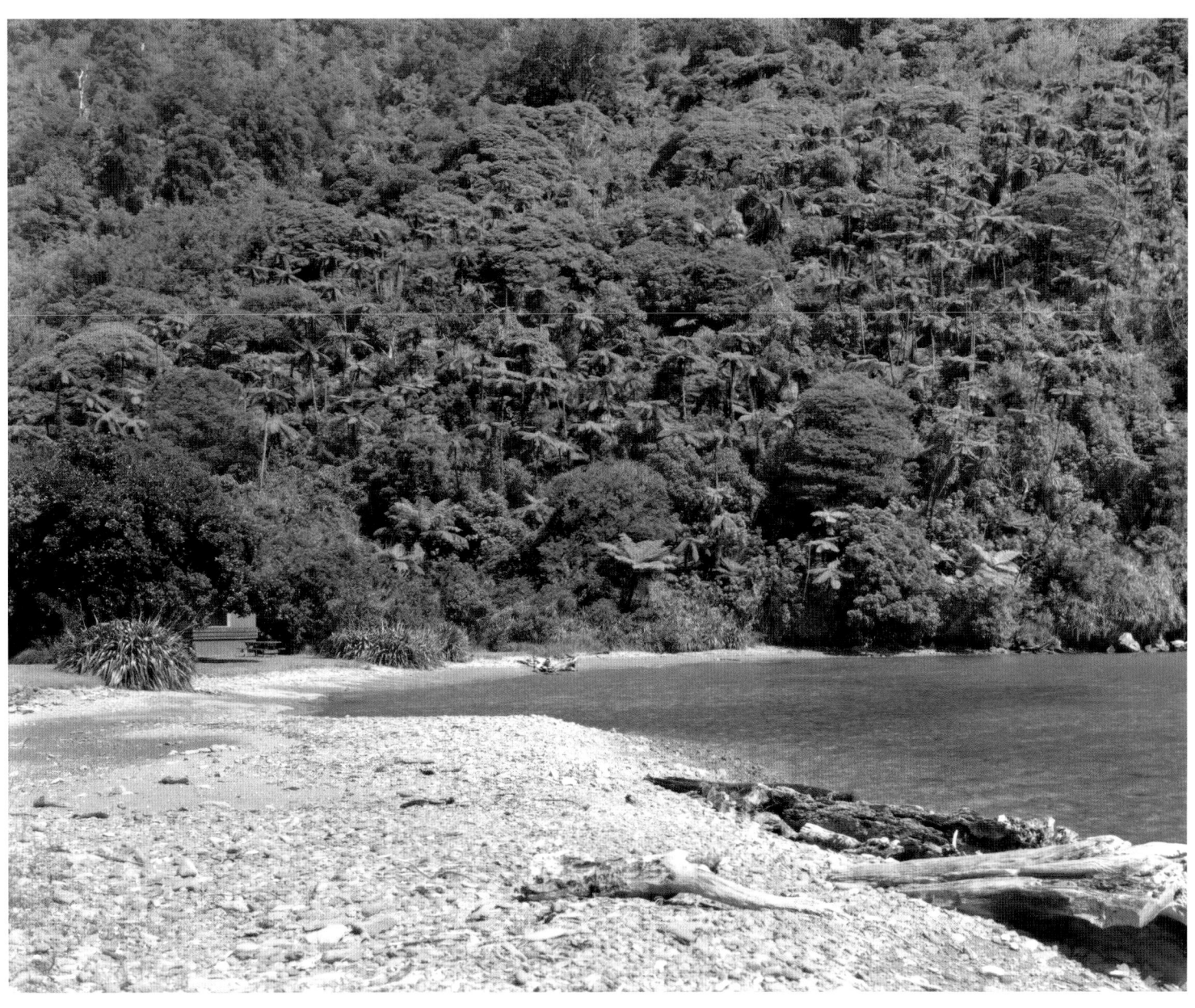

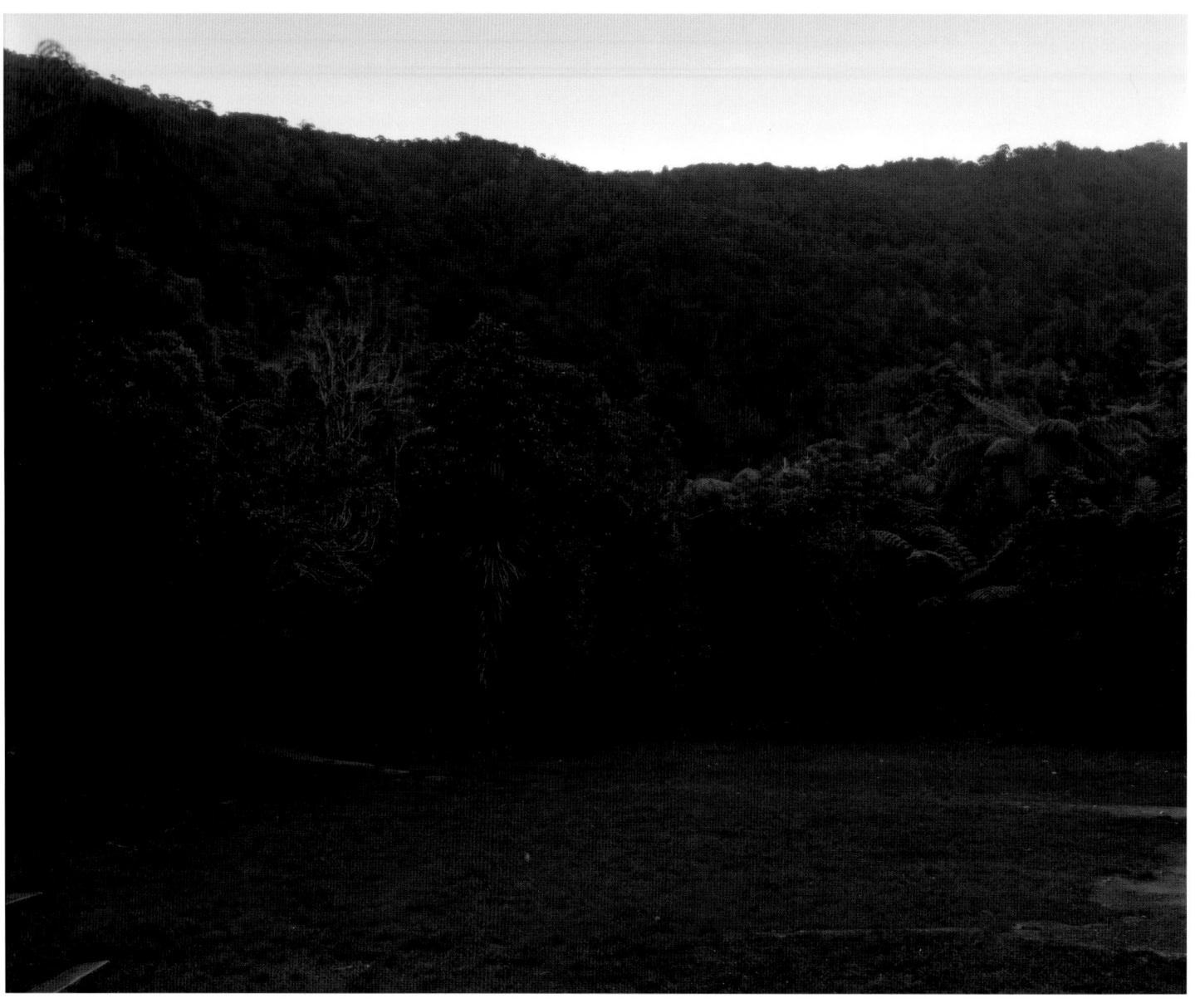

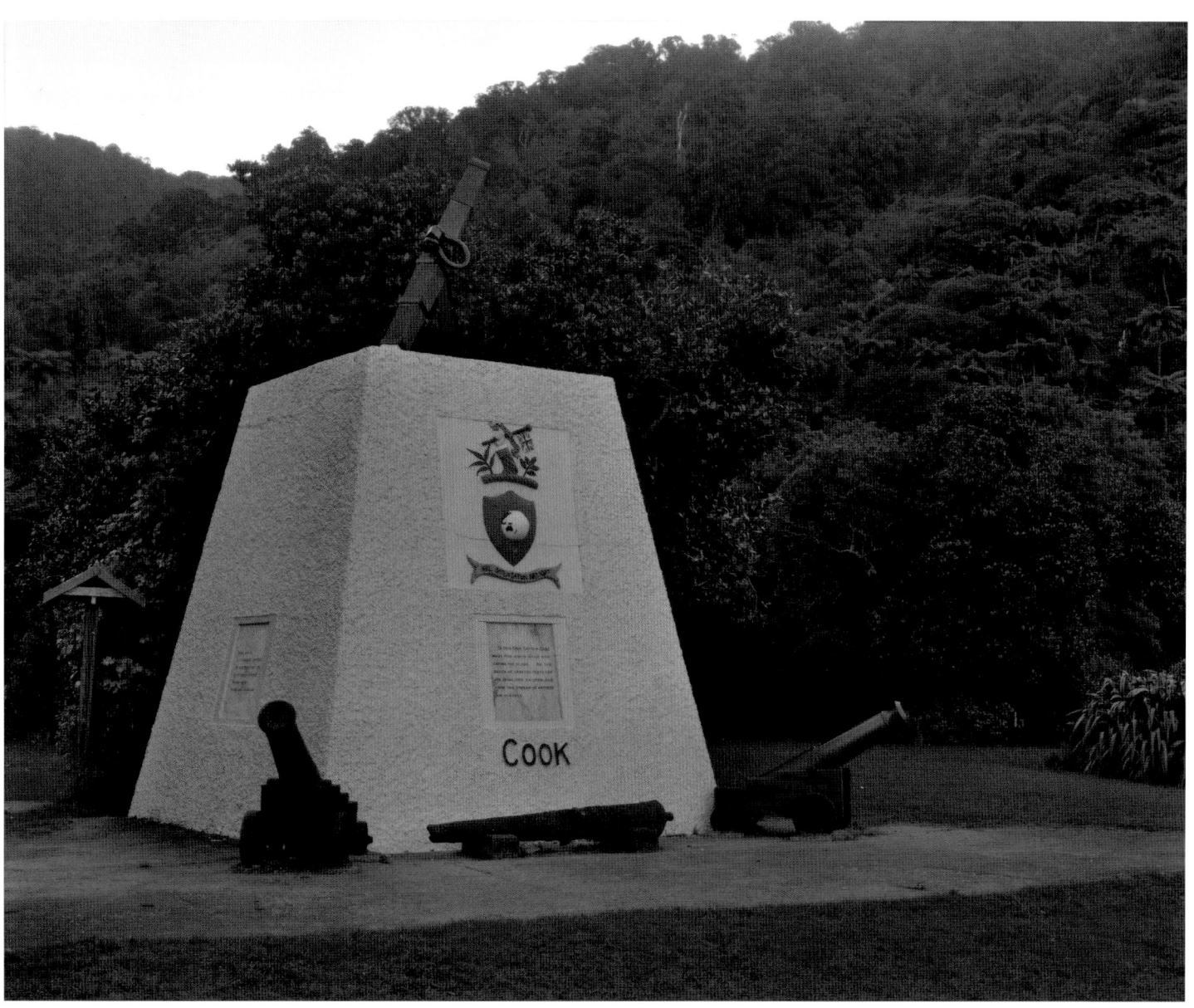

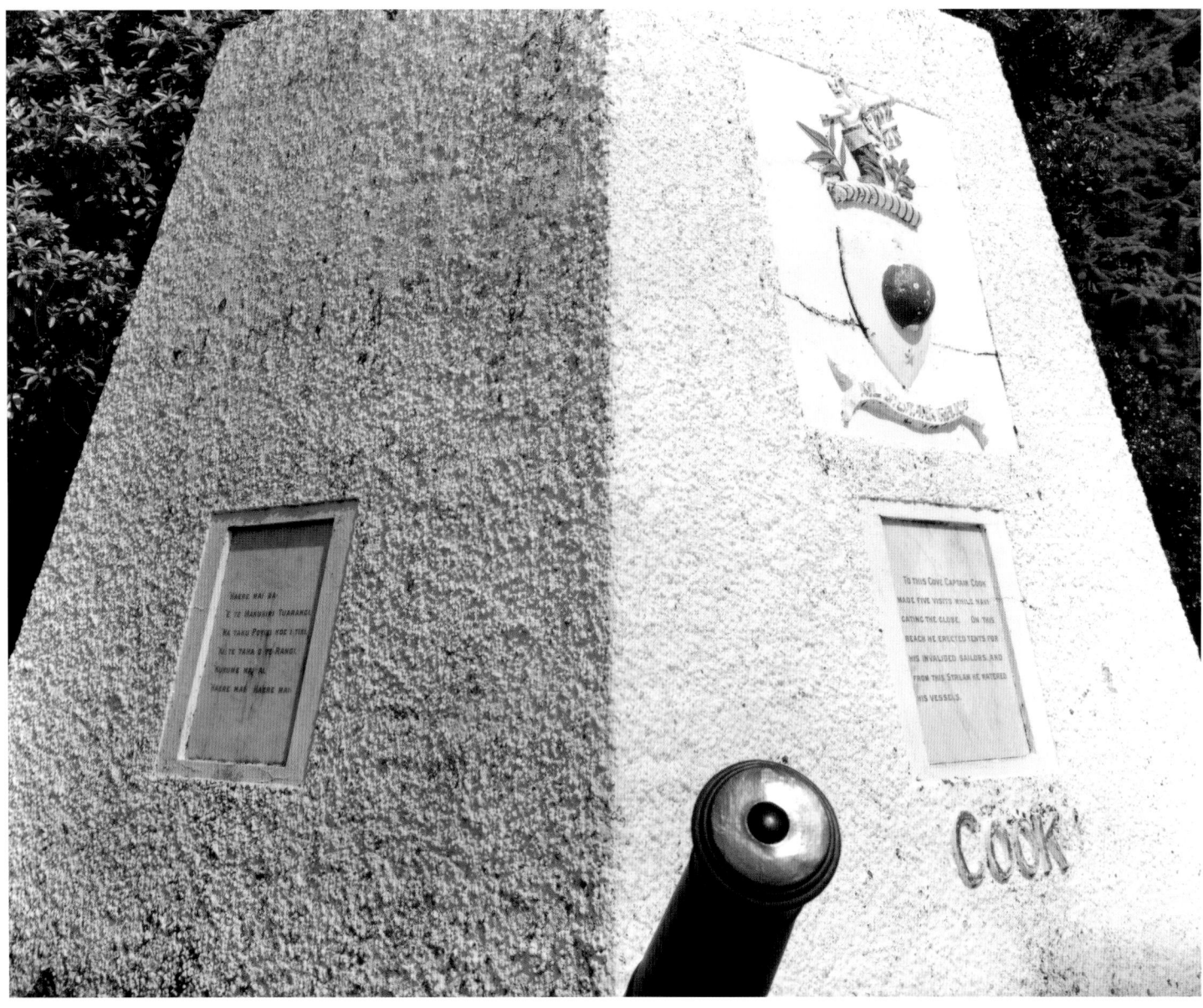

21
Meretoto/Ship Cove, the Cook Monument, 15 December 1995

22 (a,b)
Meretoto/Ship Cove, the Cook Monument, 10 December 1995

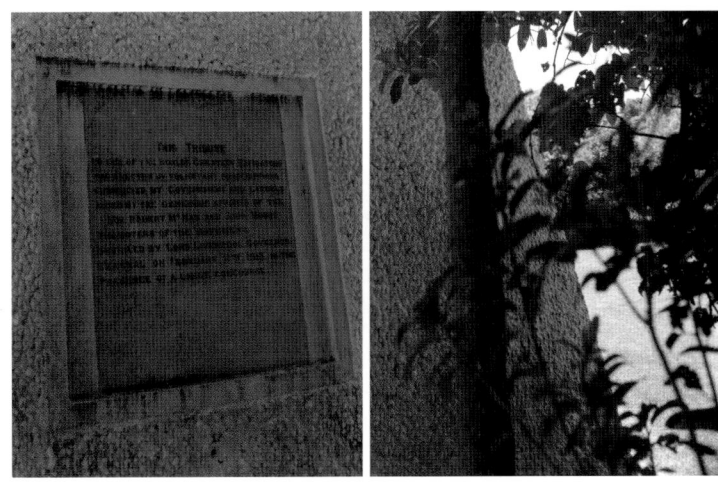

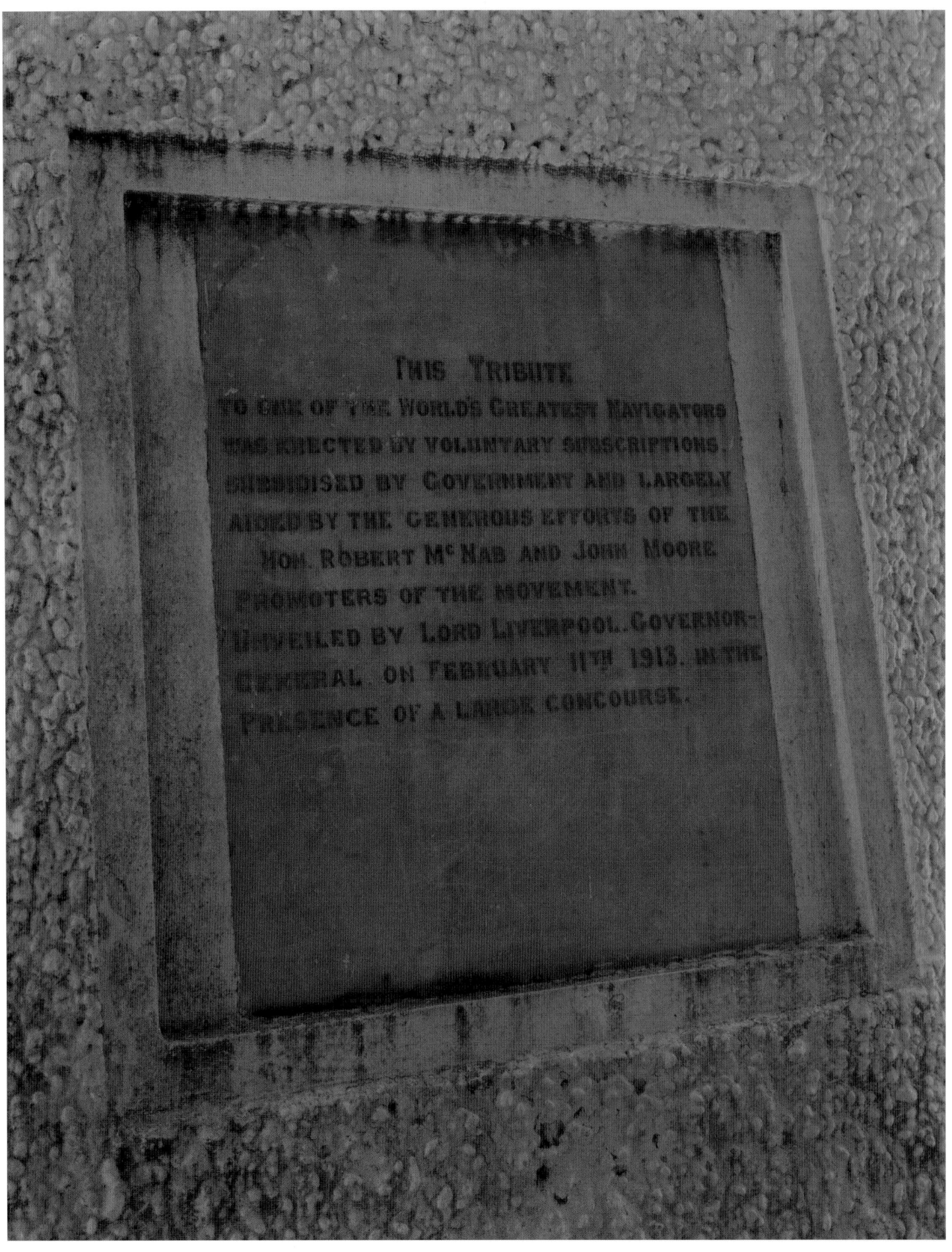

THIS TRIBUTE
TO ONE OF THE WORLD'S GREATEST NAVIGATORS
WAS ERECTED BY VOLUNTARY SUBSCRIPTIONS,
SUBSIDISED BY GOVERNMENT AND LARGELY
AIDED BY THE GENEROUS EFFORTS OF THE
HON. ROBERT MᶜNAB AND JOHN MOORE
PROMOTERS OF THE MOVEMENT.
UNVEILED BY LORD LIVERPOOL, GOVERNOR-
GENERAL ON FEBRUARY 11ᵀᴴ 1913, IN THE
PRESENCE OF A LARGE CONCOURSE.

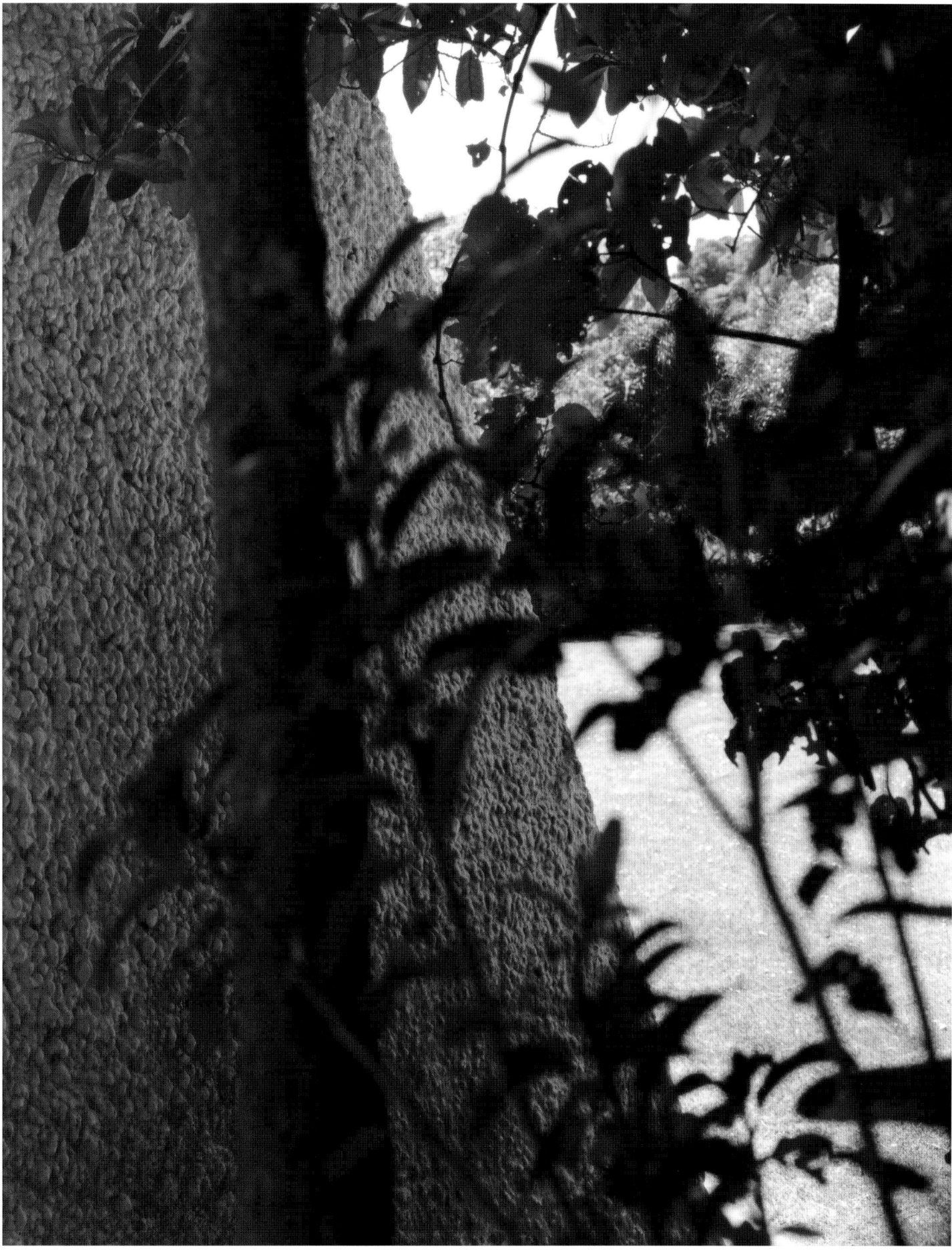

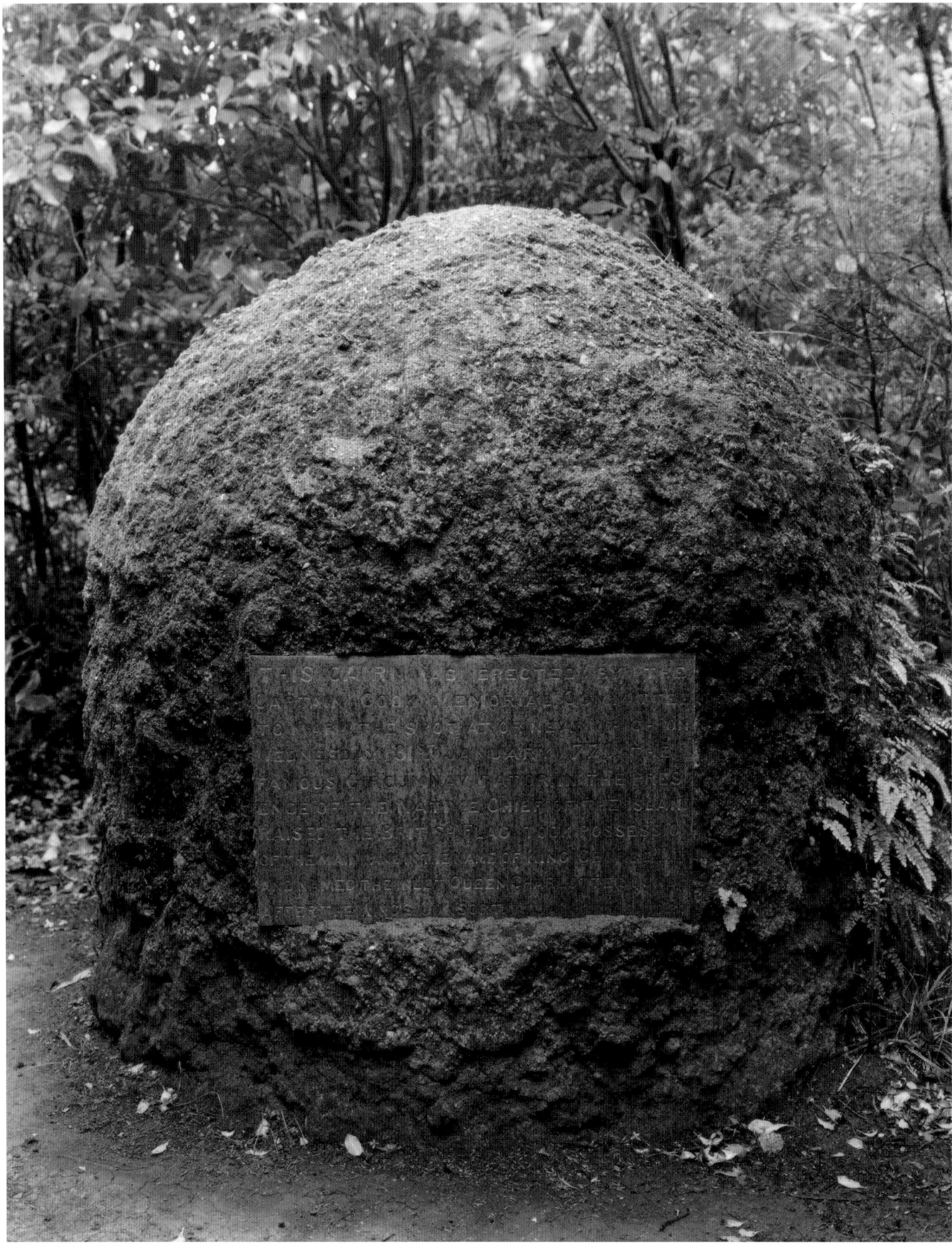

23
Motuara Island. Memorial to Cook's declaration of
possession on Wednesday 31 January 1770,
12 December 1995

24 (a,b,c)
Motuara Island. Memorial to Cook's declaration of
possession on Wednesday 31 January 1770,
18 March 1999

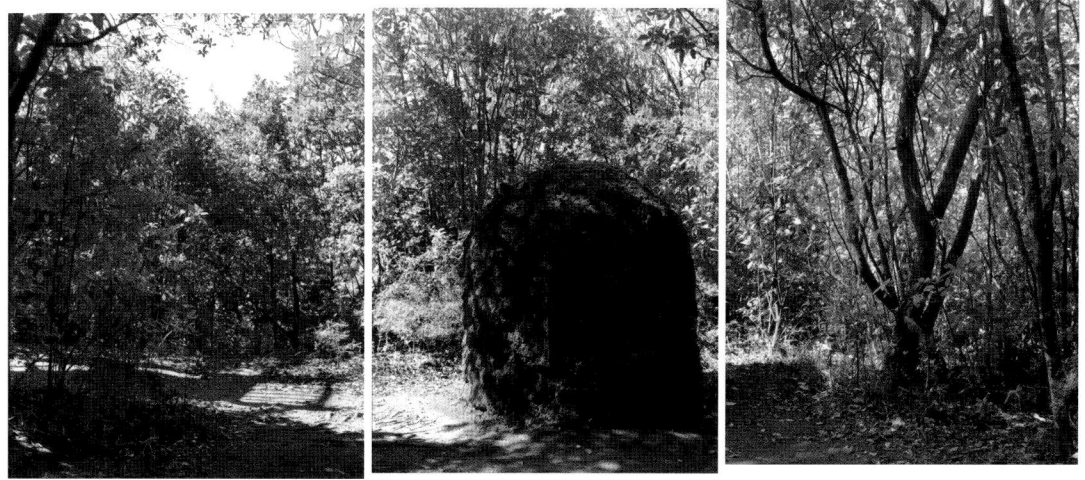

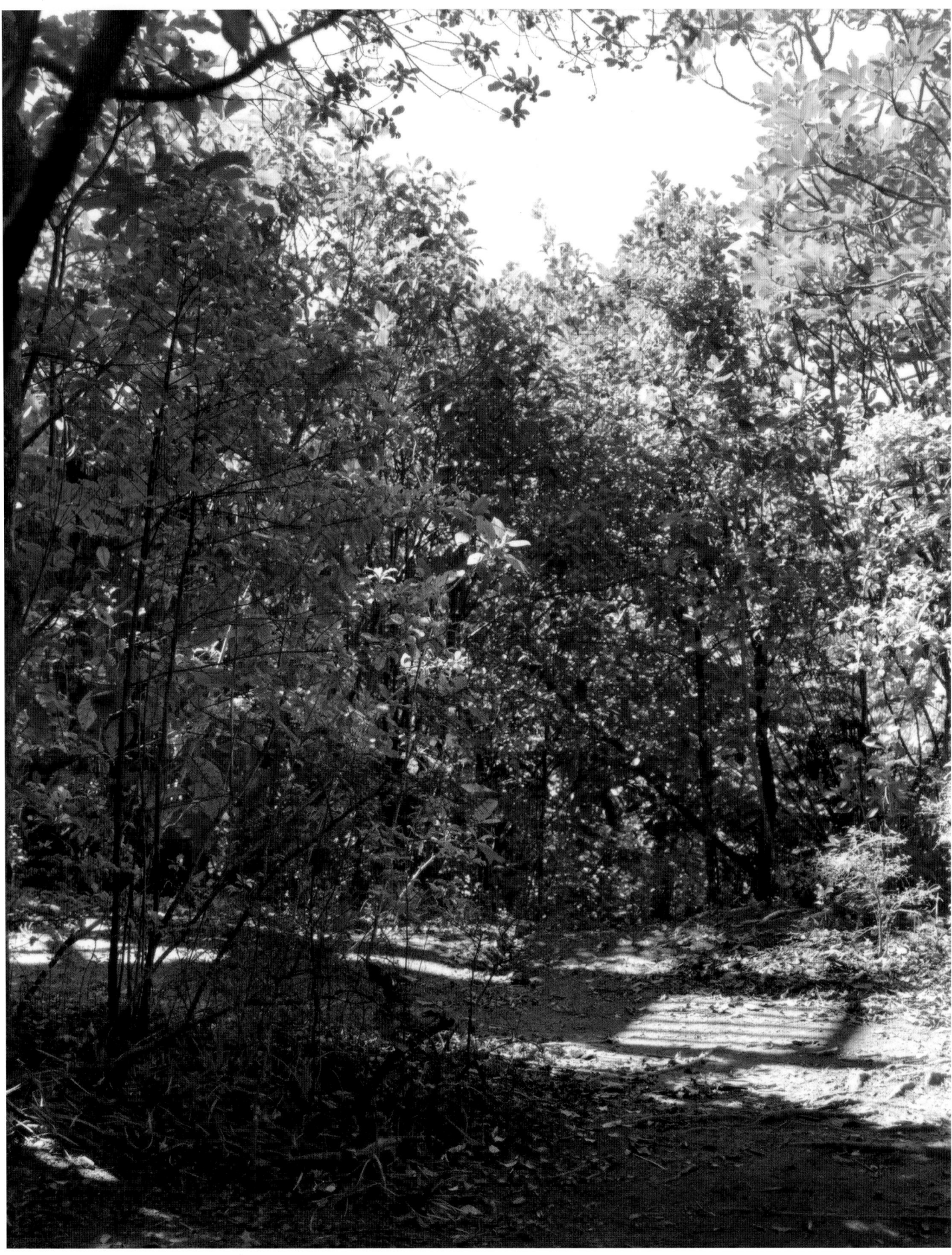

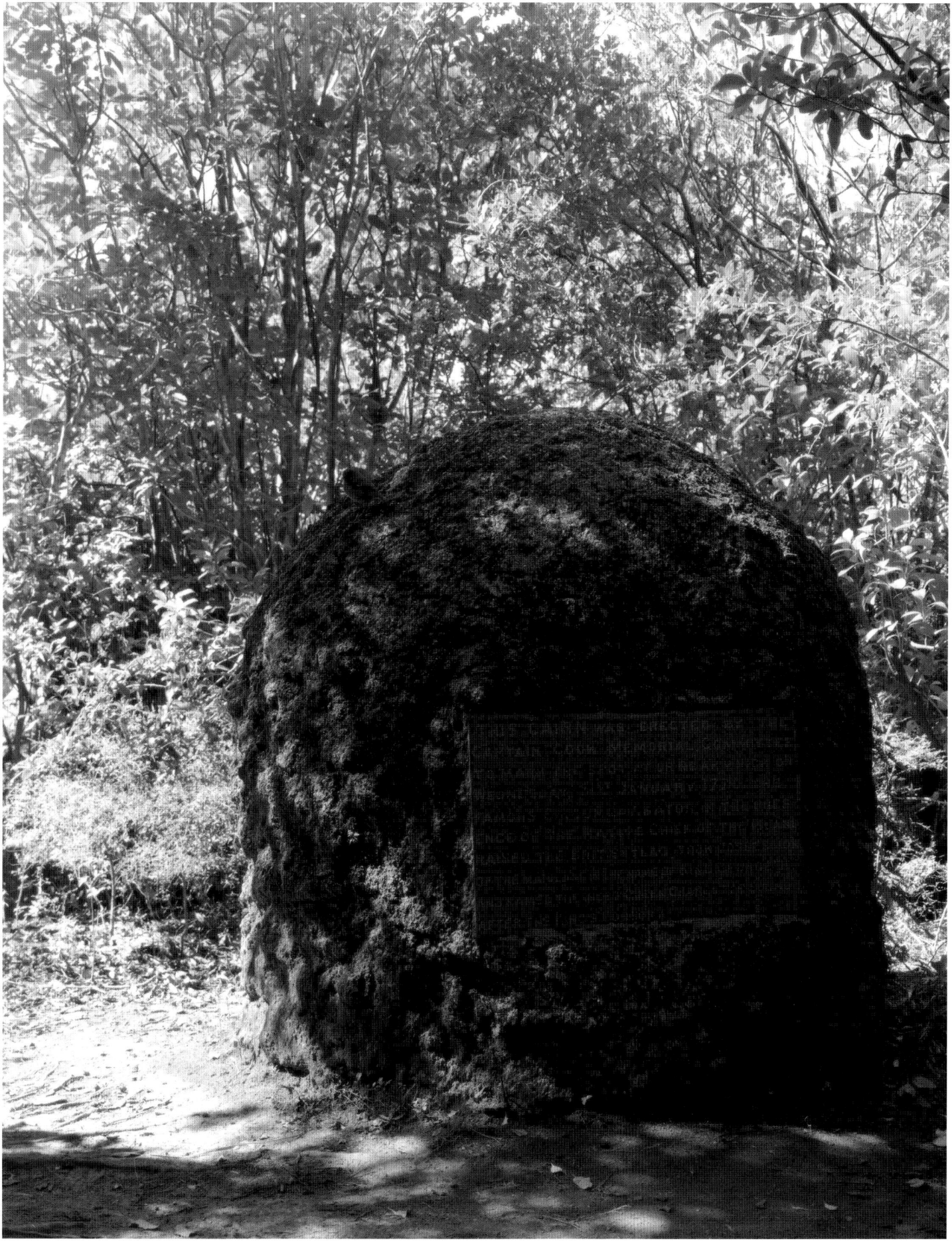

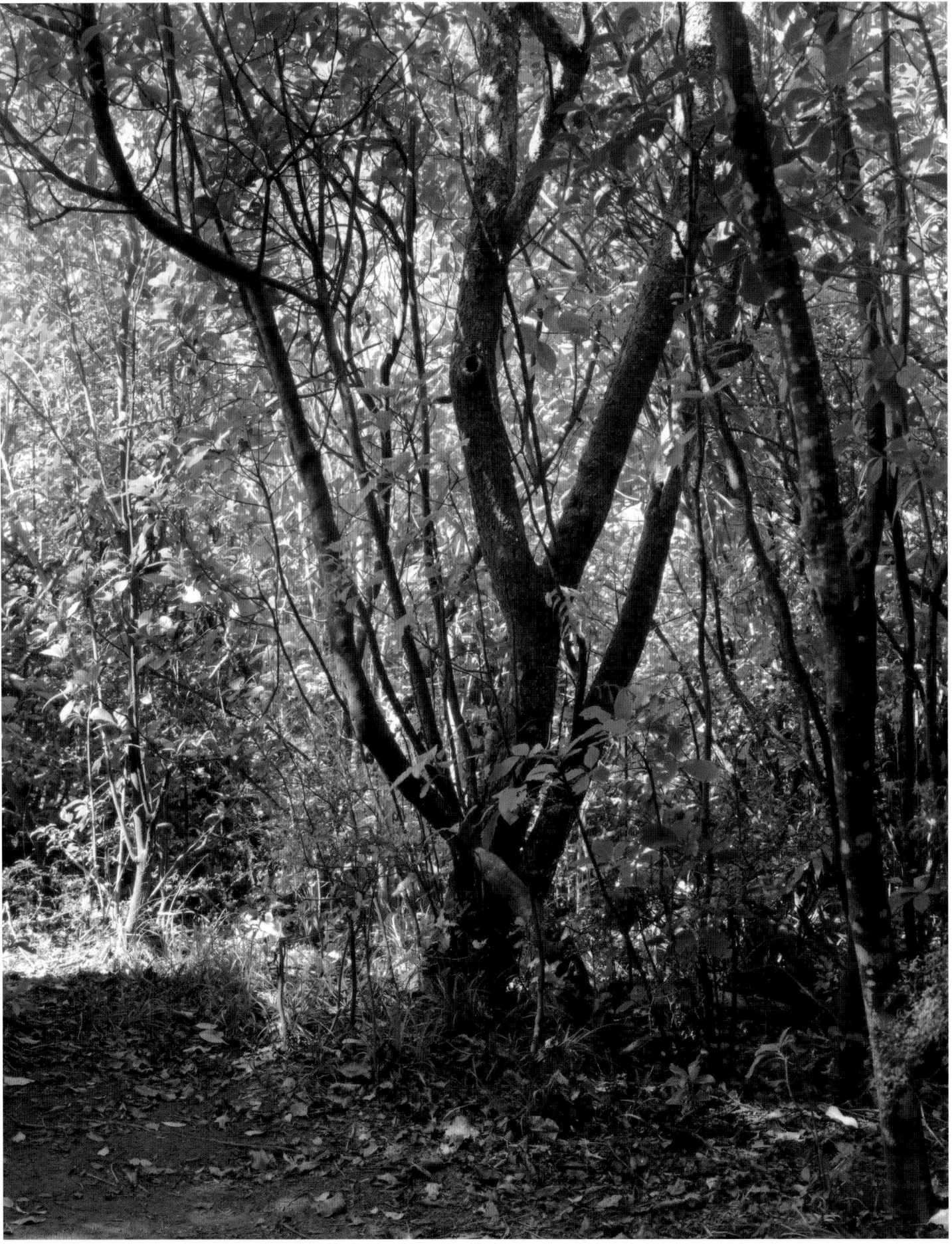

6. Berlin

The taxi wound its way in from the airport to a pretty ordinary, appallingly expensive hotel a few blocks from the Zoo, which I reached around midday. It was mid-November 1997. Mark had arrived the evening before. I showered but didn't rest, and we walked for a couple of hours around the Zoo's perimeter; I felt lightheaded and jetlagged in the bright cold. Later, we ate in a bar off the Ku'damm crammed with gratuituous polished wooden and brass fixtures, mirrors, and reproductions of hunting paintings. The cloudy lager was good, all the more so for having been chosen at random, as one does when travelling, when one has no sense of what the brands or varieties might mean.

I was in Berlin to study the Oceanic art collections in the Museum für Völkerkunde, as well as to work with Mark on Johann Reinhold Forster's journal from Cook's second voyage, which I knew as a text rather than as an artifact. I mean that I knew Forster's words well, because the journal had been edited and published by the late Michael Hoare, a generous New Zealand historian whom I'd met once, who'd done much to document Forster's life. I knew the diary through print; I knew it with the help of Hoare's transcription, his annotations, and his introduction; I did not know it 'personally'. Though I'd read other Forster manuscripts, I did not know the look of the script in this case. I did not know the journal's condition, nor had I a sense of the colour or weight of Forster's pages, the kinds of volumes that this voyage record would be bound in.

Mark's equipment was heavy, so we took a cab the next morning to the Staatsbibliothek. Getting in was difficult at first, because the senior librarian with whom I had corresponded about our visit was not easily located; eventually, however, his photographic curator arrived and proved extraordinarily co-operative. The manuscripts department was closed, which made it easier in the sense that we could arrange desks, tripod and camera to suit ourselves, without obstructing, or being obstructed, by other readers. The volumes were procured from an adjoining room, and we were left to our own devices on a sort of mezzanine level overlooking the main reading room, in which scores worked, seemingly absorbed, hunched over their papers and their laptops.

The journal, bound in vellum, had something of an aura. I mean, of course, that it possessed that historical or artifactual magic for me, and for us, as it might for other scholars and enthusiasts of the history of Cook's voyages, of Forster's life, of the encounters his writings refracted. Even the critically minded historian may lapse into antiquarian mode in the presence of a document that has this look, and this genealogy. It possessed 'authenticity', and 'authenticity' is mostly mystification. Yet the point is not that the past might seem suddenly present, nor that a myth of discovery seems real, by virtue of a manuscript. I am not sure that the experience of contact with the historical object enjoins any such naivety upon the historian, or upon any other reader who is lucky enough not merely to read, but to handle, a document written during the course of an eighteenth-century voyage to the Pacific. No doubt one might imagine that one enjoys some direct access to the truth of the past, simply because one holds and reads an object, a text, that is physically connected with that past, and indeed is a product of the past circumstances one aims to describe. But that triumphal sense of knowing is not what I felt, feeling the journal, which is both relic and text; nor is it what I imagine you might feel before the same object. Surely we all know the bad habits of memory, which make static scenes and artifacts out of happenings and confused circumstances? History is not memory but is equally inclined to make exhibits of the past. Forster's document is not false or 'constructed', but it gives us no more of the truth of a singular cross-cultural encounter than do the tree stumps that are still found in Dusky Sound today. His document is remarkable for its own presence, but also for what has been left elsewhere and unmentioned, or lost. What I felt before the journal was a sense that there was a body in the library. The manuscript is a residue of a life and a succession of happenings; it makes the past tangible, but only through a connection that is palpably tenuous. The physical fixity of the matter and the text seem belied by the murky circumstances of a murder story, a story that takes place both elsewhere and before.

~

Each of Forster's journal volumes includes a title page. The wording varies. That of the most relevant part reads 'Continuation of a Journal of a Voyage on Board his Majesties Ship Resolution Capt Cook Commander from the Cape of good Hope Nov: ye 23^d (1772 till May ye 1773 to Dusky-Bay in New-Zeeland.' The mark before '1772' is in fact a crescent, indicating the moon's phase on 23 November 1772; there is a space for a date before '1773', which Forster never filled in. The manuscript is replete with intriguing little sketches – botanical, ethnographic, and cartographic; one or two of the maps are scored over, seemingly impatiently; there are doodles and ink blots, and Forster's signature on one page.

Mark and I talked, but rarely in great detail, about the kinds of images we were looking for when we were confronted by landscapes, monuments, artifacts and situations, in one place or another. I felt that the right response was his business; I knew that he needed time to absorb a place, to stand around, taking in (I imagine) the feel of the light, and a space's shapes and edges. I could do this too, and needed to do it, up to a point, a point that stopped short of the visual acclimatisation that the photographer needed to work himself through. Both in New Zealand and in Germany I would stand about with Mark at a site, but retreat after a time to a novel or a notebook, leaving him in the dusk.

In Berlin, in any event, we had already worked something out: we had established that a certain approach to the voyage's relics made sense, or made as much sense as we were able to make of this history. We needed to study both objects and their situations. This meant that we needed to produce two kinds of images that were on the one hand close, and on the other contextual – hence a set of photographs of the pages of the journal itself, and a panoramic view of its environment. In this case, the environment was itself famous, consisting as it did of the light-filled, high modernist expanse of the main reading room of Hans Scharoun's Staatsbibliothek, designed and built between 1967 and 1972. Forster's voyage, it seemed, could be rediscovered in an archivist's spaceship.

Late in the afternoon, we left the gear in the same locked room as the manuscript and walked back to the Zoo, along Kurfürstenstrasse. Posters advertised a tattooing convention and the New Zealand film, *Topless Women Talk About Their Lives*. The movie opens with a scene on the west Auckland beach Piha, where a German tourist asks locals if this was where *The Piano* was made. He is told it was in fact shot at Karekare, the next beach to the south, but he nevertheless hands over his camera and asks them to take his photograph: the visitor can fudge the geographic subtlety and say 'I was there' when he shows the snapshot to friends at home. We stumble upon the Café Einstein, which has high ceilings and polished wooden floors; it is as stylish and pricey as my guidebook, I realise later, has told me; the white wine is good but not dry; there are still a few leaves on the august trees that line the street, which are no doubt common, but for which I do not have a name.

I spent a couple of days in the exhibition halls and in the storage basement of the museum in Dahlem. It was a time of highs and lows, of finding wonderful things, and of depression amidst the sheer mass of overmodelled skulls from the Sepik, of New Ireland malanggan crammed into cabinets, of racks of spears and arrows. Too much of this stuff was uncontextualised, uncontextualisable, displaced, and useless; it left me dispirited. In other German museums, I had often been struck by the gulf between the former importance of the Pacific Islands and of Pacific cultures to Germans, and the present sense of their relevance. There had been German colonies in New Guinea, Samoa, and Micronesia; planters and traders were active; and in the cultural domain, Oceania had a tremendous impact on German expressionism, and particularly on painters like Max Pechstein and Emil Nolde who emulated Gauguin, travelling to Palau and New Guinea respectively. Museum ethnologists had gone out in force; hence the vast collections in Hamburg, Dresden, Leipzig, and Bremen, as well as in Berlin, that seem today as rich as they are undervisited, and in some places simply neglected, in dusty and unrenovated stores and displays. Once so suggestively and powerfully exotic, the expanse of the Pacific now seemed irrelevantly large, and too far away.

I forget now whether it was on a Wednesday or Thursday that I was finished. I had exposed my rolls of film, made notes that later seemed inadequate, foregone expensive book purchases in the museum shop, and walked out into the patches of ice and harsh sunlight of the street. The next morning it was colder and seemed still more brilliant. We walked down Unter der Linden toward the Nationalgalerie, passing the Humboldt-Universitat; I remembered that Alexander von Humboldt had cited George Forster's voyage to the South Seas as one of his inspirations to study natural history. So – there were certain connections between the institutions and great names of German intellectual history and science, and the antipodean chill of the waters of Dusky Sound. Yet all these resonances of place, aesthetics, and thought, the monumental statues of the Humboldts (Alexander and his linguist brother, Wilhelm) and Forster's 'body' in the library, seemed equally irrelevant to the new Germany and its troubled modern historical consciousness. Contending with the past means contending with the Holocaust, and with everything exemplified by the construction and deconstruction of the Wall. It does not mean engagement with Germany's colonial past, which is marked in its own way in the museum collections. Nor does it mean engaging with the extra-European history of German travel and knowledge documented in such artifacts as Forster's journal.

The location of the journal had also been that of the opening sequences in Wim Wenders' *Wings of Desire* (*Der Himmel über Berlin*, 1984), a film 'in and about Berlin' that (its director had written) aspired to 'convey something of the history of the city since 1945'.[18] *Wings of Desire* had long been an important film for me. Watching it was unlike any other cinematic experience. On the first viewing, and even subsequently, I felt that I was merely sitting in the shallows at the edge of a sea, letting its images of angels over Berlin, the library, the circus, and the trapeze wash over me like gentle waves. The odd coincidence of the 'location' that I knew slightly through a film I knew intimately, and the situation of a document that I knew as well as I knew any, only underlined the strangeness of the migrations that objects undergo. In places such as Tamatea – or, if you like, Dusky Sound – I was, and perhaps you would be, overwhelmed by the particularity of place, by temperate humidity, tangled vegetation, slippery stone, and the seal's splash. The journal seemed profoundly connected with that locality, among others in the South Pacific, and with great grey oceans and ice floes. I found its connection with the Staatsbibliothek harder to grasp, despite the fact that a German state library is a 'natural' location for the papers of a German scientist. What is now, for those who know Wenders' film, a library of Angels has its own environmental specificity; it is in the midst of a city undergoing a new reconstruction consequent on reunification. It is a site that speaks a history 'since 1945'.

25 (a–d)
View in Berlin State Library, 18 November 1997

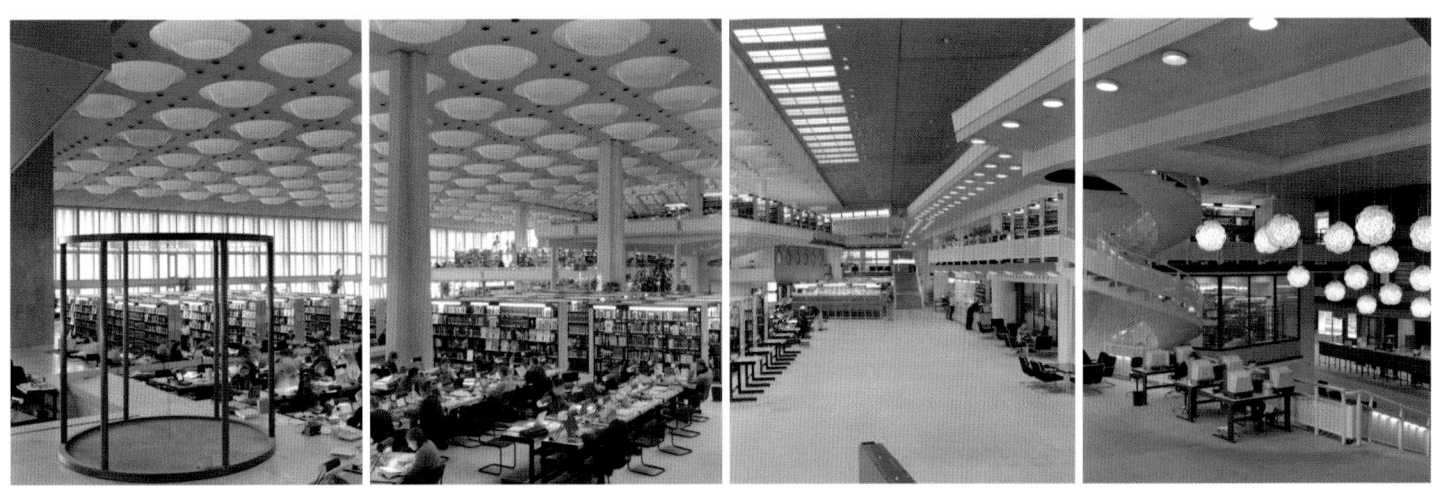

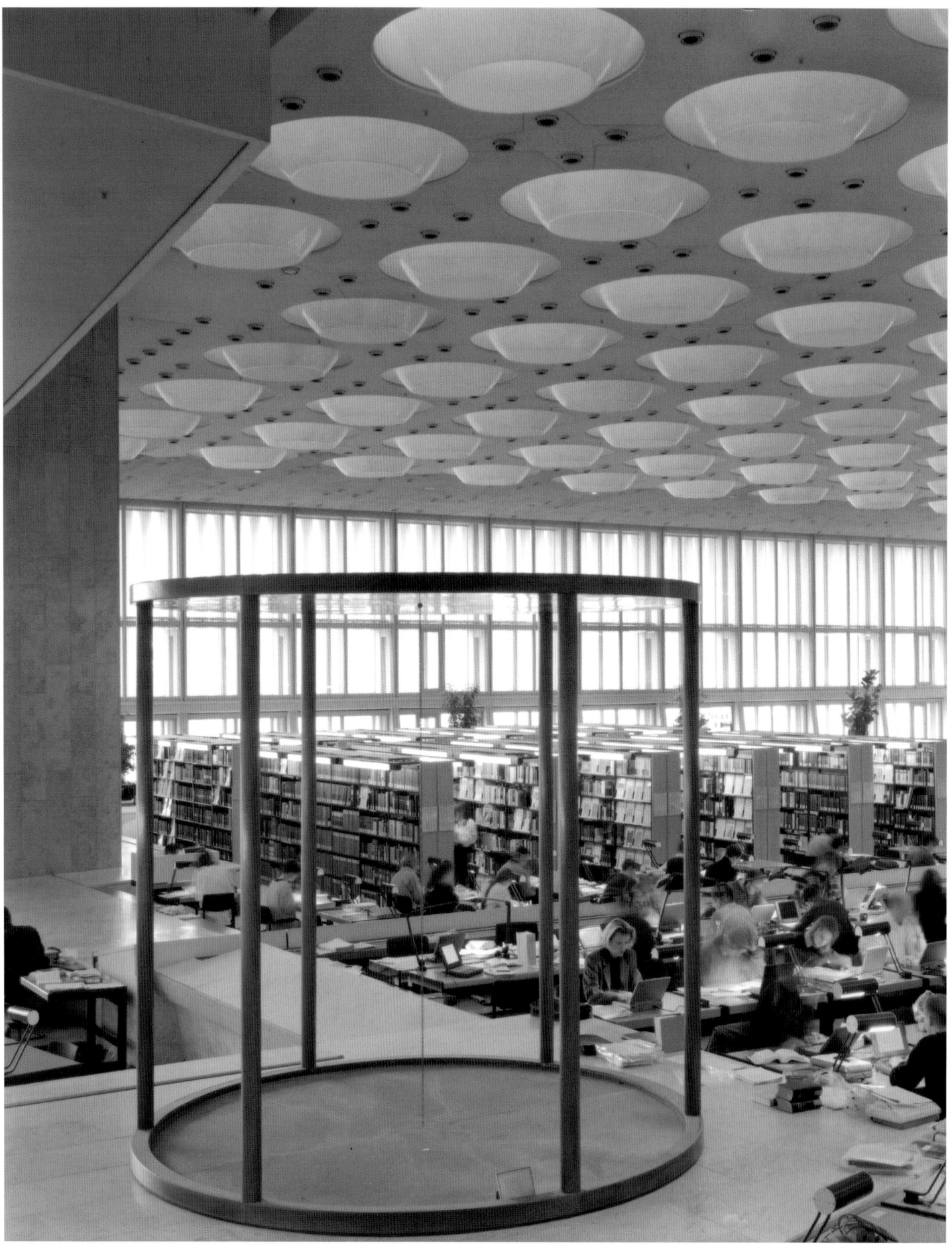

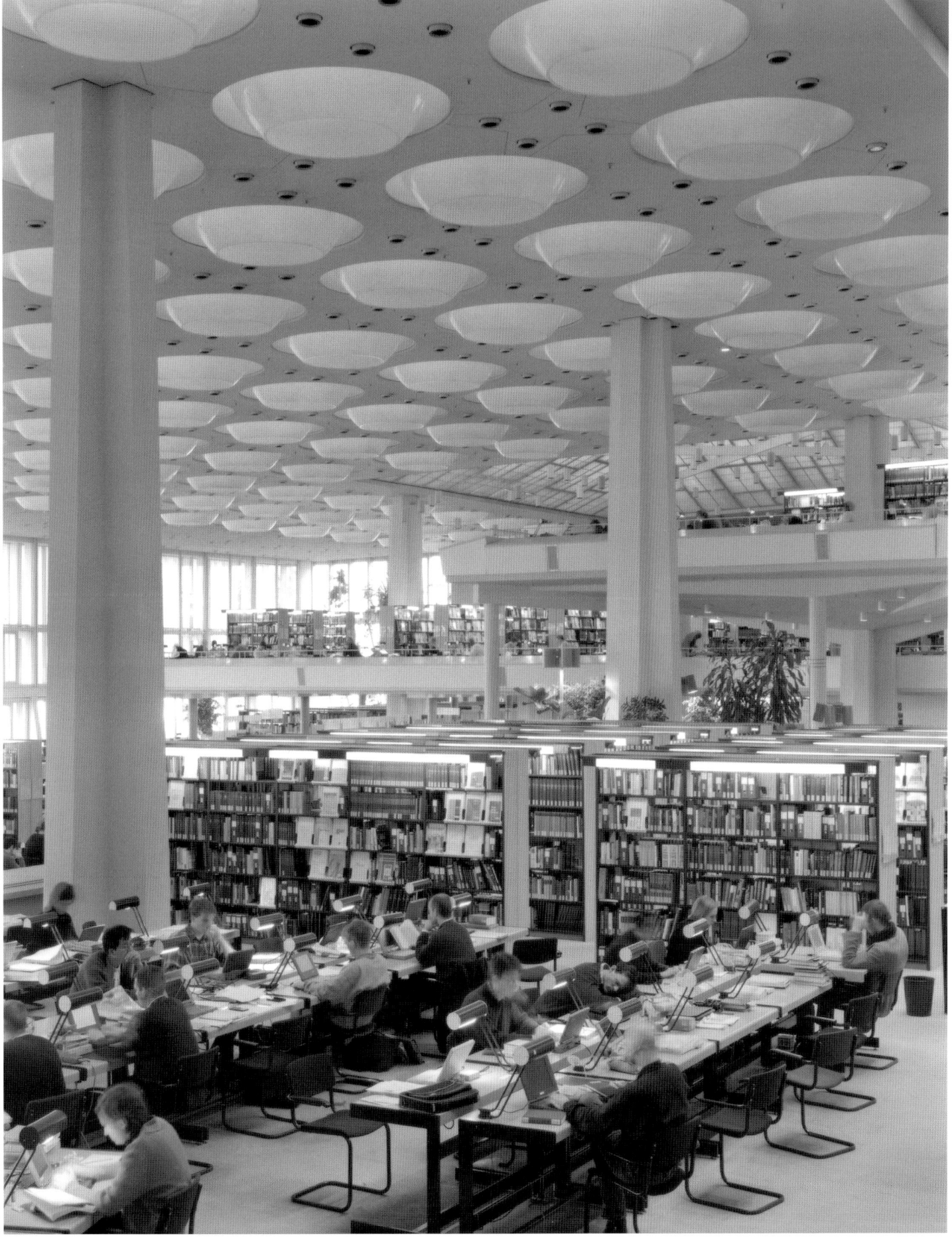

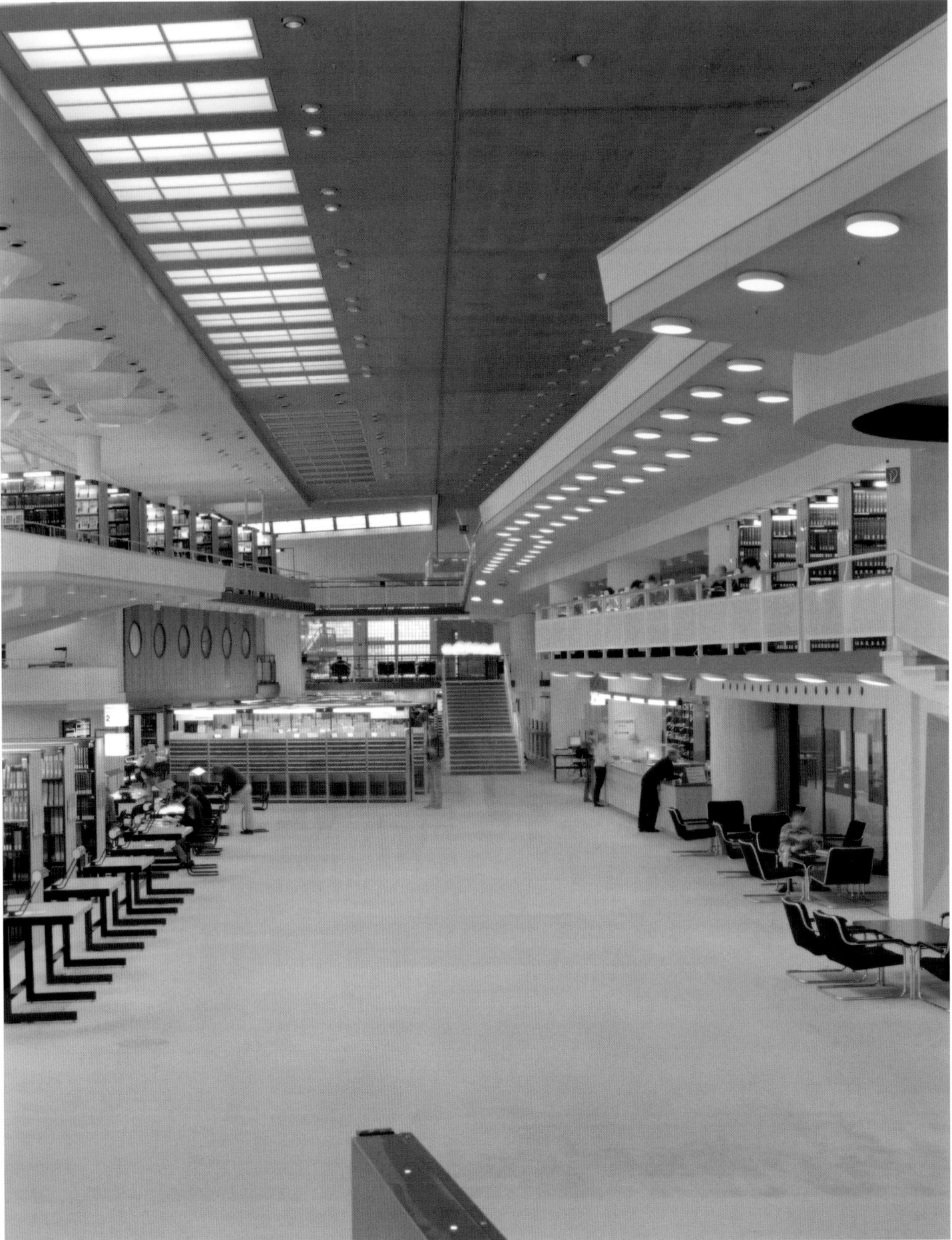

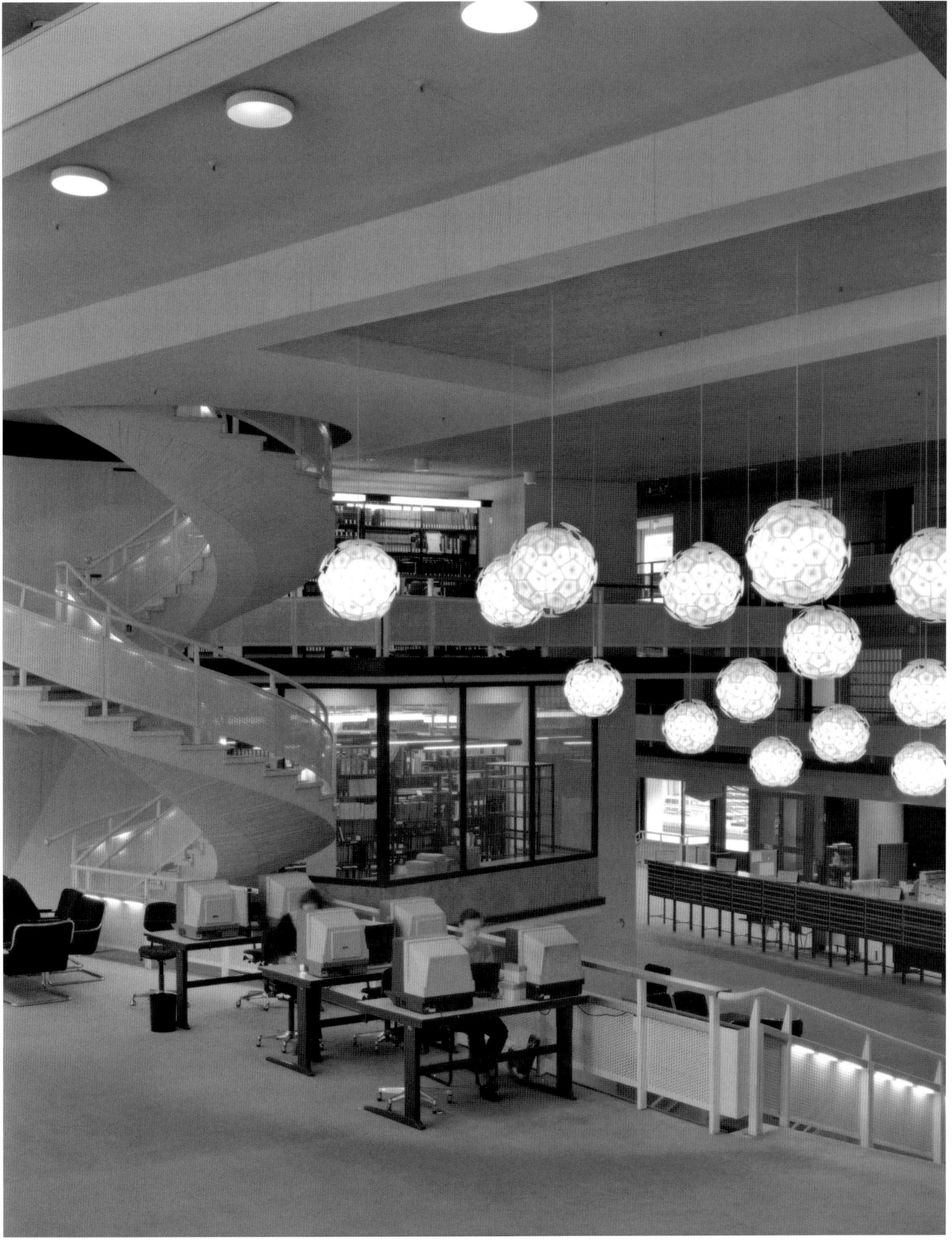

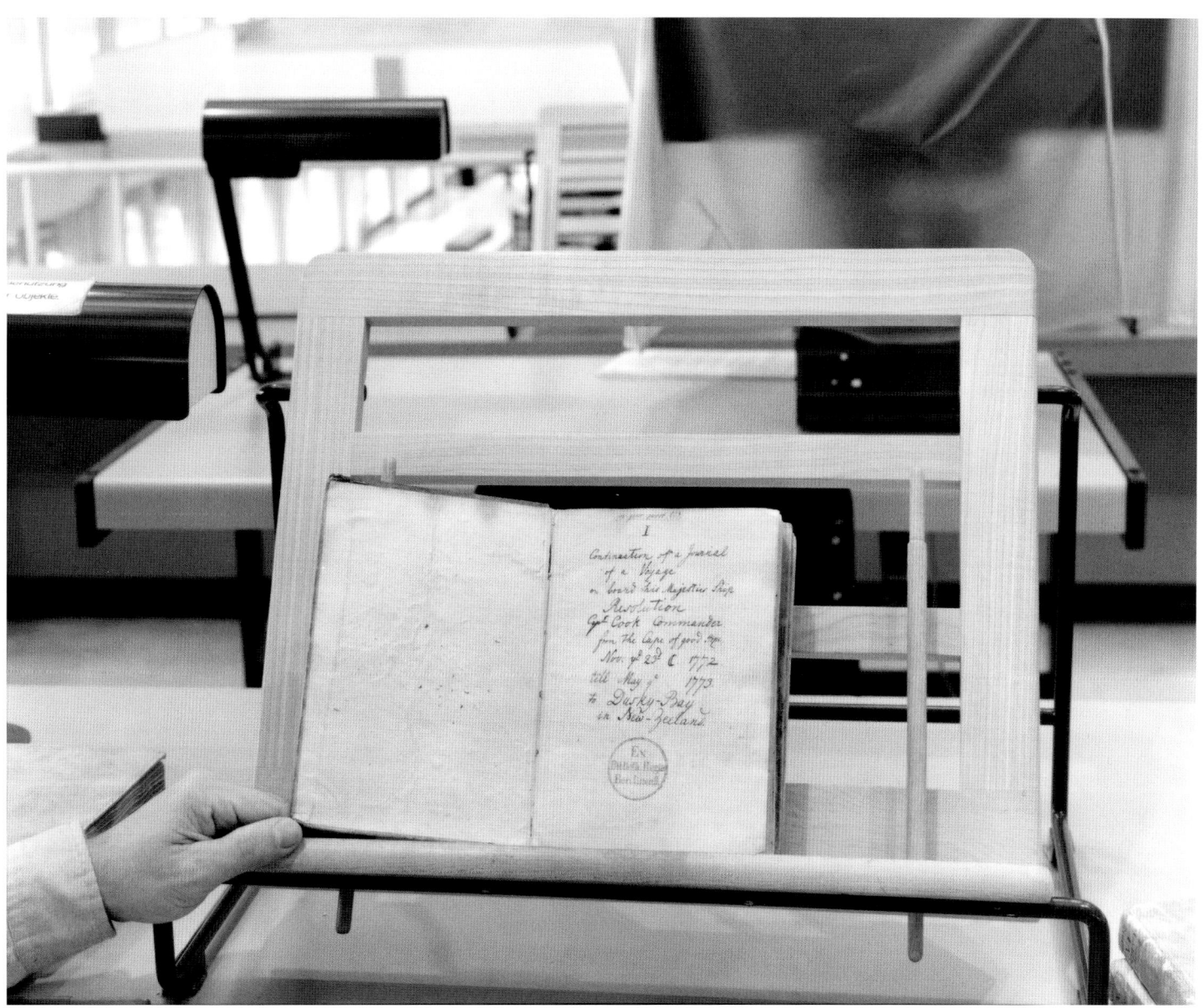

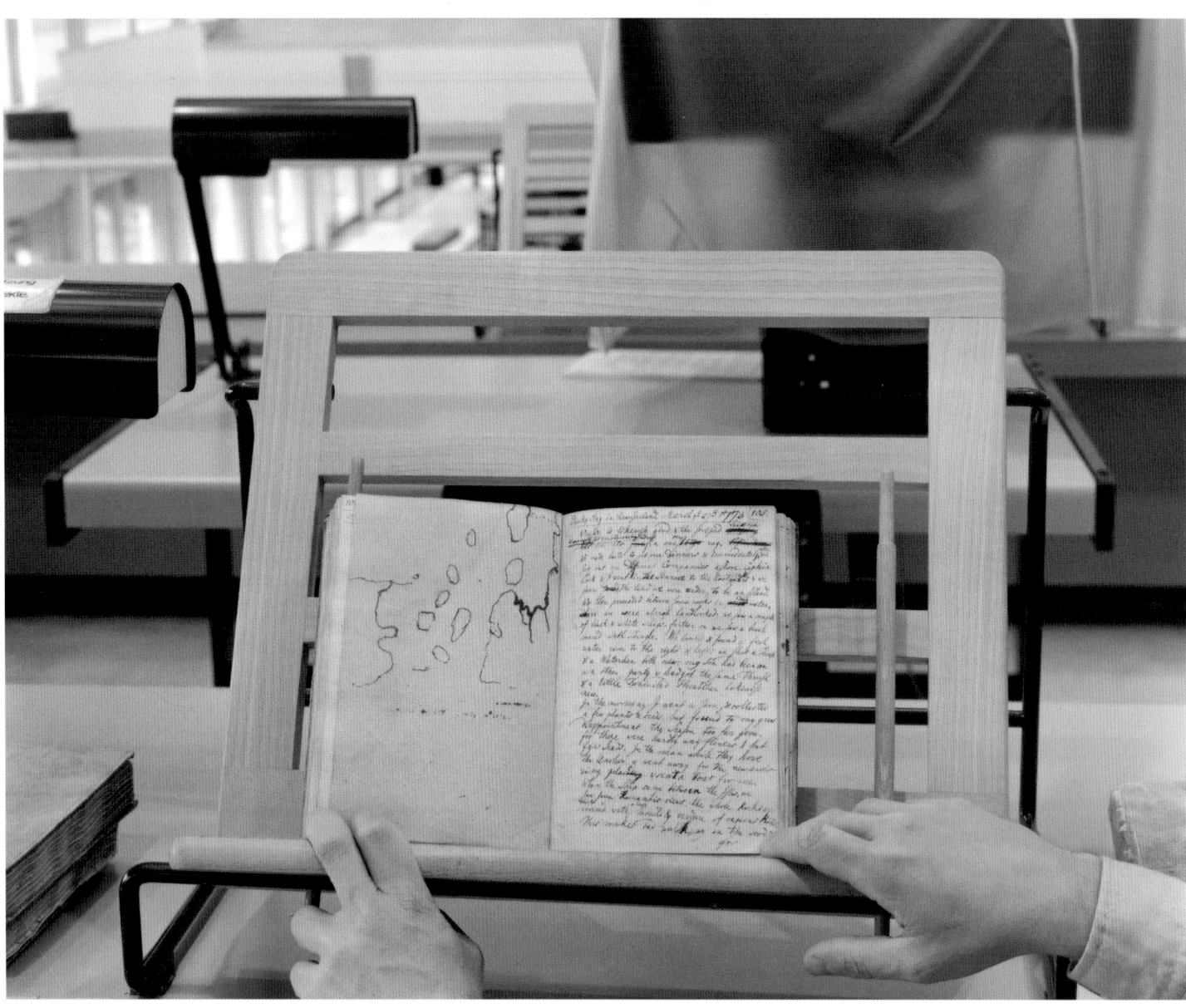

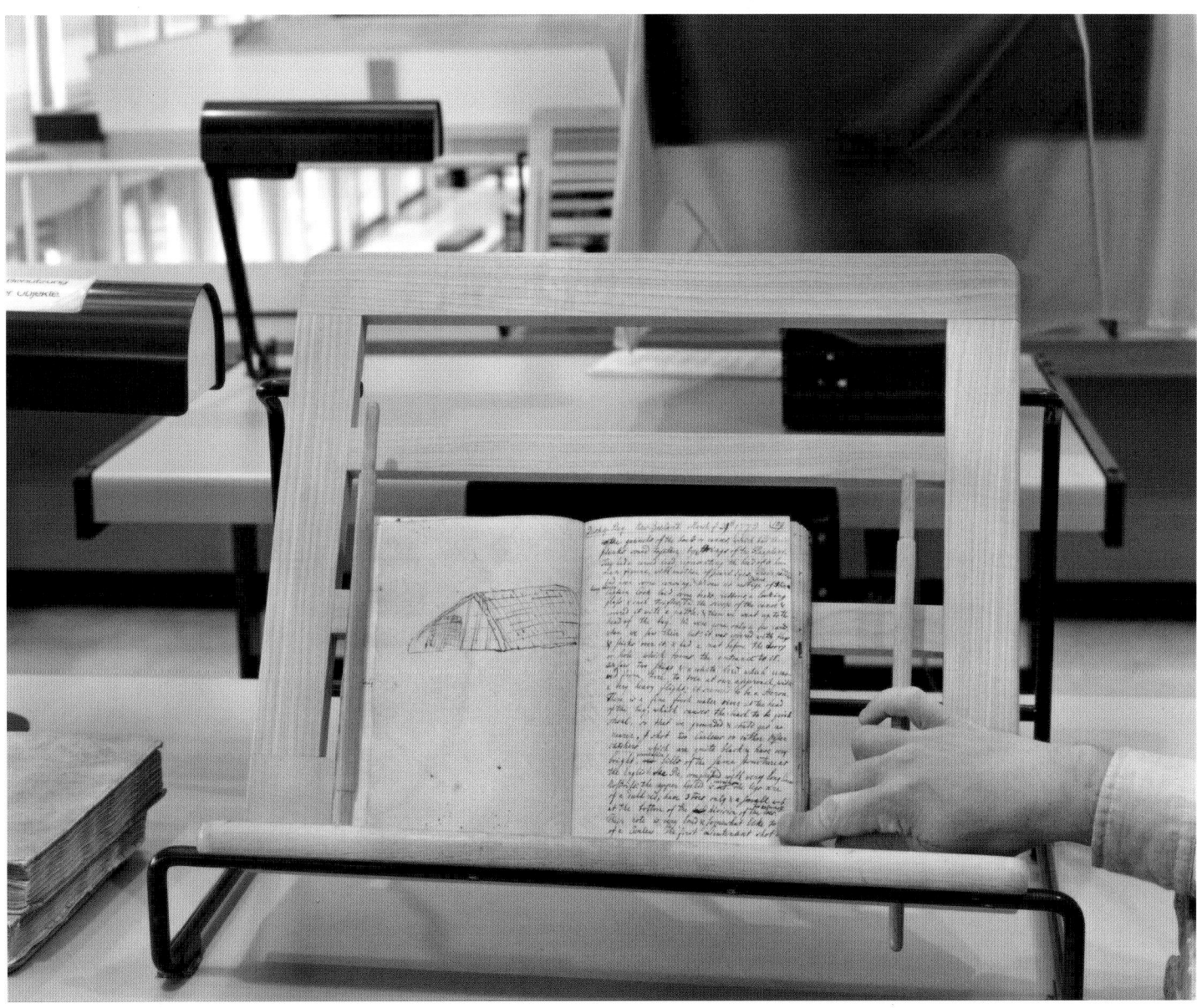

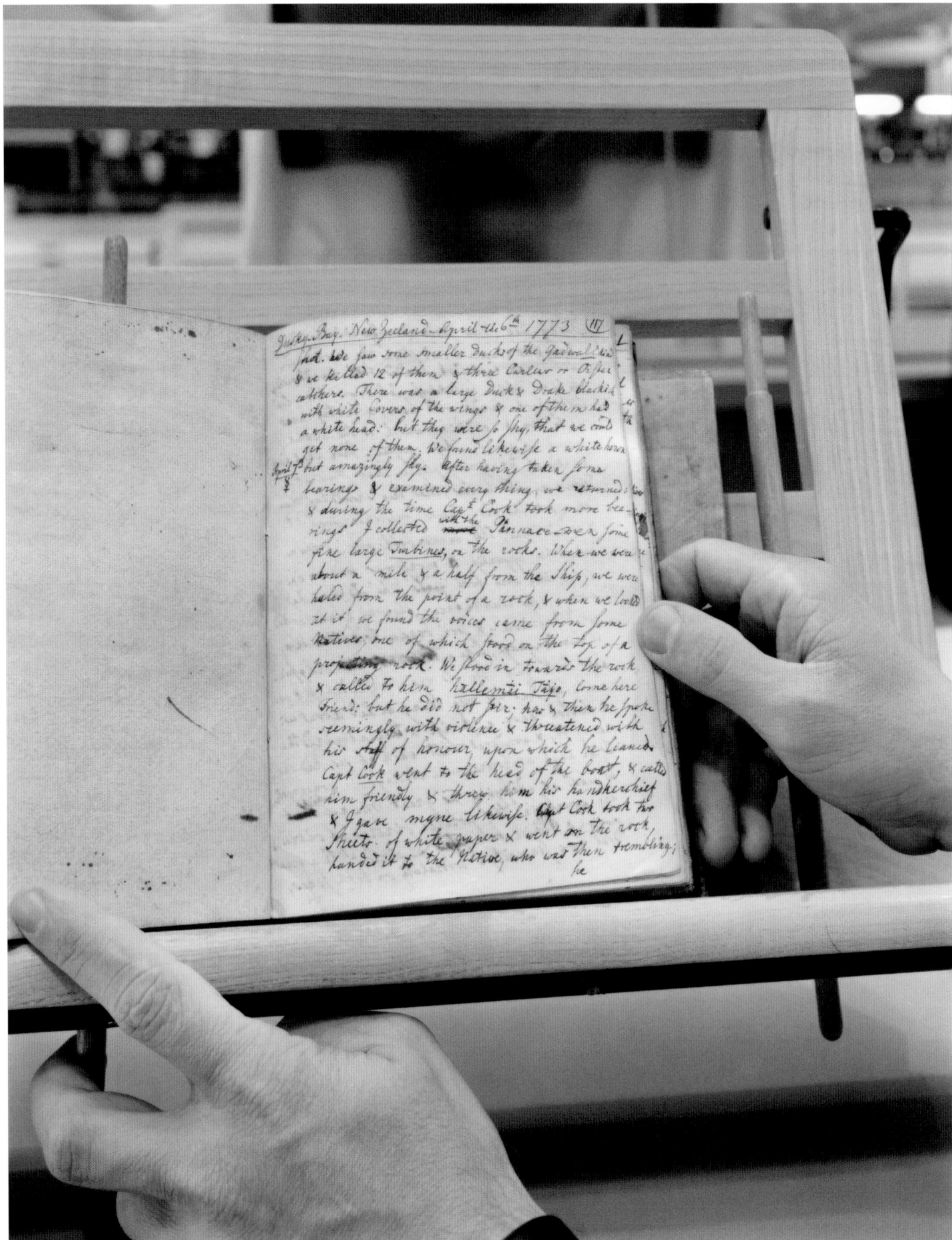

Dusky Bay, New Zeeland. April 16th 1773 (17)

shot. We saw some smaller ducks of the Gadwall kind
& we killed 12 of them & three Curlew or Cooper
others. There was a large Duck & Drake blackish
with white Covers of the wings & one of them had
a white head: but they were so shy, that we could
get none of them. We found likewise a white heron
but amazingly shy. After having taken some
bearings & examined every thing, we returned
& during the time Capt. Cook took more bearings I collected with the Pinnace over some
fine large Turbines, on the rocks. When we were
about a mile & a half from the Ship, we were
haled from the point of a rock, & when we looked
at it we found the voices came from some
Natives; one of which stood on the top of a
projecting rock. We stood in towards the rock
& called to him hallemäi Tajo, come here
friend: but he did not stir; now & then he spoke
seemingly with violence & threatened with
his Staff of honour upon which he leaned.
Capt. Cook went to the head of the boat, & called
him friendly & threw him his handkerchief
& I gave myne likewise. Capt. Cook took two
Sheets of white paper & went on the rock,
handed it to the Native, who was then trembling;
he

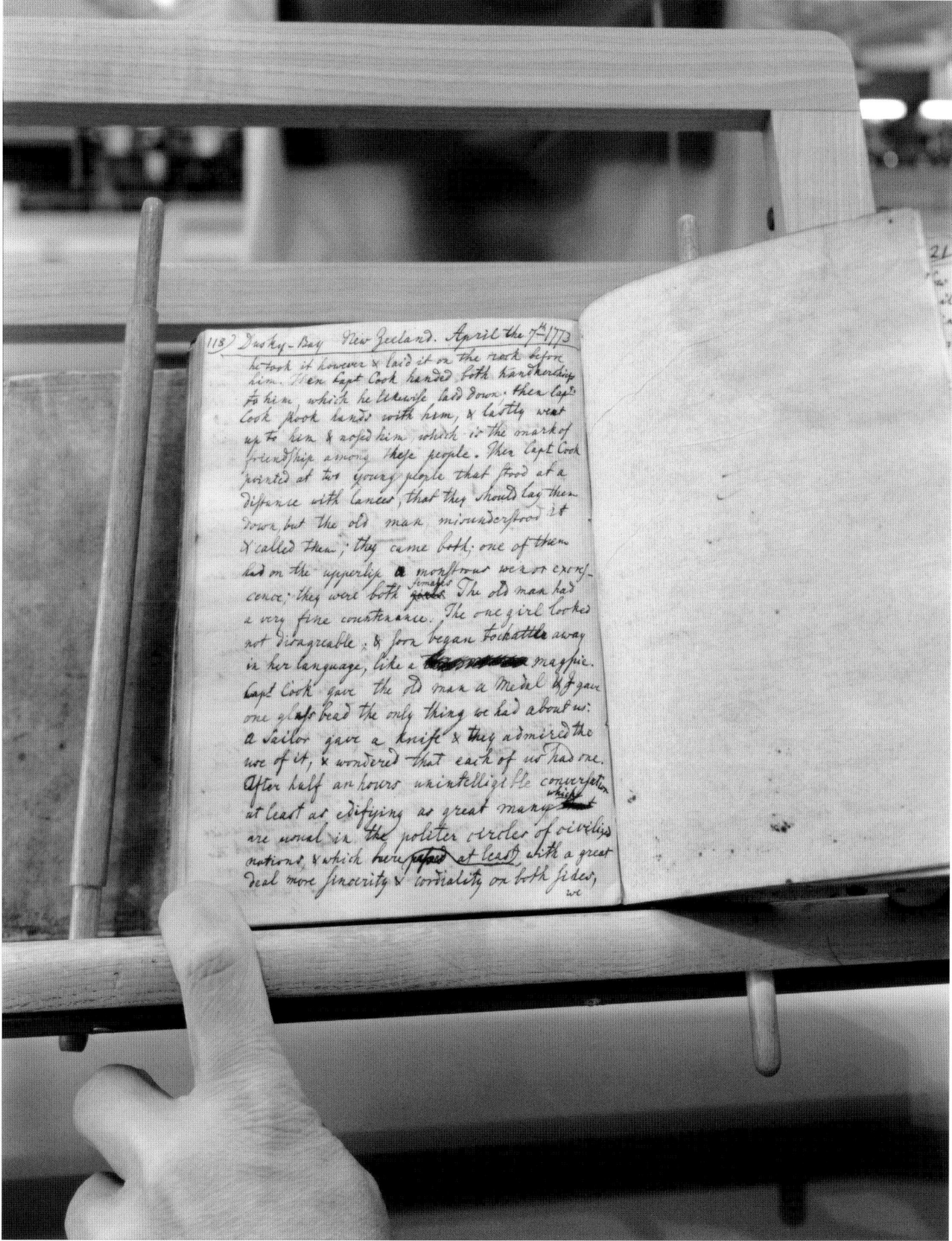

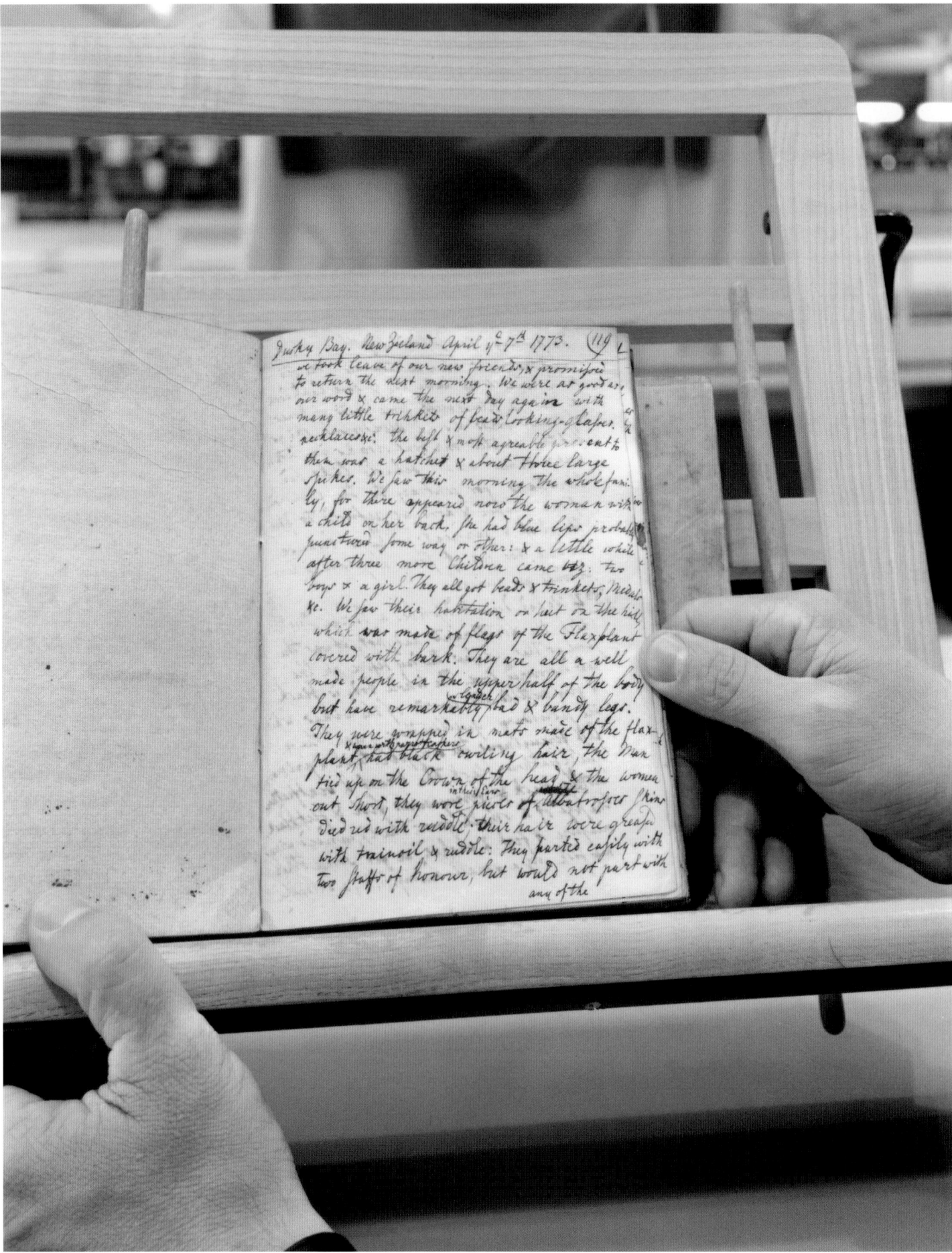

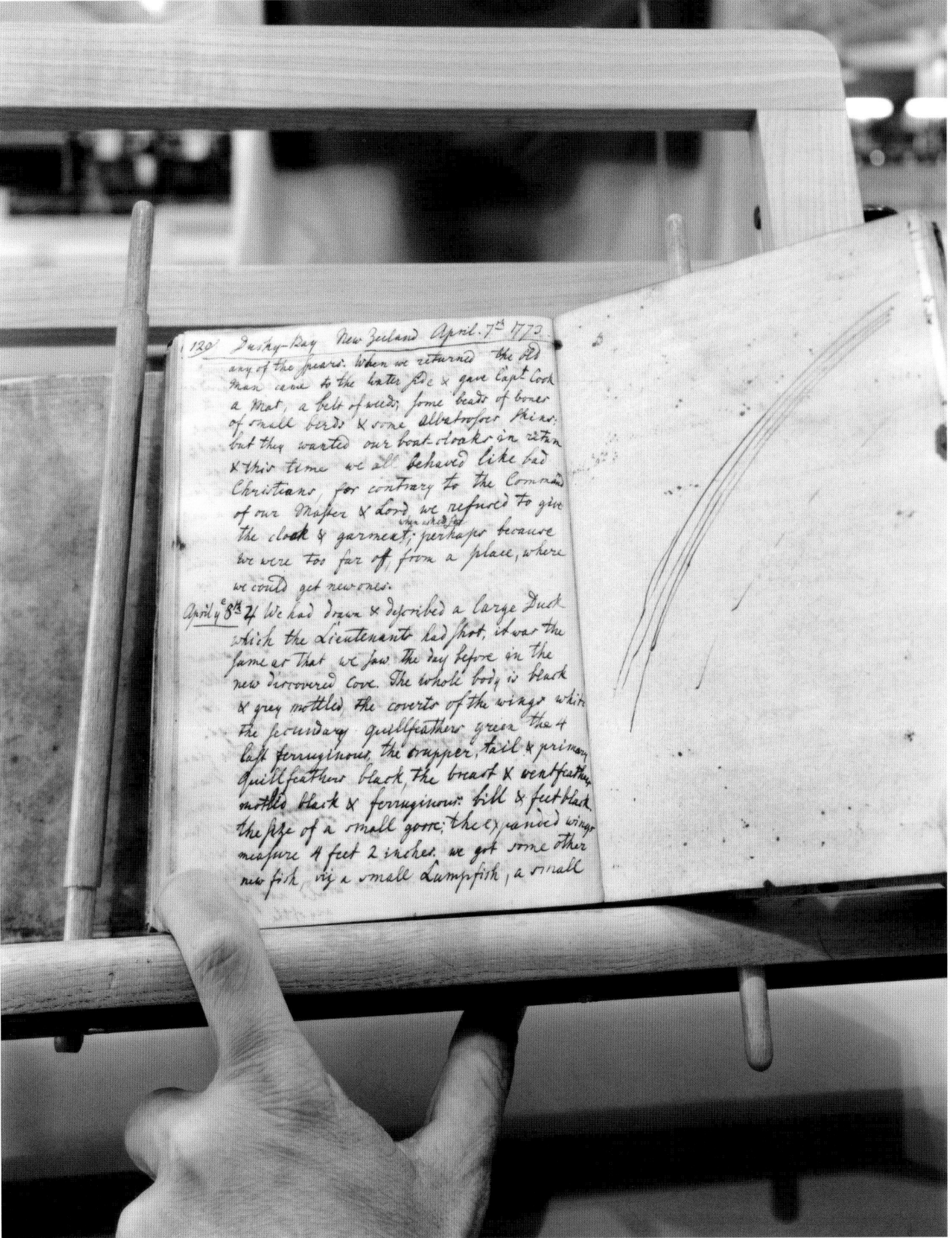

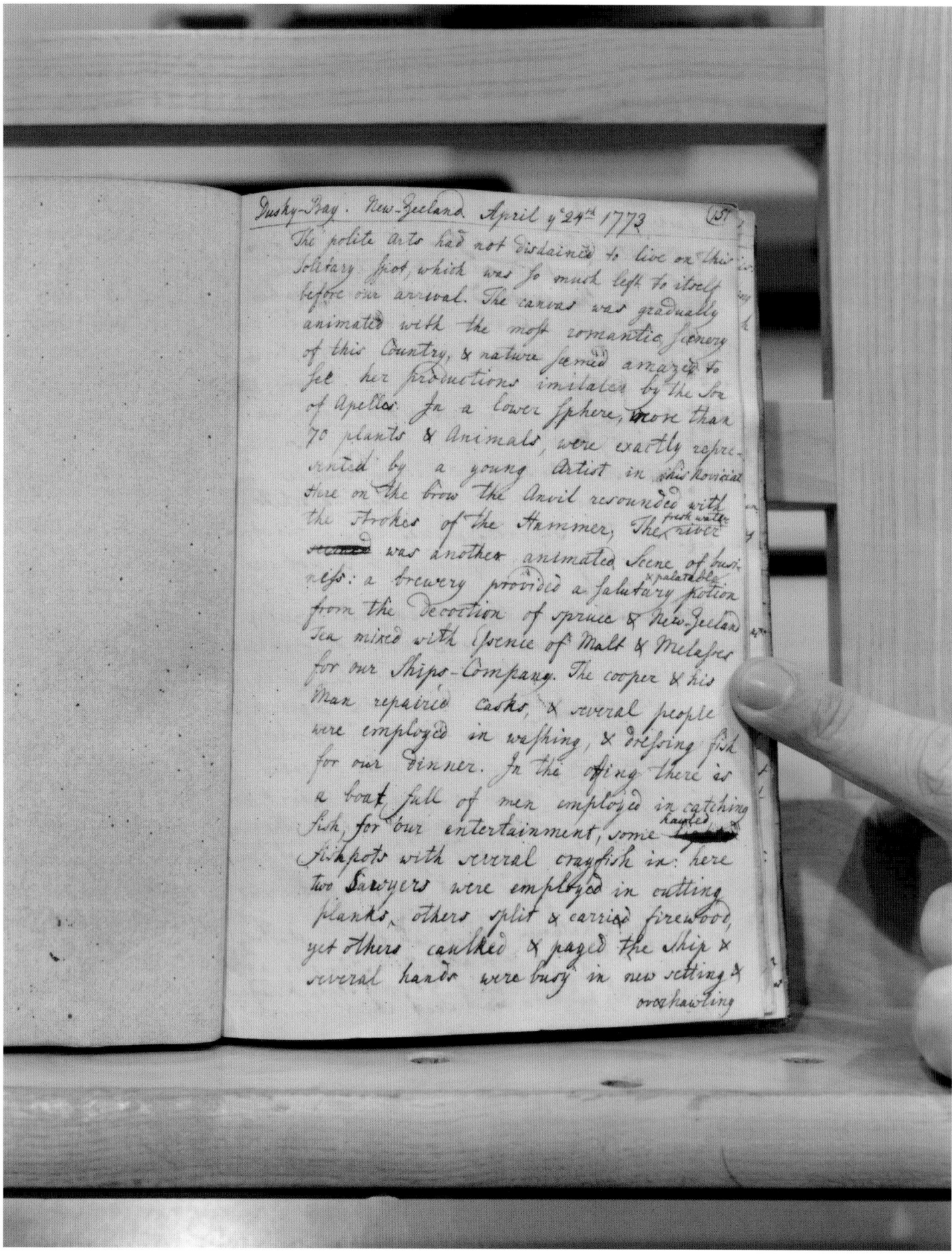

Dusky-Bay. New-Zeeland April y 24th 1773   [51]

The polite arts had not disdained to live on this
solitary spot, which was so much left to itself
before our arrival. The canvas was gradually
animated with the most romantic scenery
of this Country, & nature seemed amazed to
see her productions imitated by the Son
of Apelles. In a lower sphere, more than
70 plants & Animals, were exactly repre-
sented by a young Artist in this novitiate
there on the brow the Anvil resounded with
the strokes of the Hammer, The fresh water river
was another animated Scene of busi-
ness: a brewery provided a salutary & palatable potion
from the decoction of spruce & New-Zeeland
Tea mixed with Essence of Malt & Melasses
for our Ships-Company. The cooper & his
Man repaired casks, & several people
were employed in washing, & dressing fish
for our dinner. In the offing there is
a boat full of men employed in catching
fish, for our entertainment, some hauled
fishpots with several crayfish in: here
two Sawyers were employed in cutting
planks, others split & carried firewood,
yet others caulked & payed the Ship &
several hands were busy in new setting &
         overhawling

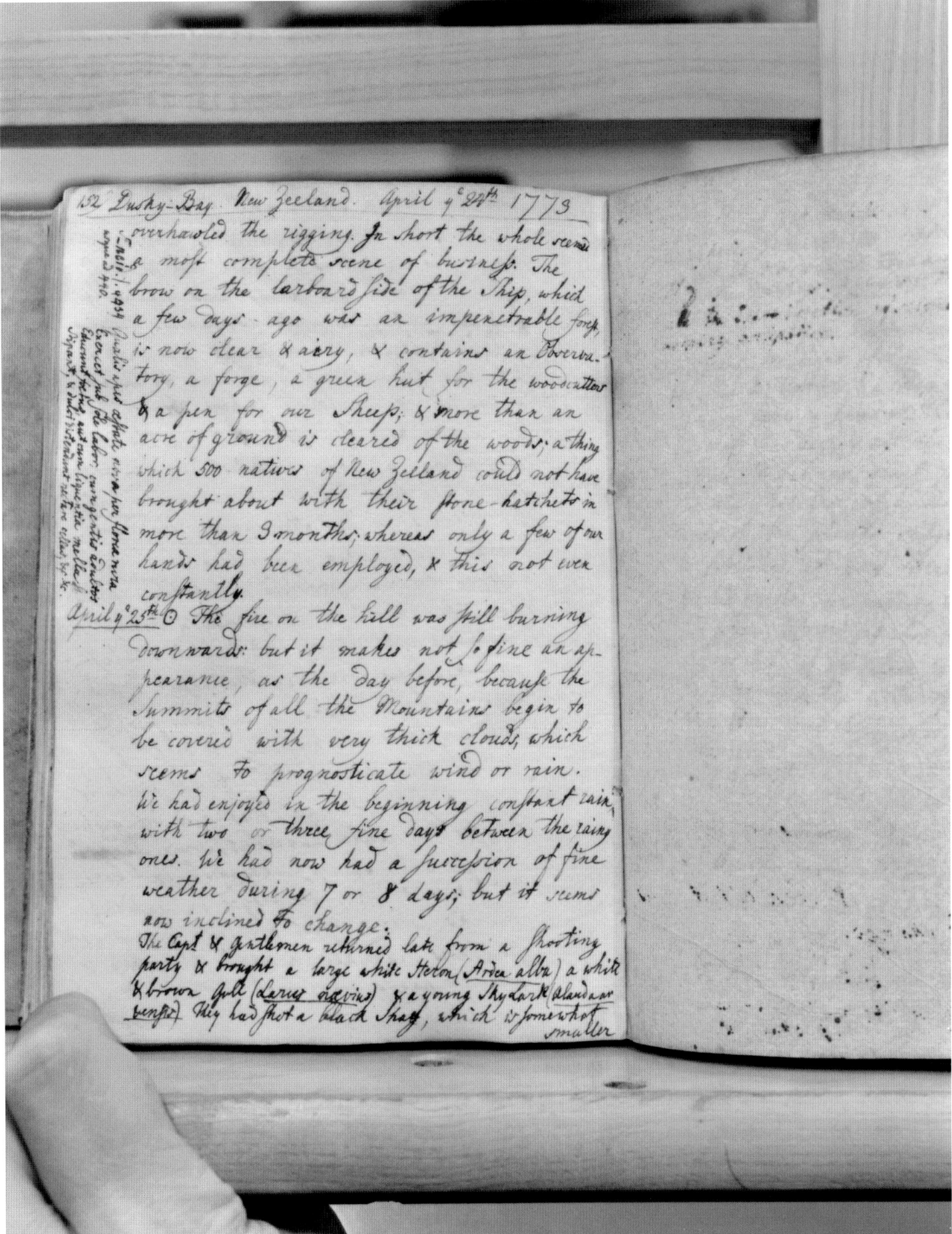

152 Dusky-Bay. New Zeeland. April y.e 24.th 1773

overhauled the rigging. In short the whole scene
a most complete scene of business. The
brow on the larboard side of the Ship, which
a few days ago was an impenetrable forest,
is now clear & airy, & contains an Observatory, a forge, a green hut for the woodcutters
& a pen for our Sheep; & more than an
acre of ground is cleared of the woods; a thing
which 500 natives of New Zeeland could not have
brought about with their stone-hatchets in
more than 3 months; whereas only a few of our
hands had been employed, & this not even
constantly.

April y.e 25.th ☉ The fire on the hill was still burning
downwards: but it makes not so fine an appearance, as the day before, because the
Summits of all the Mountains begin to
be covered with very thick clouds, which
seems to prognosticate wind or rain.
We had enjoyed in the beginning constant rain,
with two or three fine days between the rainy
ones. We had now had a succession of fine
weather during 7 or 8 days; but it seems
now inclined to change.
The Capt & gentlemen returned late from a shooting
party & brought a large white Heron (Ardea alba) a white
& brown Gull (Larus ridibus) & a young SkyLark (Alauda
sensis) They had shot a black Shag, which is somewhat
smaller

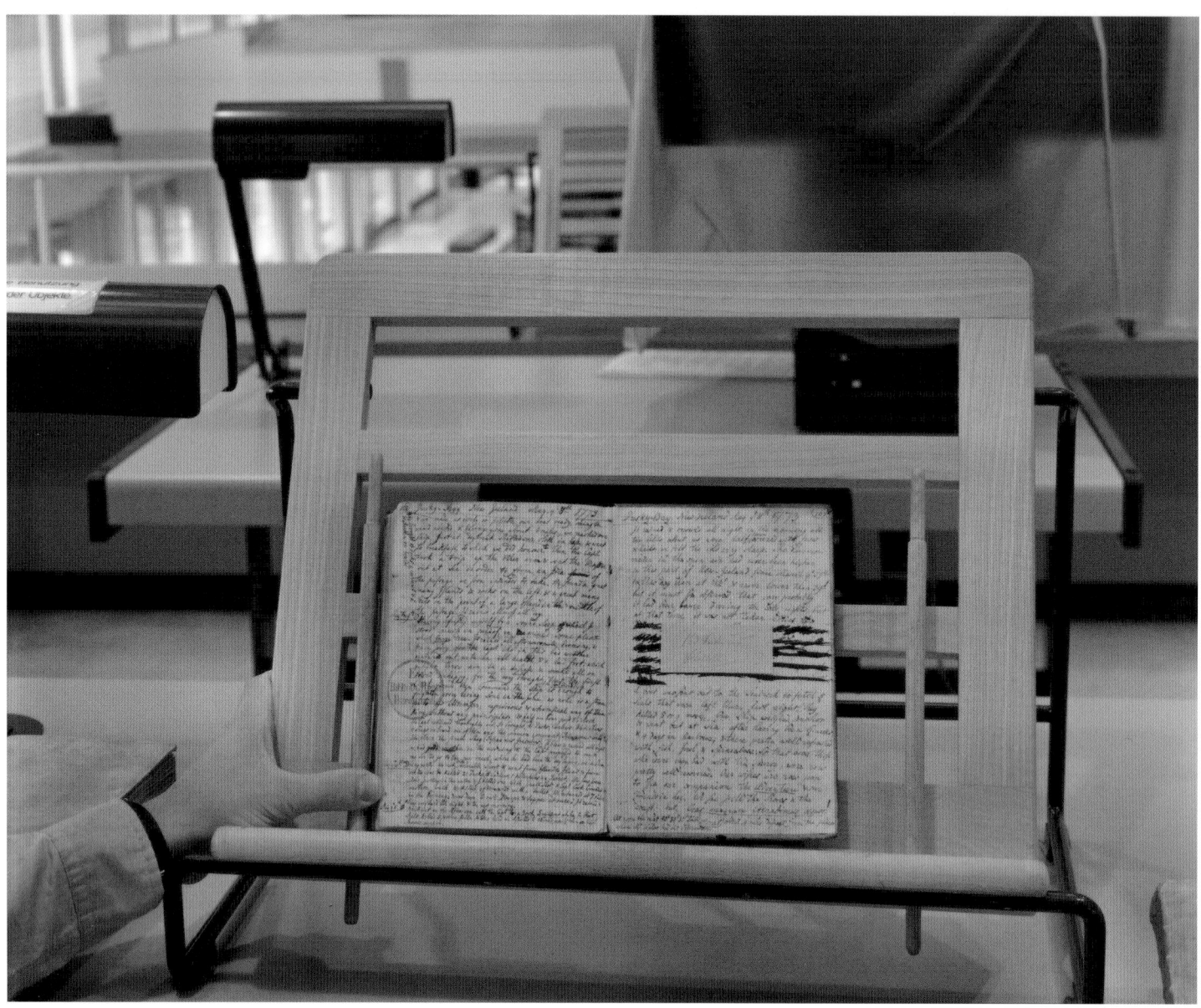

7. Göttingen

The dilute sun flickers through the winter trees. We're taking an afternoon intercity express from Berlin to Göttingen that rides indecently smoothly, given its speed. Most of the country is open, and is occupied by fields dedicated to one sort of industrial agriculture or another, but here and there a power station – I suppose a nuclear power station – emits clouds of steam; there are odd patches of forest, and occasional stands of trees alongside the railway line. It is as we pass these, and the sunlight is abruptly filtered before the copse is left behind, that we are conscious of the train's rapidity. It's as if one is flying low, rather than travelling overland: there's no irregularity, there are no bends, no awkwardness: this is travel without tactility.

You – if you come from New Zealand or Australia – are struck by a kind of confinement in the skies here. It's awkward, since one feels that a myth, indeed a set of clichés, concerning new and old worlds are confirmed by one's own experience. The pioneer vision that saw antipodean environments as bright and limitless was more than a nationalist or colonialist ideology, if you and I are right now, in being amazed, a couple of days off the plane from Auckland or Sydney, by the horizon's contraction here. The light is misty, diffuse, and soft; the sun, on a Thursday afternoon in the middle of November, is low in the sky; already the charcoal evening is gathering.

By the time we arrive in Göttingen it is raining softly. At a kiosk I buy a map and a guide to local museums, and we take a taxi to the hotel. I had left it late to make reservations, and the preferred albeit more expensive options nearer the centre of town were fully booked. I feel a twinge of disappointment and oddly even fear as the driver skirts around what appears to be a congenial, intimate old town, and takes us out toward some sort of periphery. I am not worried by the prospect of somewhere down-market or sleazy – not much chance of that, given that we've got the hotel's number from the city's official web site – but of what Marc Augé calls *non-lieux*, those domains and sites in which identity is evacuated, and through which so much travel consists in passing. I don't mind airports, but the aseptic standardisation of corporate hotels gets me down. And the hotel is indeed bland and white in the mist, and caters, it appears, for people who were once called commercial travellers; it is not far from a major freeway junction, and it evidently hosts business meetings and small conventions. We check in; there are already a couple of faxes from Canberra; what figures as a relief, though, is that the overheated and immaculate white rooms are irregular shapes, and this somehow makes it comfortable after all. We shower; Mark loads film in his room, while I collapse in mine, onto the enveloping duvet, and read a few chapters of Henry Handel Richardson's great novel of antipodean and expatriate identity, *The Fortunes of Richard Mahony*. Outside, the rain dissolves into mist.

Later on, we catch a cab into town and walk around the cobbled streets; it is cold, on the point of snow, I think; but the place is talkative and full of students; the bars are crowded, and the shops all open late. We eat in a classic German restaurant in the basement of the old Rathaus, a huge place full of dark wood, mounted stags heads, hunting pictures, and other weird relics. What with the sharp transition from the frosty air outside to the open fires, what with the schnitzel and good red wine, you too would have found it hard to imagine that we – or you – were there to look at relics that belonged to other histories altogether.

⌒

The museum dates back to the late eighteenth century, when Enlightenment philosophers, natural historians, and proto-anthropologists such as G.C. Lichtenberg and Johann Friedrich Blumenbach established a university cabinet, which incorporated both the natural specimens they used for reference purposes in teaching, and artificial curiosities from the South Seas and elsewhere. Some of the latter were obtained through dealers; the material was not yet tribal art but it was avidly sought after and trafficked in; as a result of Blumenbach's lobbying, the Hannoverian councillors made a direct request to George III, the upshot of which was that Göttingen obtained an important collection for just over £100. This had been assembled for the university by the London dealer George Humphrey, who himself collected ethnographic objects and shells, perhaps too enthusiastically: he had already been compelled by his creditors to send his own curiosities to the auction room. Soon after the main consignment of material arrived, Humphrey was good enough to supply further pieces, including a feather mask of the Hawaiian god Kuka'ilimoku and one of the ritual costumes of the Tahitian 'chief mourner'; the former remains absolutely arresting, the latter is a spectacularly complex assemblage of feathers, barkcloth, netting, tortoise-shell, wood, and a number of types of shell. The mourner's costumes were the Polynesian curiosities that Europeans from Joseph Banks onward had found fantastical and fascinating: the museum was singularly fortunate to acquire this example, at a time when it was already being said that they could not be obtained at any price. The Humphrey collection included many New Zealand pieces, including flax capes, greenstone artifacts, the handclubs known generically as *patu*, fish-hooks, paddles, combs, and flutes; though all these were certainly obtained during one or other of Cook's voyages, it is not known when, where exactly, or by or from whom.[19]

After the death of Johann Reinhold Forster, Blumenbach was again able to obtain university funds to purchase what remained of his collection (much of which had already been dispersed, most significantly through a gift to the University of Oxford, otherwise to various prospective patrons and others). The pieces most likely to have been collected by one or other Forster, probably in Queen Charlotte Sound rather than in the far south, include whalebone and basalt *patu*, a two-metre *taiaha*, and a beautiful *kete*.

This is a small museum, and one that is very much part of an anthropology teaching department: there are the usual things like noticeboards with lecture and scholarship announcements, and people frowning over aged photocopiers. There is the informality of the academy; there are big maps of Africa in the classrooms. The Cook/Forster display is in old but refurbished cases. The objects are well illuminated. The captions are correct if cursory. Naming nods toward native precedence: 'Aotearoa' in large letters stands above the subscript '(Neuseeland)'.

The 'glass case' now has a certain notoriety, implying as it does that what it contains has been irretrievably removed from the world of life. Before it, in the small and comparatively intimate museum, you may be distracted by reflection. You might dwell, as I did, on the question of whether these objects, these taonga, are sad to be so far from their lands of origin. Let us not be too hasty, though, in presuming that a European location is necessarily a sign of an evil, that nothing is attested to here apart from loss and displacement. These *taonga* may, perhaps, also be proud to represent their lands and peoples, as they stand at the endpoints of both Polynesian and European voyages. It is not as though the original condition of the Oceanic object – whether treasure, tool, or both – was ever one of static attachment to place or person. Things always moved, and lived because they moved, as gift and debt. So there is no simple sense in which these things *should* be elsewhere rather than here. Today, Polynesian people belong in the United States, Germany, and Australia, as well as all the other places to which they have migrated; perhaps Polynesian things likewise belong in the places to which they have been trafficked or sent. We peer through the glass, into the weave of the flax, and into the involuted spiral and residual ochre of the 'Canoe prow ornament(?)' – the (?) indexes somebody's, rather than everybody's, loss of knowledge, I suppose.

One dwells on the complexities and tries to avoid a simple condemnation of a collection of this kind. One thinks of the question of repatriation, which can never be far from the mind of any curator of an ethnographic museum today, and tries to avoid presuming that there is only one right answer. Nevertheless, one comes back to a sense that these costumes, gods, and clubs are weirdly placed, and may be just out of place.

The glass also bears reflection in a literal sense. We face not the objects themselves, but reflections of the other cases, of Cook's portrait, of the room as a whole, of the rank of venetian blinds. That rank of immaculate blinds suddenly looks like nothing so much as a minimalist white-on-white installation. It's hard to say whether the many interrupted horizontal bands, or the few continuous vertical ones, dominate this austere work, which even the Forsters seem to study reverentially from within the frame of their portrait. Cook, it has to be said, looks a little askance. Kukaʻilimoku, who knows and serves an art of blood and feathers, not form, is unmoved, still intransigently ferocious.

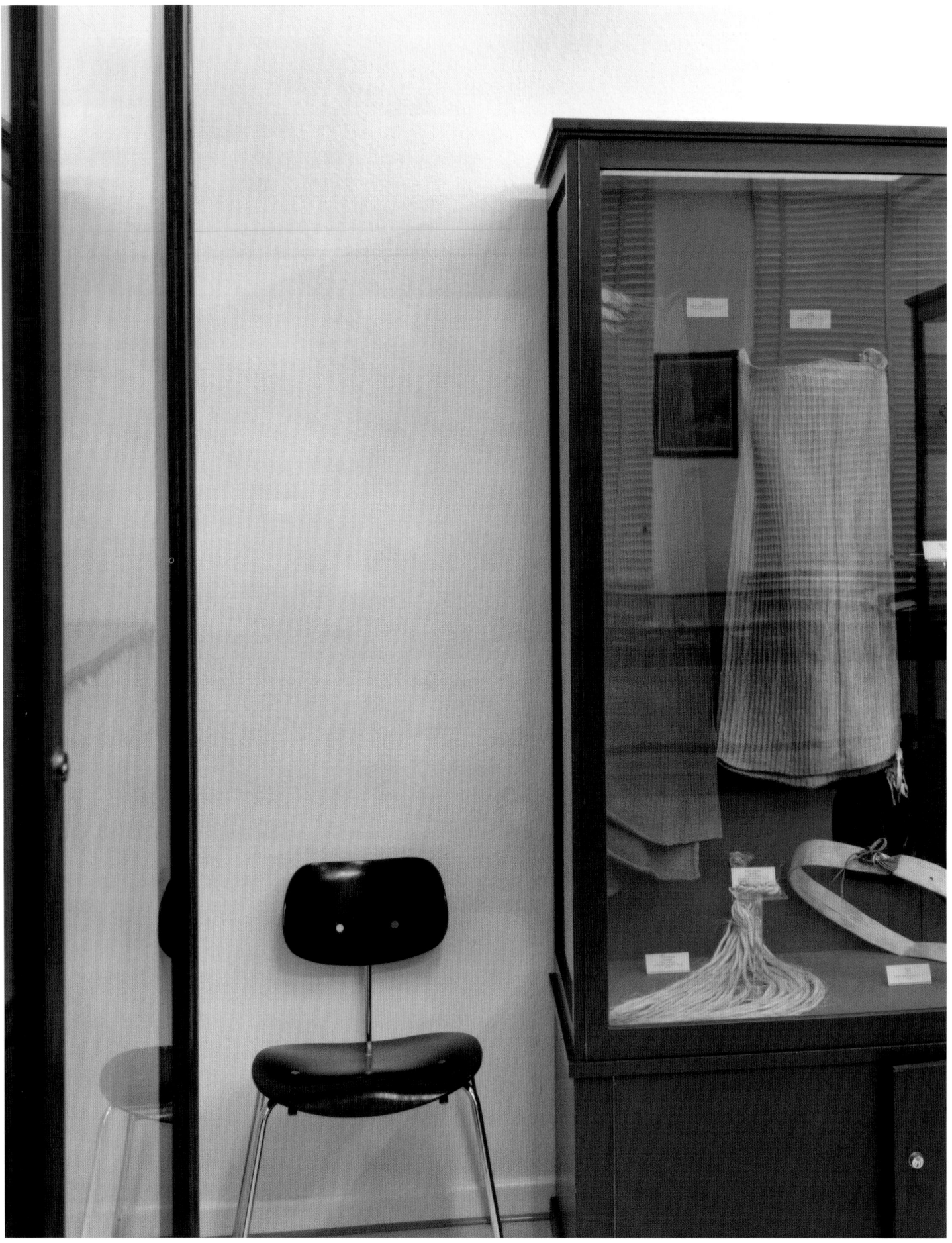

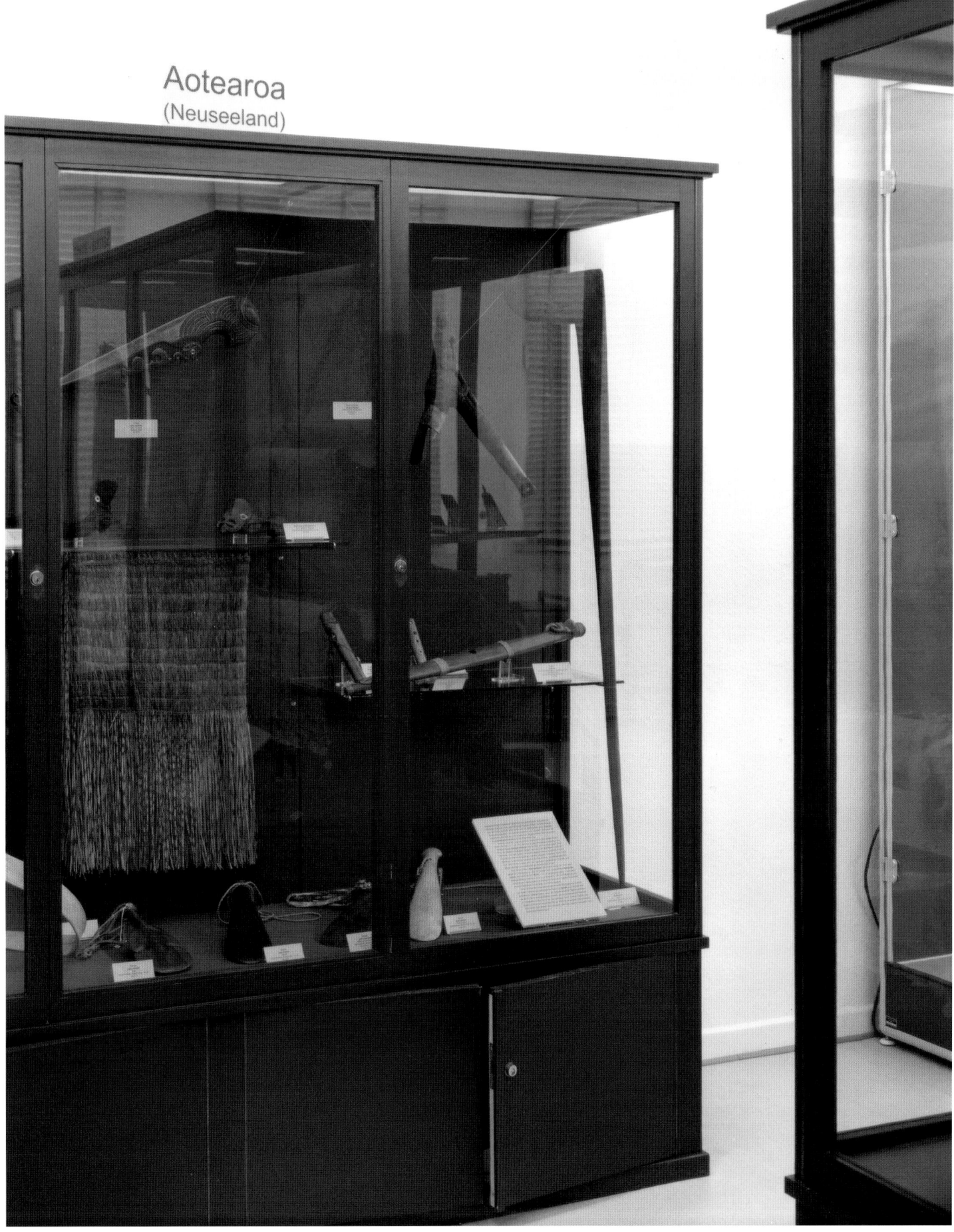

Aotearoa
(Neuseeland)

36 (a, b)
Aotearoa case, Institute of Ethnology Museum,
University of Göttingen, 21 November 1997

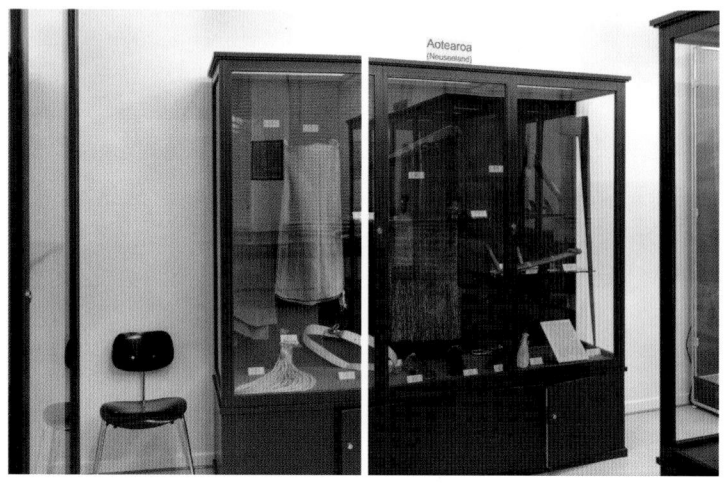

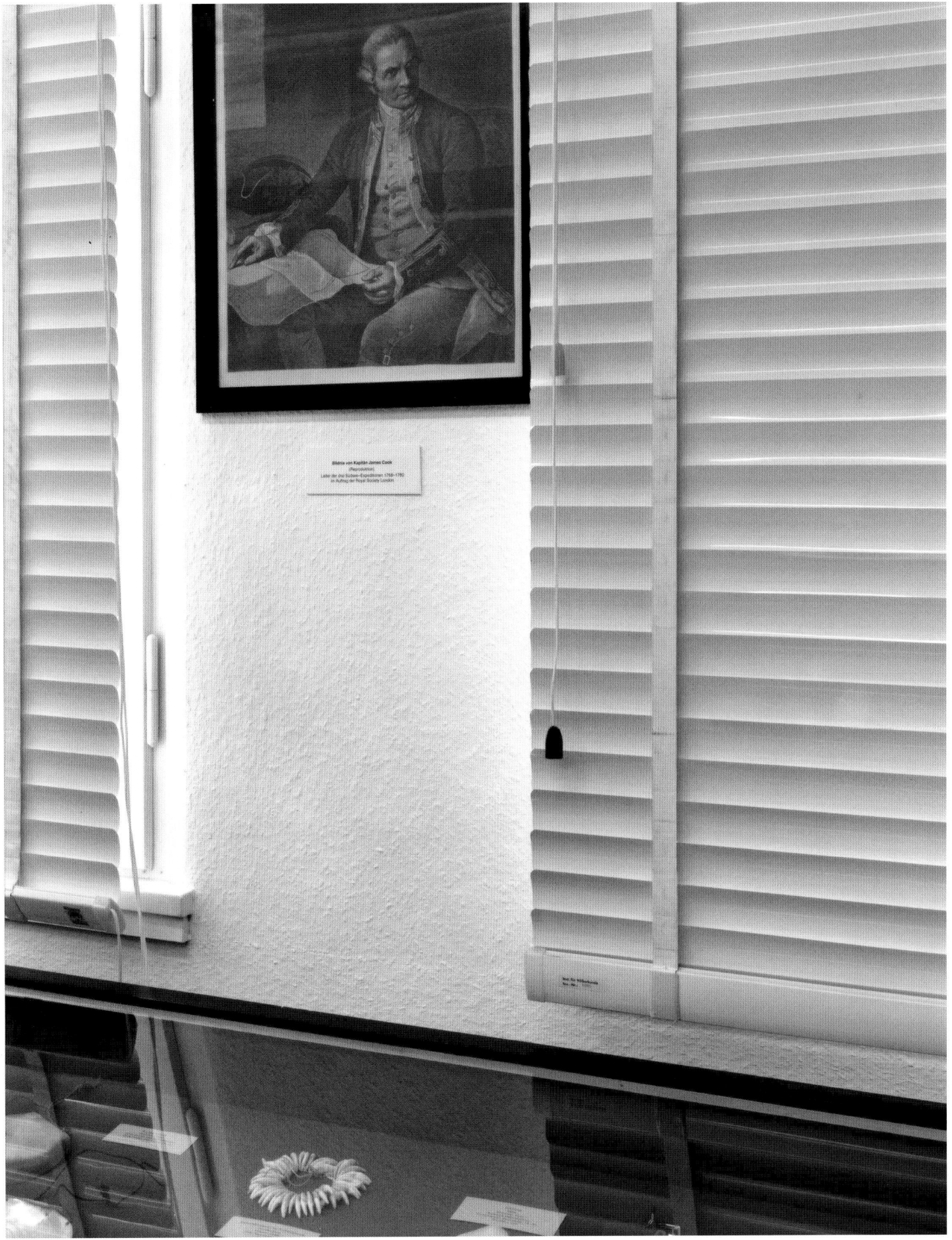

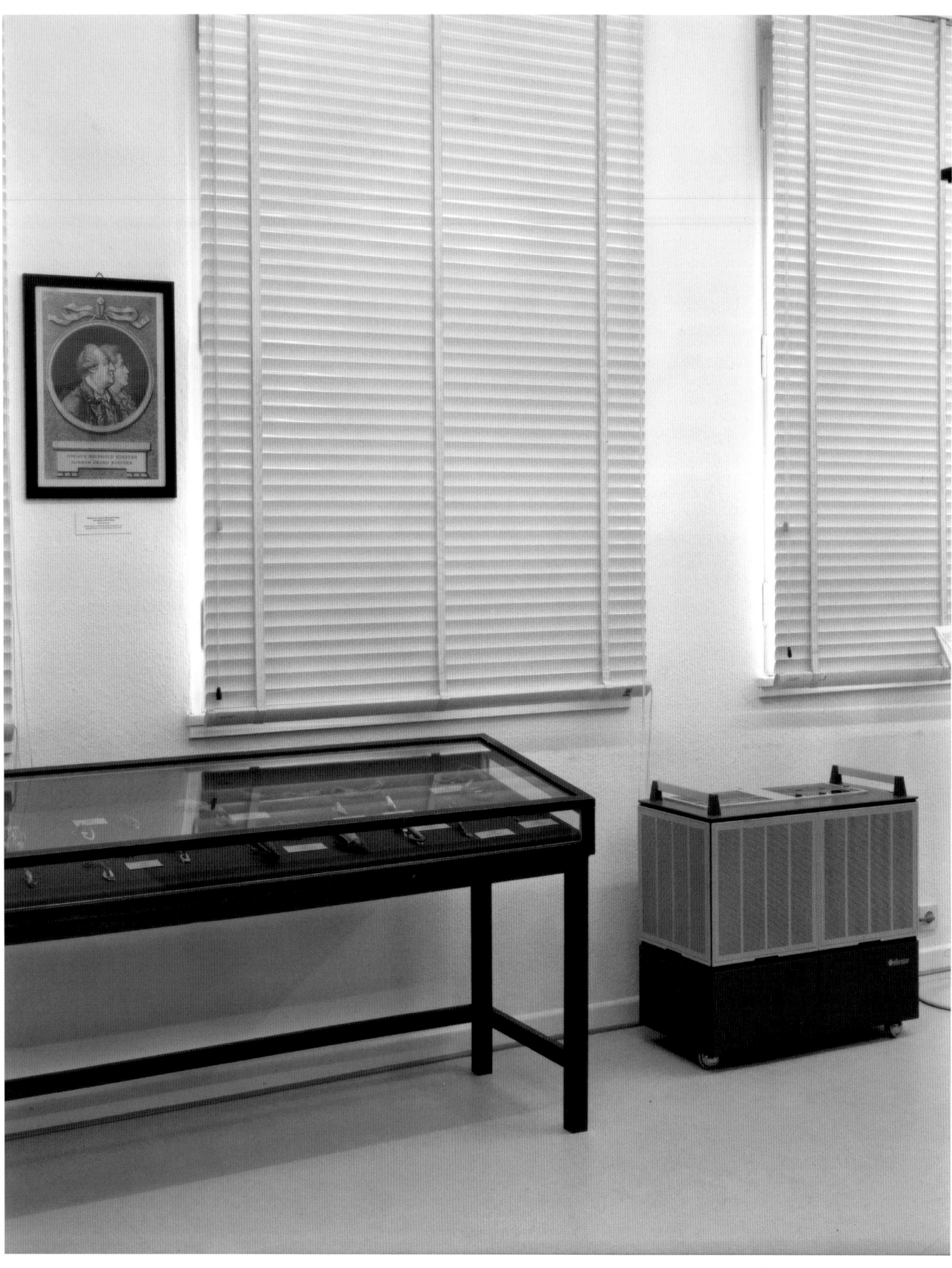

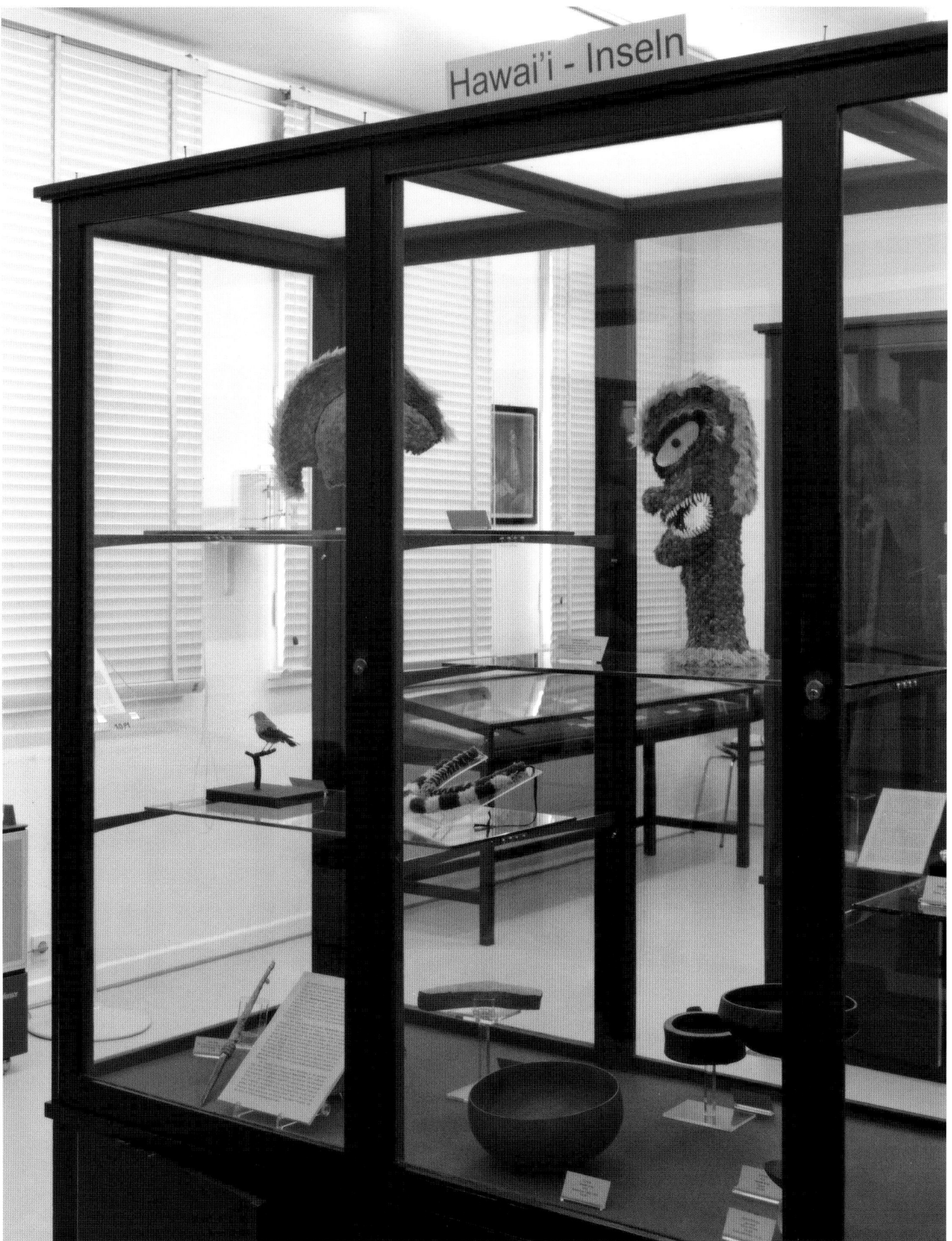

38 (a,b)
Hawaii case, Institute of Ethnology Museum, University of Göttingen,
21 November 1997

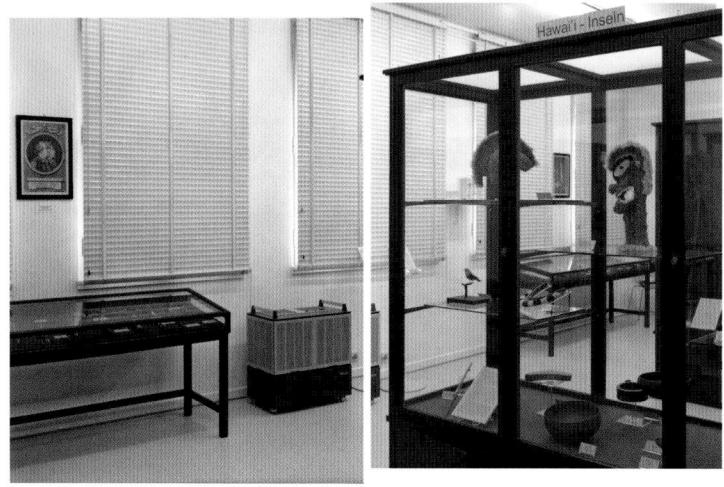

8. Oxford

I am foolish enough to choose a four o'clock train from Paddington to Oxford: though we find seats, the carriage is crammed with standing commuters. I am still more foolish in failing to avoid the Virgin Trains service, which is said to be the object of more complaints than all the other privatised British rail companies put together. Admittedly this particular train runs on time, but the carriage is ankle-deep in polystyrene cups, junk food wrappers, and other detritus.

It is early summer. Oxford is crowded. Tourists and students are milling around the pubs on the stone pavements. There are boards up for Inspector Morse tours guided by undergraduates in academic dress. I remember previous trips here: in the late seventies, as a young tourist; in the early eighties, as a nervous graduate student, to call on a senior Pacific historian; and later, mostly fleeting visits – for conferences, to do archival work among the colonial records in Rhodes House, to meet Oxford friends, who mostly now live elsewhere; and on various occasions to do research in the Pitt Rivers Museum. I take a cab to a hotel on the Banbury Road; we stop and start through the city centre. The hotel is staffed by Italians; its driveway features a copy of a Minoan fresco from Knossos, the bull-vaulting image, more restoration than original, which is on all the postcards. I intend, but forget, to ask staff what it is doing there. My room is above the street; that night, I am woken intermittently by heavy trucks.

The Pitt Rivers Museum is an icon of Victorian anthropology. A.H.L.F. Pitt Rivers was a wealthy scientific amateur, actively involved in the debates about technology and evolutionism that animated the British ethnological world in the Victorian period. From the 1850s onward, he collected first weapons and then material culture on a much broader scale. In the early 1880s, after inheriting a huge estate, he attempted to donate his collection to government, subject to it being established in a London museum. Negotiations broke down, and in the end Pitt Rivers gave it to the University of Oxford.

There were once many museums organised like this, with symmetrically arranged dark wooden cases jammed with objects from Africa, Asia, Oceania, Australia, and the Americas. Since the turn of the century, most of these institutions have been renovated not once but several times, even if many today have an antiquated feel: once-fresh exhibits in the 1960s today seem as dated or more dated than some older displays. It was a provision of Pitt Rivers' bequest that his system of organising the collection was preserved. Though this did not, in fact, absolutely require later curators to leave the museum as it was, one is grateful that they have done so. The exhibits here are not geographically organised, as has happened in most anthropological museums since; there is no parcelling out of continents and islands within the hall. Here, instead, the arrangement is functional: smoking equipment from all parts of the world is found together, as are fabrics, containers, shields, arrows, and many other things. The display is a strangely powerful one that can be responded to in many ways. Pitt Rivers, and the inaugural keeper, Henry Balfour, intended the exhibits to exemplify what they saw as the evolutionary principles that had governed human development. On the one hand, the diverse materials manifested the unity of the species and suggested a variety of historical relationships between populations; on the other, they made it clear that humanity was ranked, and that successive technological advances could be noted from one population to another.

Yet this invidious message may easily be lost on viewers at the end of the twentieth century and the beginning of the twenty-first. What you or I encounter is instead an extraordinary expression of the rapacious appetite for specimens, and for knowledge in the form of artifacts, that nineteenth-century natural science exhibited. The aura this site possesses is that of the power of this effort of imperial antiquarianism. The power of the place is indefinably punctuated, however. The arrangement makes the effect of the museum and the main exhibition hall overwhelming: this is a place in which the whole and the enclosing case dominate the part and the thing contained. Yet the part and the things break into one's appreciation of the site. Most obviously, the totem pole from the American northwest coast is strangely grand, and certainly powerful in itself, in ways that precede and resist the power of Victorian ethnology. Here and there, also, one finds something small or seemingly decorative, reminding you and I that the things in this collection may have been assimilated into an anthropological institution, but they come from other places and bear other values that the institution, in displaying them, unavoidably draws attention to. It is as if the museum threw a spotlight onto its very strangeness, illuminating the fact that its grand narratives of social and technological development told us at best a little about the ways these various things were used, still less about their diverse significances, in their places of origin. The Pitt Rivers Museum has become not just a museum of itself, but almost an anti-museum.

After Cook's second voyage, Johann Reinhold Forster was awarded an honorary doctorate by Oxford, and he presented a collection of over a hundred Oceanic artifacts to the Ashmolean Museum. These were transferred to the Pitt Rivers Museum in 1886, and were incorporated into the larger, typologically arranged collection. In 1970, however, the museum organised a Cook bicentenary exhibition. The collection, which includes Tahitian barkcloth and one of the famous 'mourner's costumes', Tongan clubs and baskets, a Maori flax cape, *taiaha* and other *taonga*, was reassembled as a distinct entity. This small display on one of the balconies was thus at odds with the organisation of the Pitt Rivers Museum as a whole. It reunited things, not with the diverse indigenous values and practices from which they ultimately derived, but with the voyage and Forster's practice of collecting – hence the model of Cook's *Resolution*, the historical notes, and the reproductions of familiar portraits of the great navigator and his natural historian. The exhibit amounts to an historical monument, which seems to have crept, almost surreptitiously, into this museum of classical anthropology. A collection which presented itself once as something without a history, and as nothing other than an expression of imperial truth, is re-connected, in an awkward and implicit sort of way, with an admittedly almost amateurish commemoration of a voyage of discovery, of one of the beginnings of imperial history. This is no subversion or contradiction of the larger message of the museum. It is rather a reminder that that larger story – the grand narrative of the evolution of civilisation – was intimately connected with privileged national histories. The whole of humanity could be seen, we need to remember, only from particular places at particular times. What we can see in this museum is not that whole history, which Pitt Rivers and Balfour saw; but we can see them seeing it; and I guess see their Great Britain, overshadowed by a totem pole.

39 (a,b,c)
Pitt Rivers Museum, Oxford, 27 November 1995

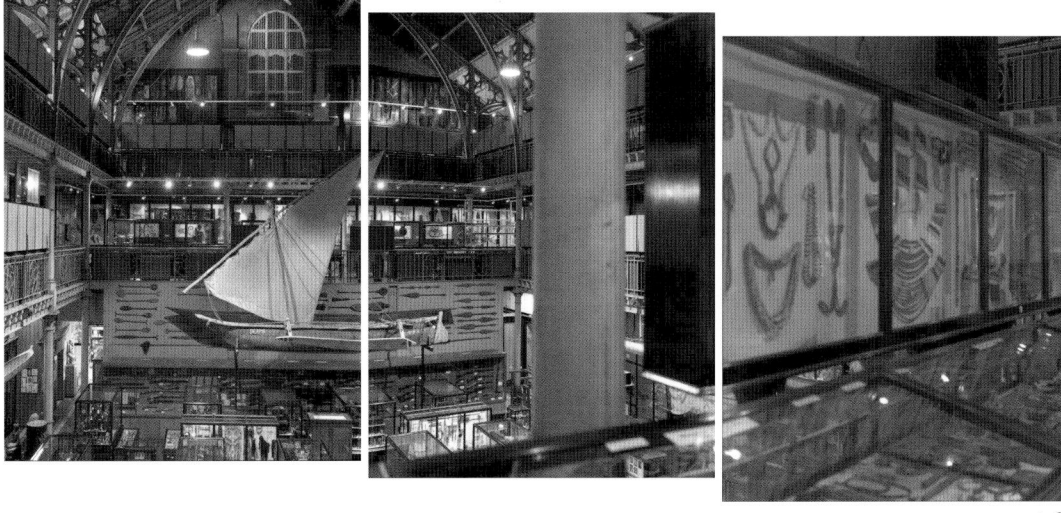

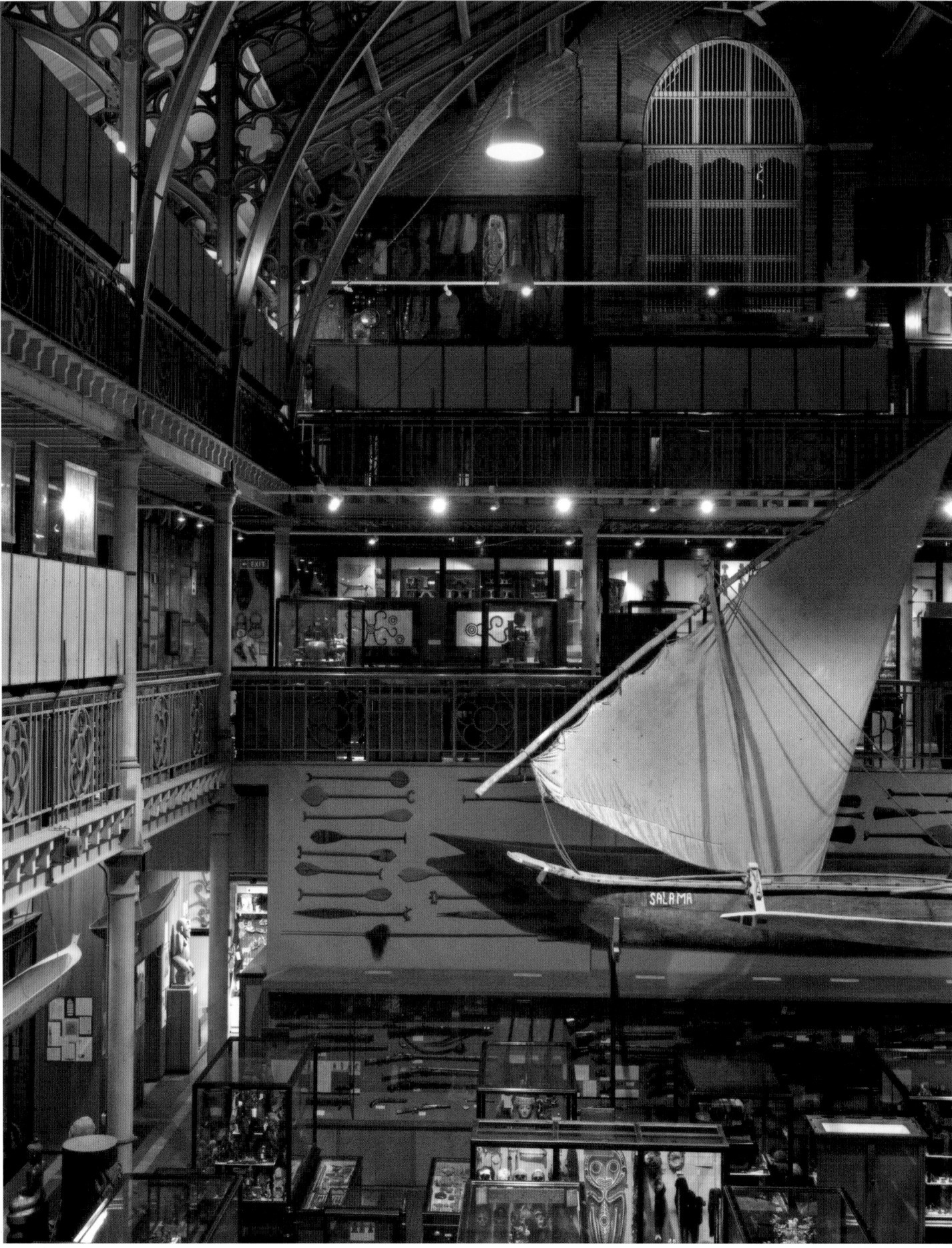

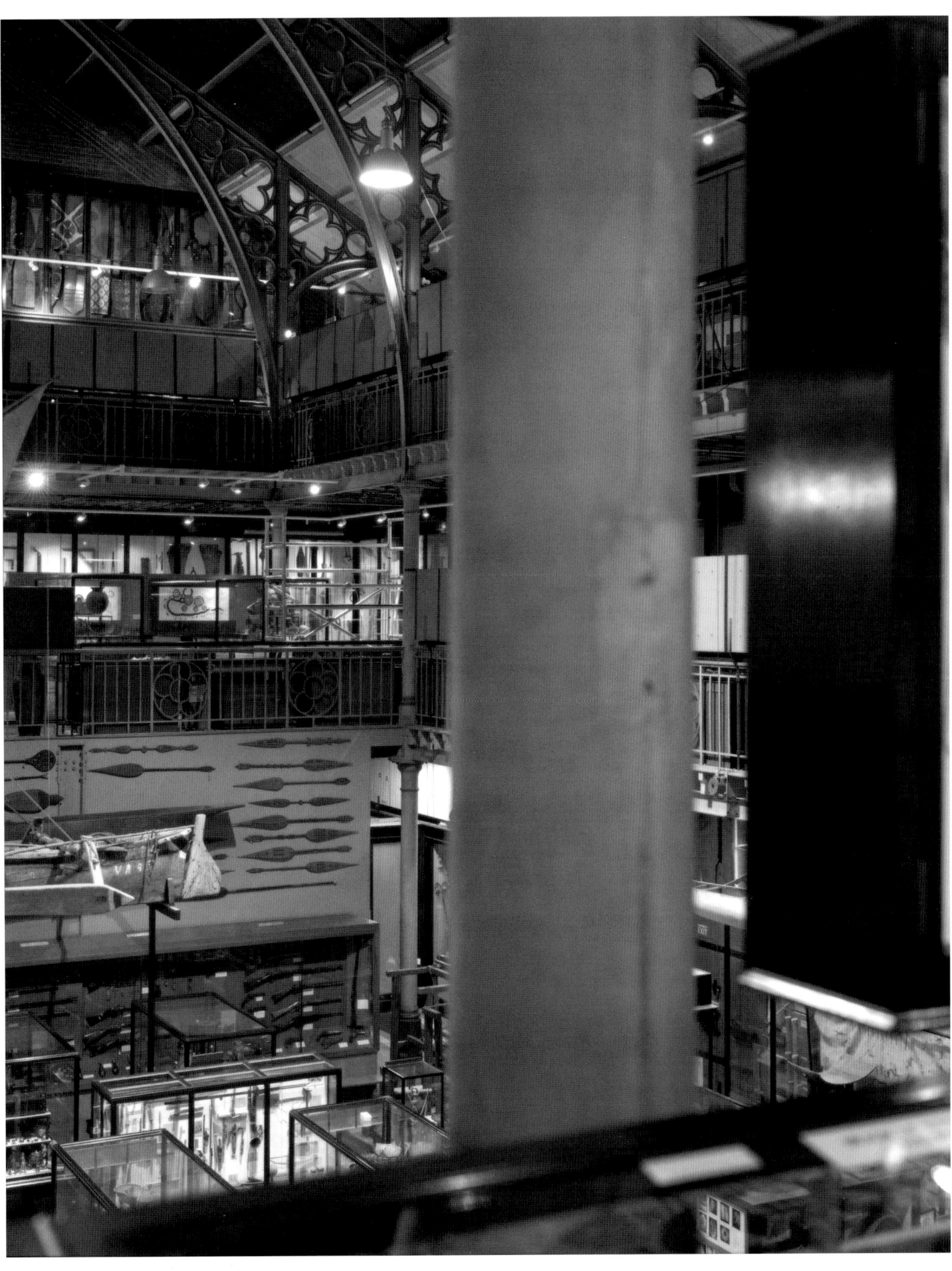

40 (a,b)
Cook display, Johann Reinhold Forster collection,
Pitt Rivers Museum, Oxford, 28 November 1995

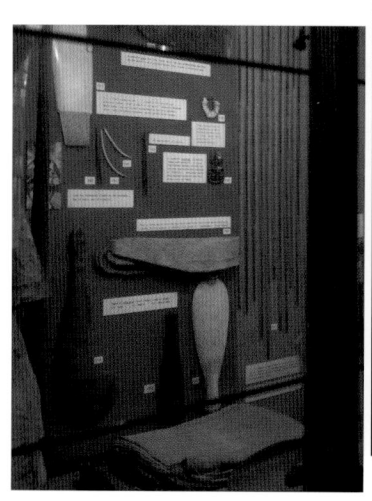 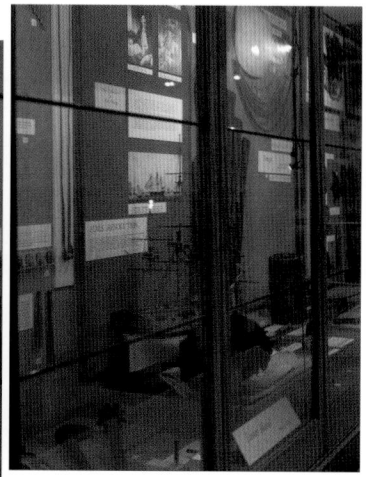

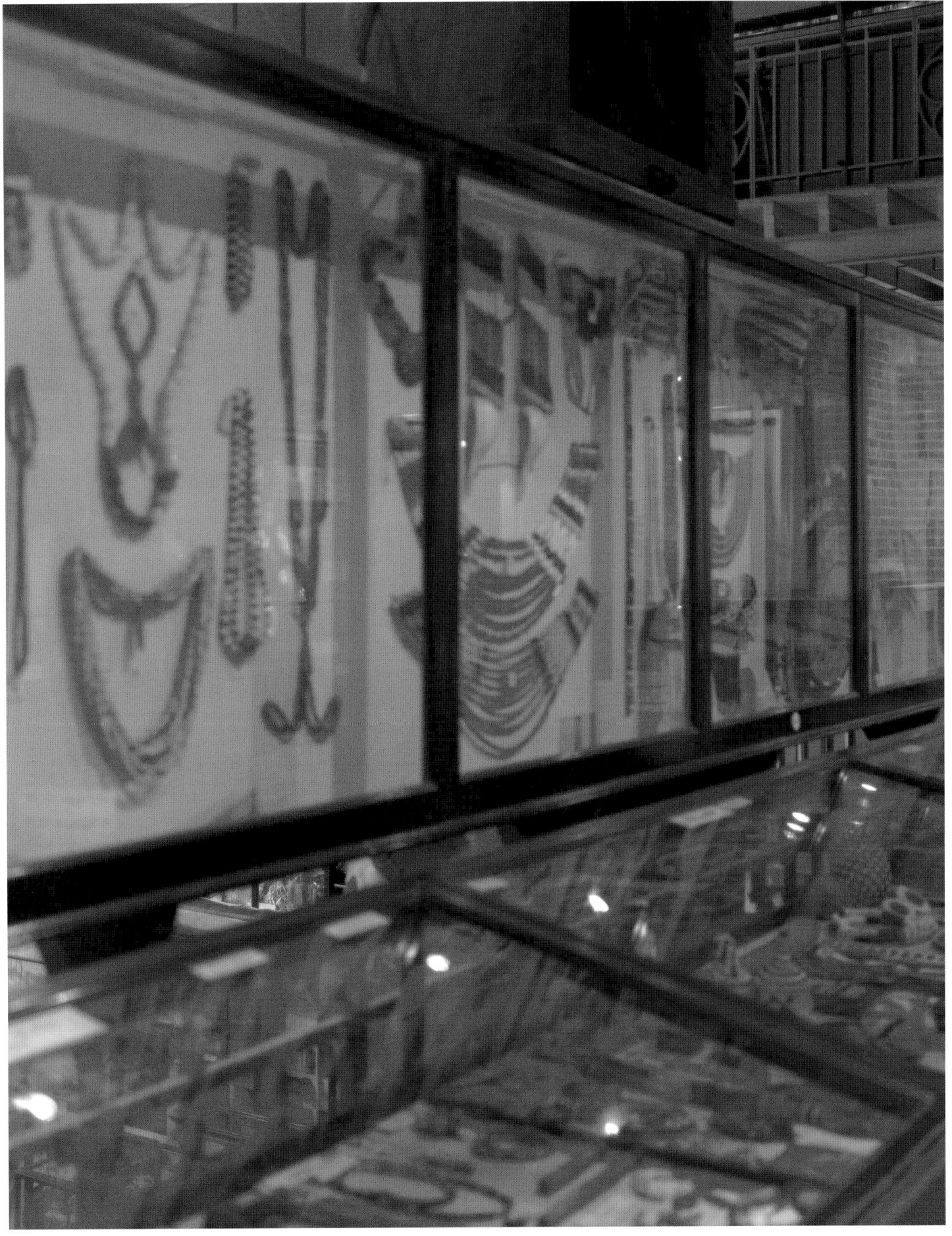

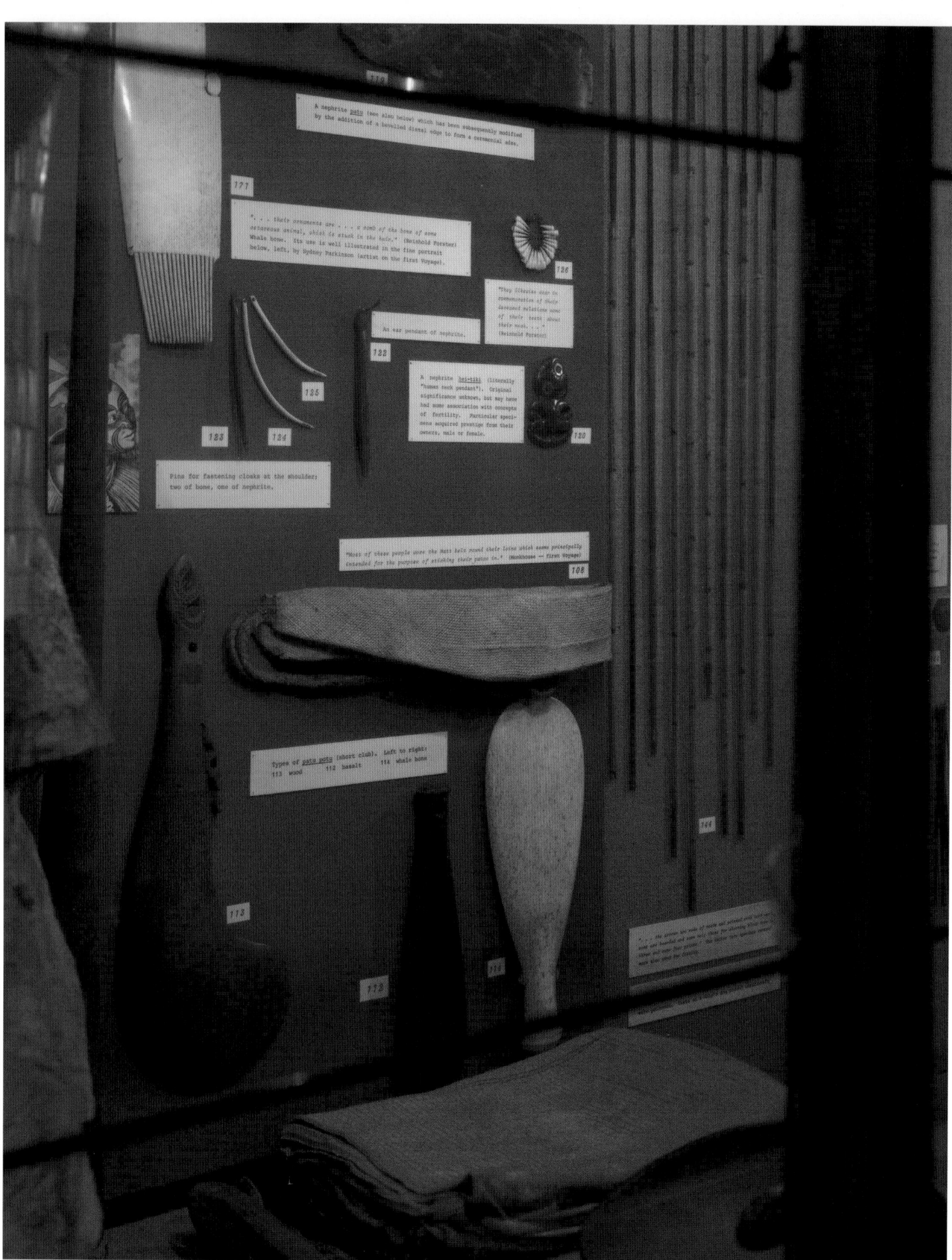

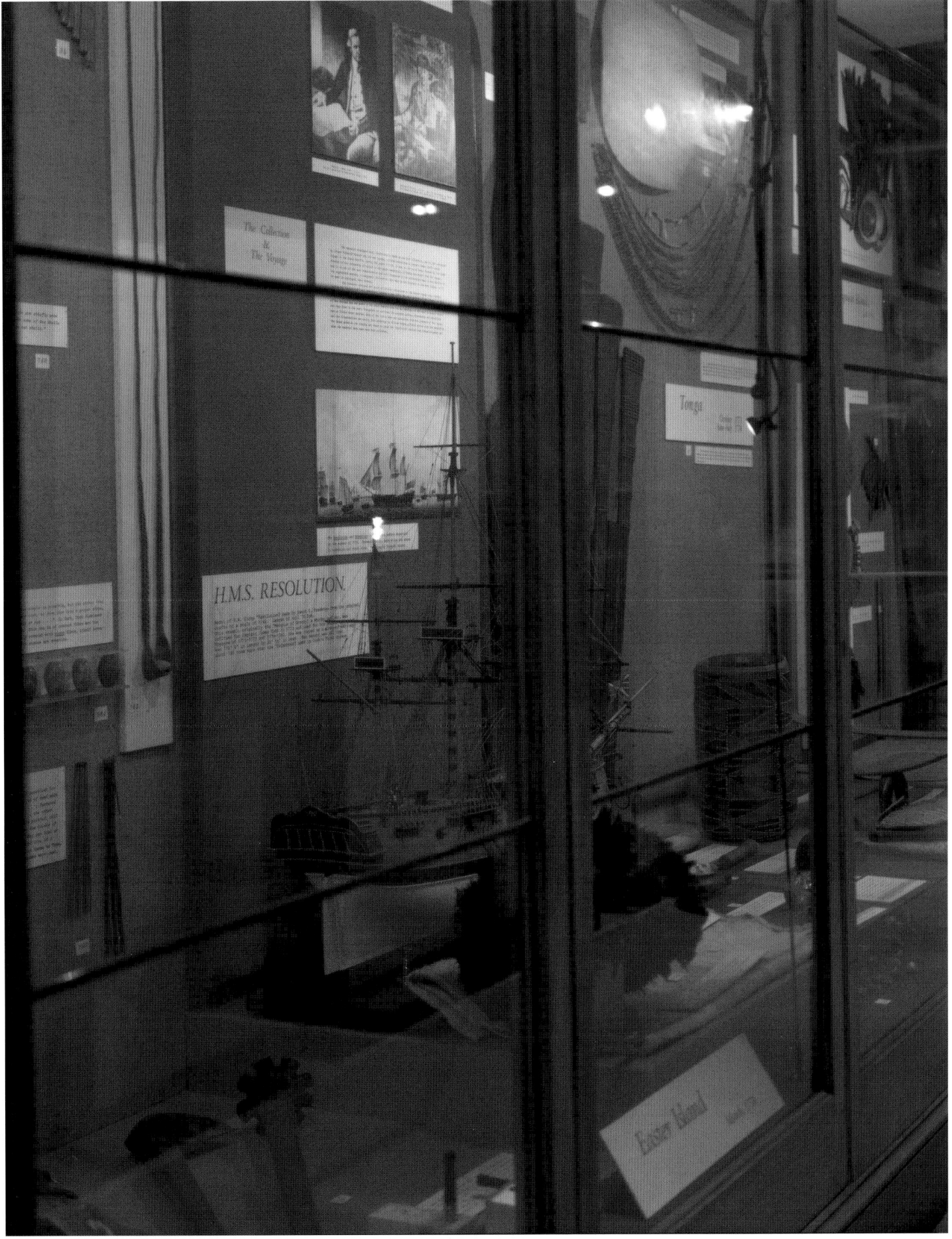

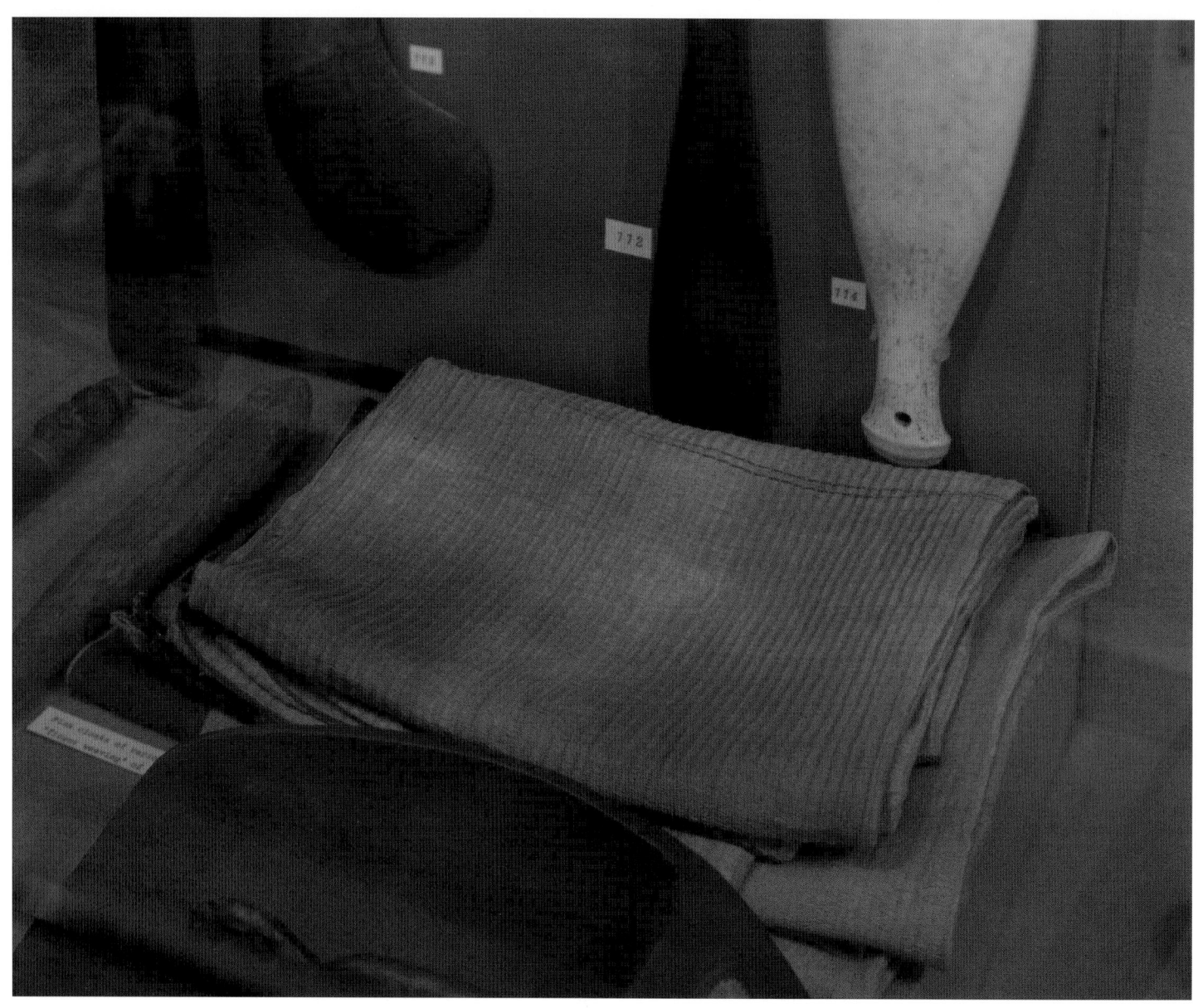

41 *Maori flax cape, Johann Reinhold Forster collection, Pitt Rivers Museum, Oxford, 28 November 1995*

Epilogue

Like the Pitt Rivers Museum, the Royal Botanic Gardens at Kew is nothing if not an imperial institution, and moreover also one intimately connected with voyages and collecting, and with one of the most famous participants in Cook's first voyage.

After returning from the Pacific, Joseph Banks established major personal botanical collections, but also became involved in what had been Princess Augusta's garden at Kew, which assumed more and more of a scientific character after Banks became a kind of unofficial director. He aimed to make it nothing less than the pre-eminent botanical institution in the world, and naturalists were despatched to collect plants from the Americas, Africa, Australia, and elsewhere. Kew became the centre of a global flow of specimens, new species, horticulture, and commerce. Banks was interested particularly in the scope for transplanting economically useful plants to colonies. In his vision, the growth of scientific knowledge was thus intimately connected with the prosperity of the empire. In this economic sense, the empire seems scarcely to have touched Dusky Sound, where Forster collected the kidney ferns that are preserved in the herbarium at Kew, together with his specimens from elsewhere in New Zealand and the Pacific.

Tamatea's waters are roughly at the opposite end of the world to this remarkable institution; each represents the other's antipodes. In the south, a few people visit an extraordinary environment, which is less purely natural, and more historical, than they imagine. In the north, millions of Londoners and tourists a year traipse around the botanical world, stopping only to feed the ducks and buy ice-creams; the educational panels referring to the intrepid botanists who made the collections seem not much read. In one place, history is manifest in the unmarked vestiges of a few trees; in the other, the history of science has made a whole natural world visible. At Kew, Forster's ferns rest intact. On a dim winter afternoon, just outside the Gardens, a Christmas tree is wired up; its bulbs come alive amidst the traffic. At the opposite end of the world, stumps of the trees felled by Cook's crew decay slowly in the rain and brilliant light of Dusky Sound.

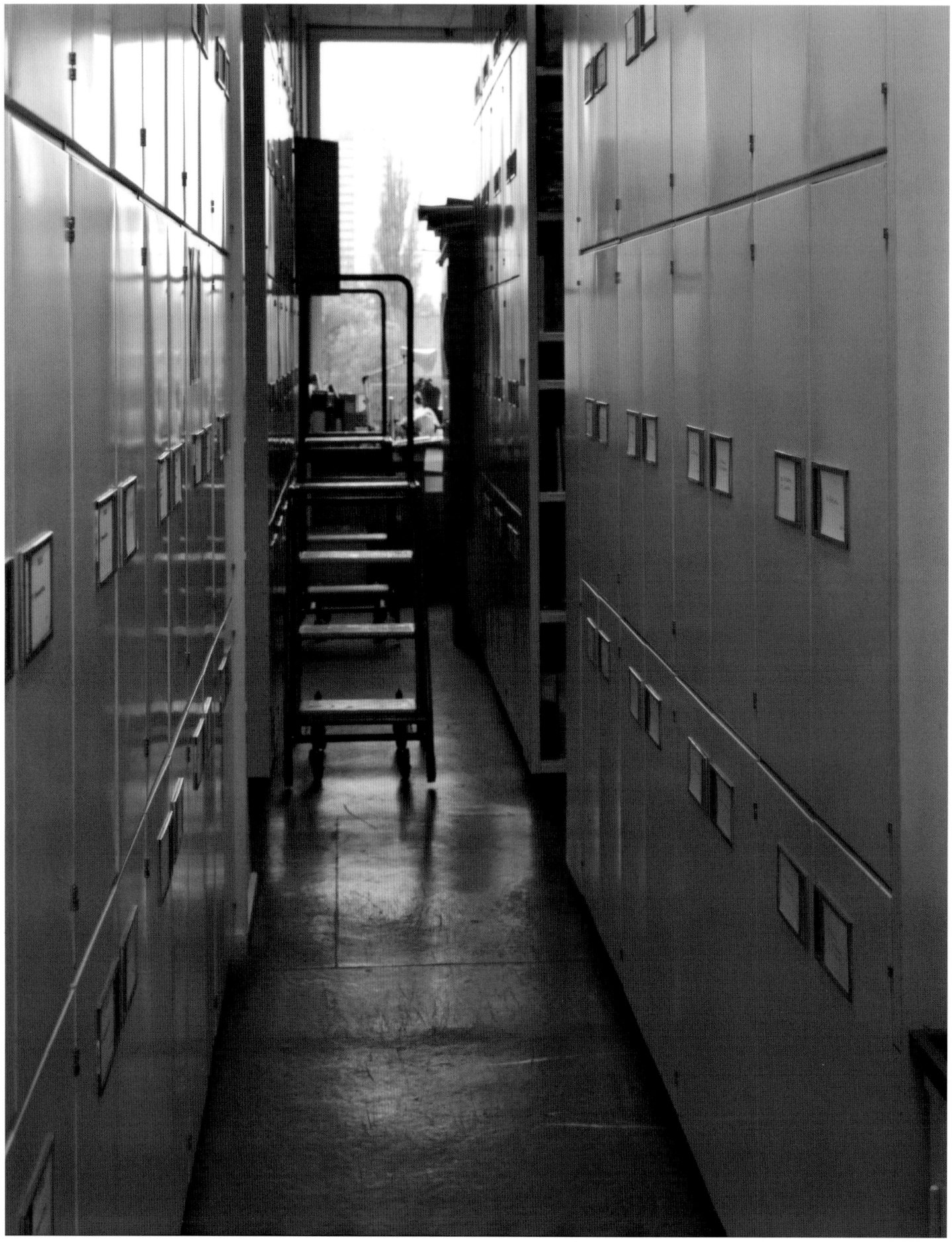

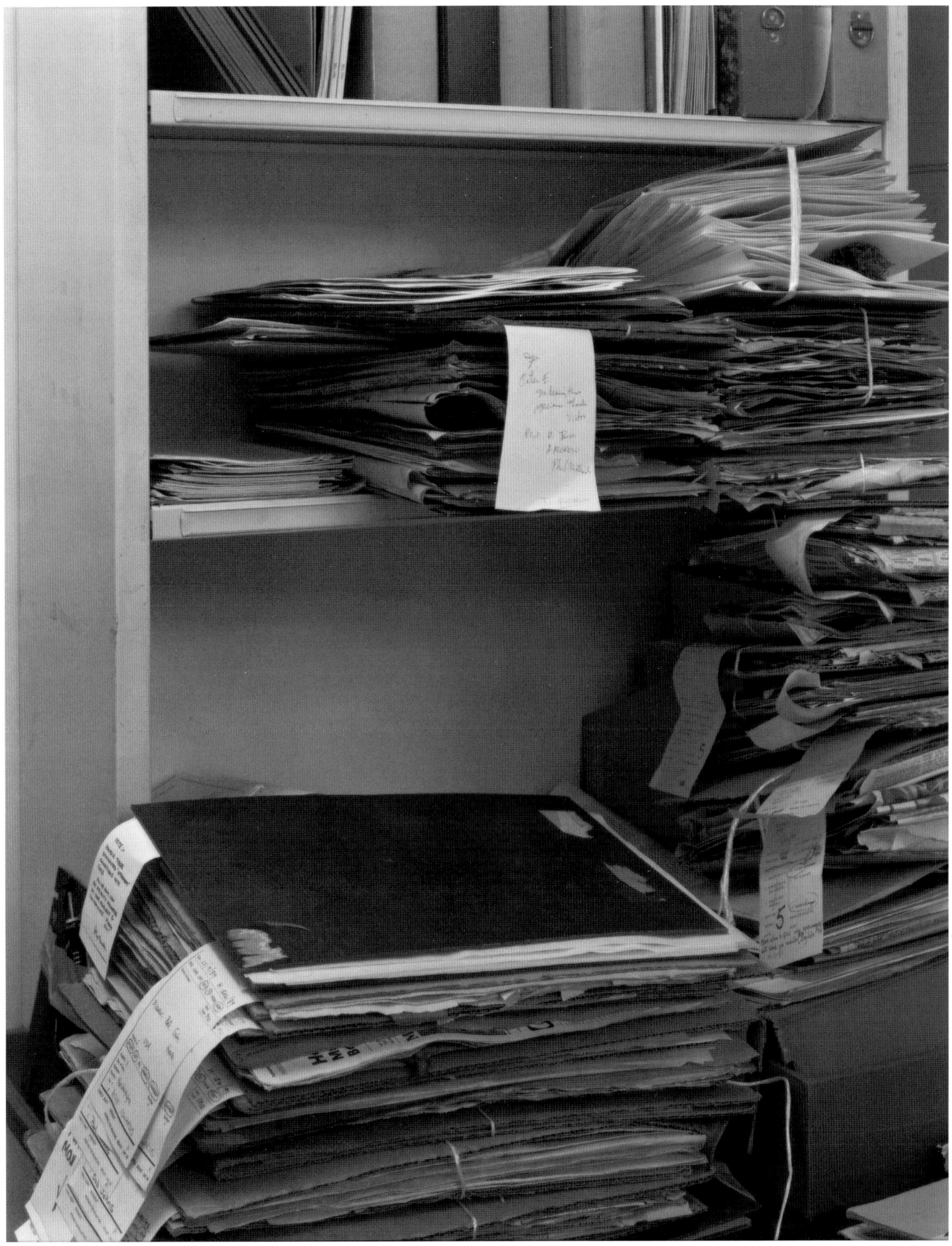

42 (a-c)
A View in the Herbarium, Royal Botanic Gardens, Kew, London, 1 December 1995

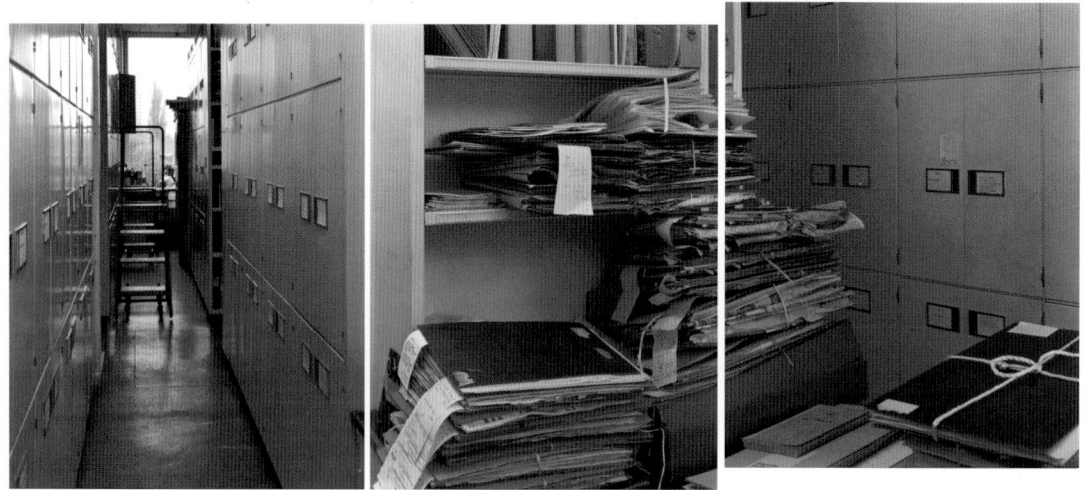

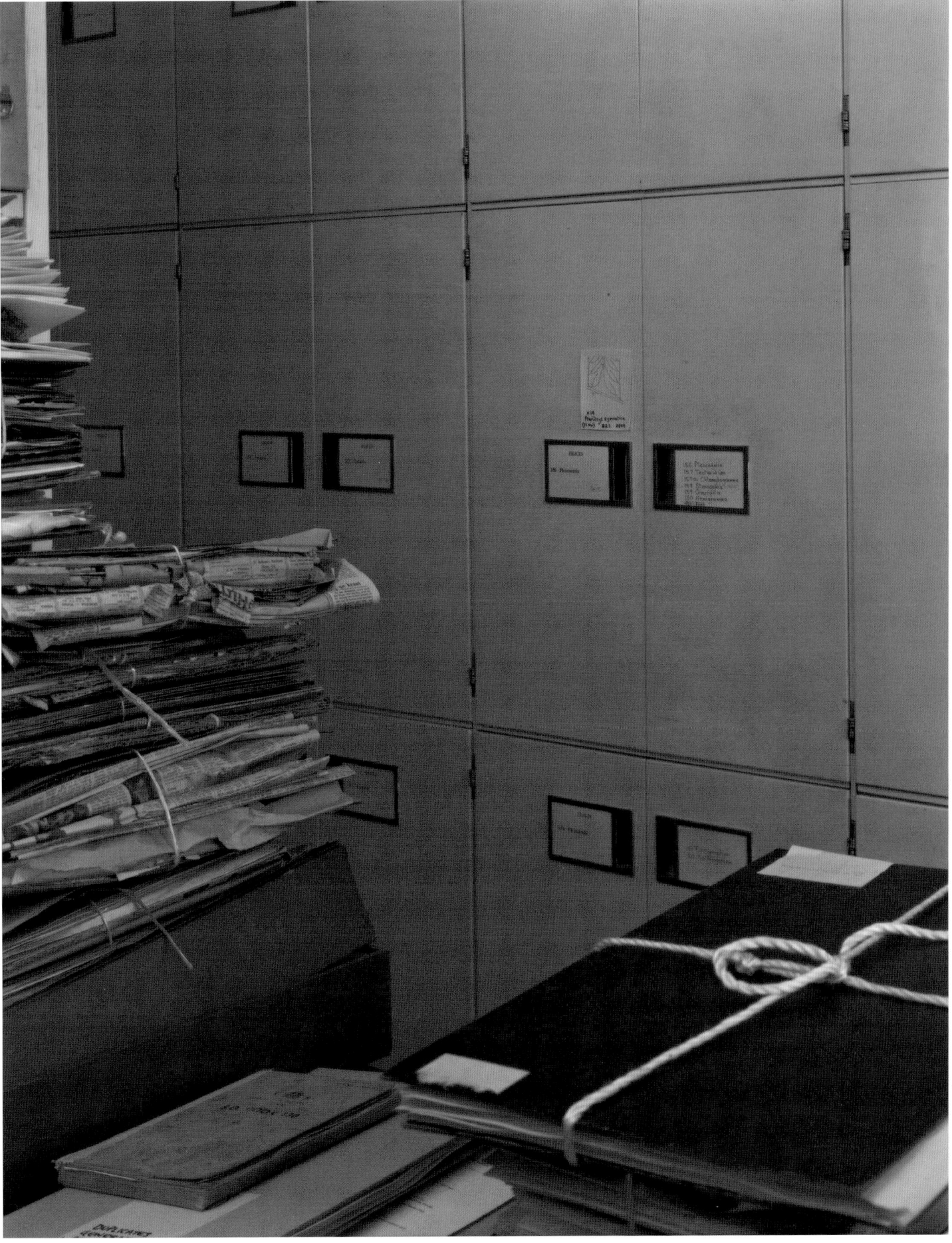

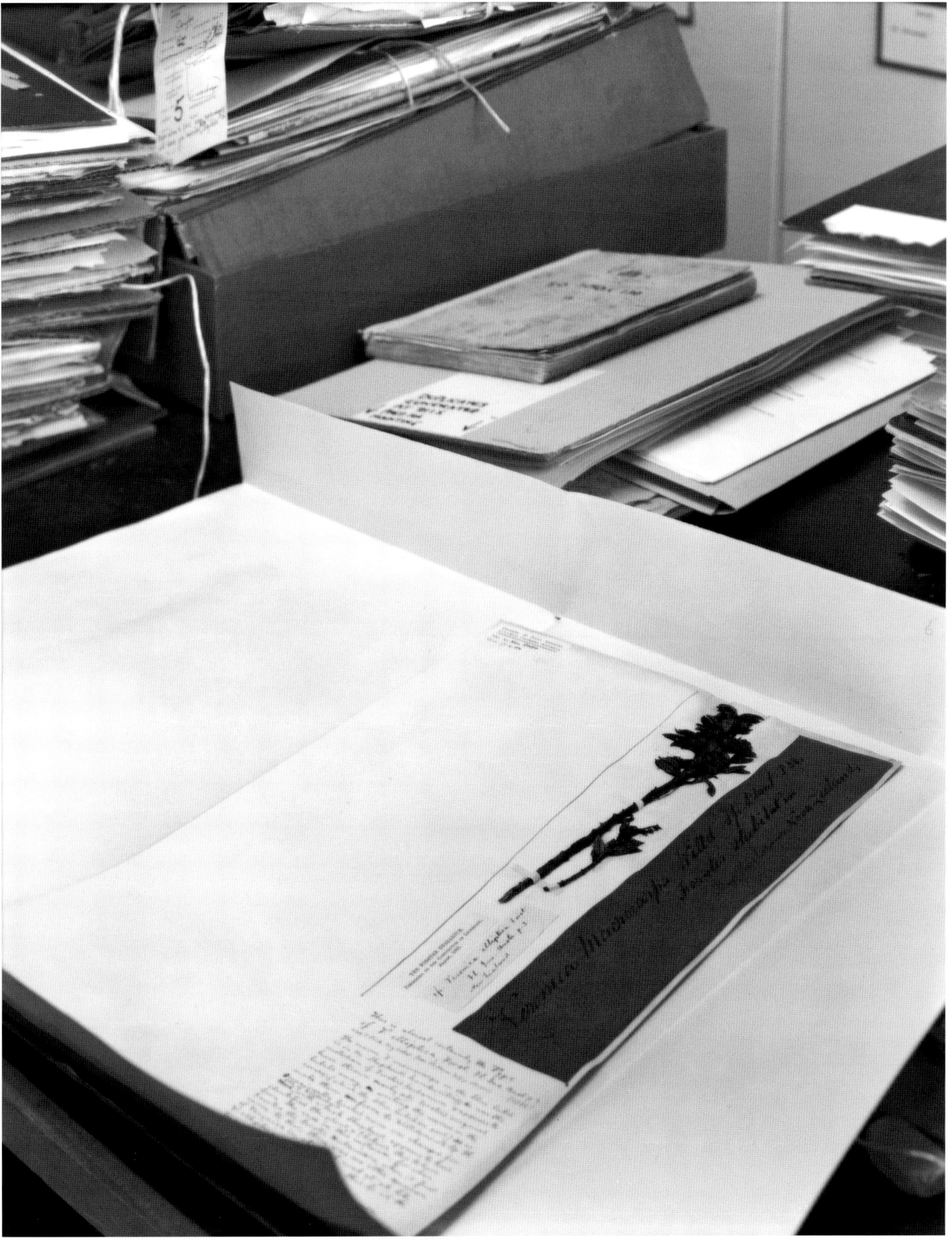

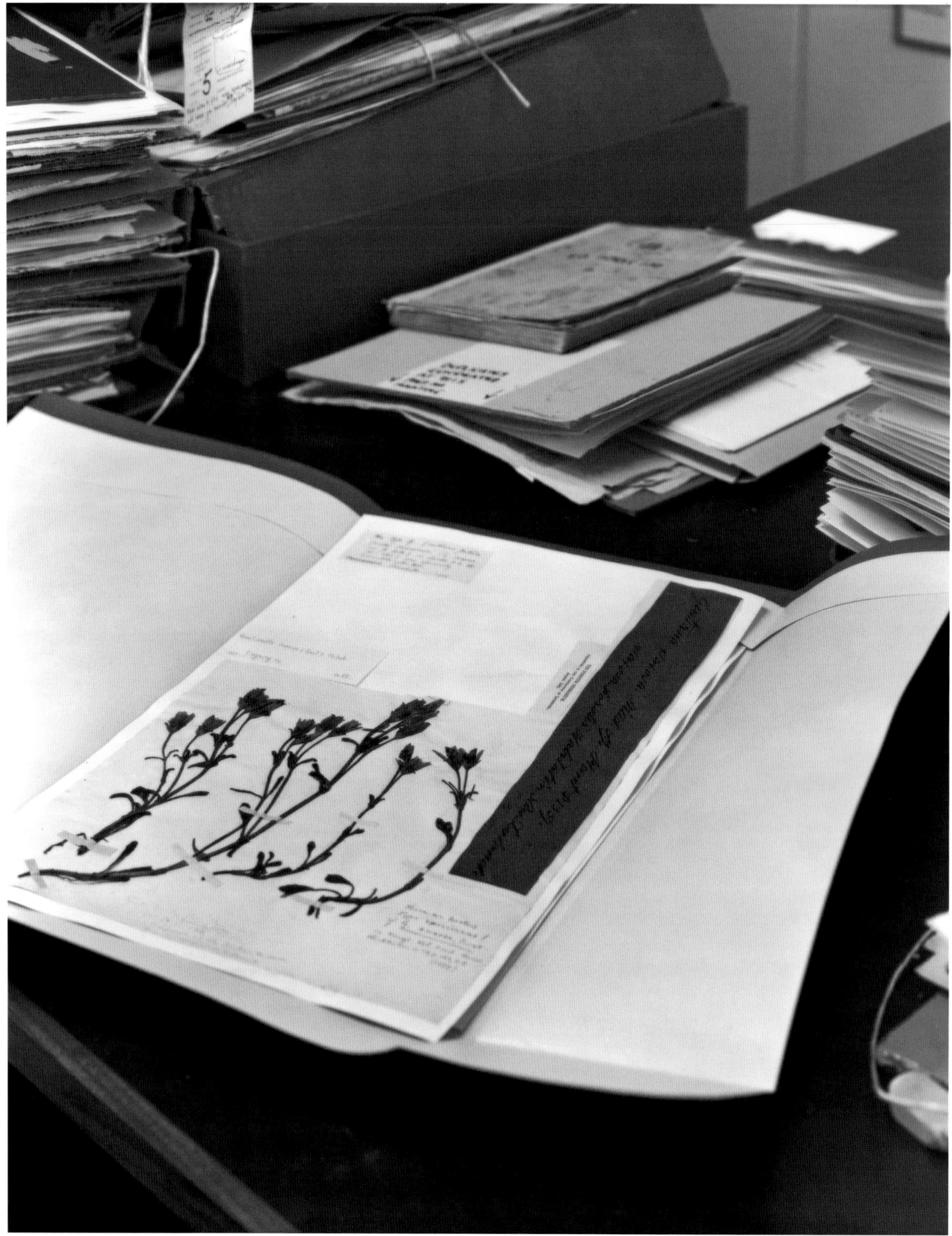

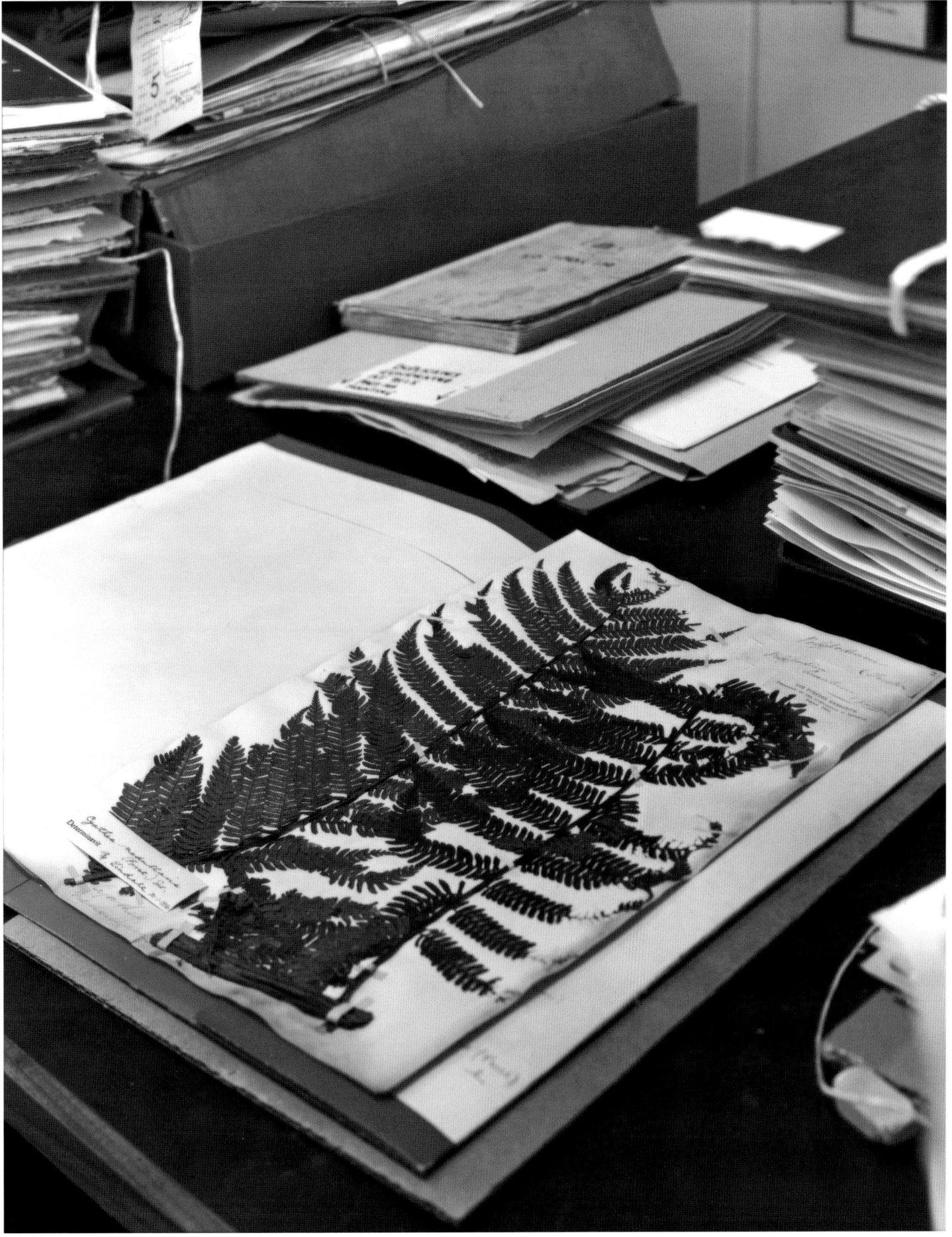

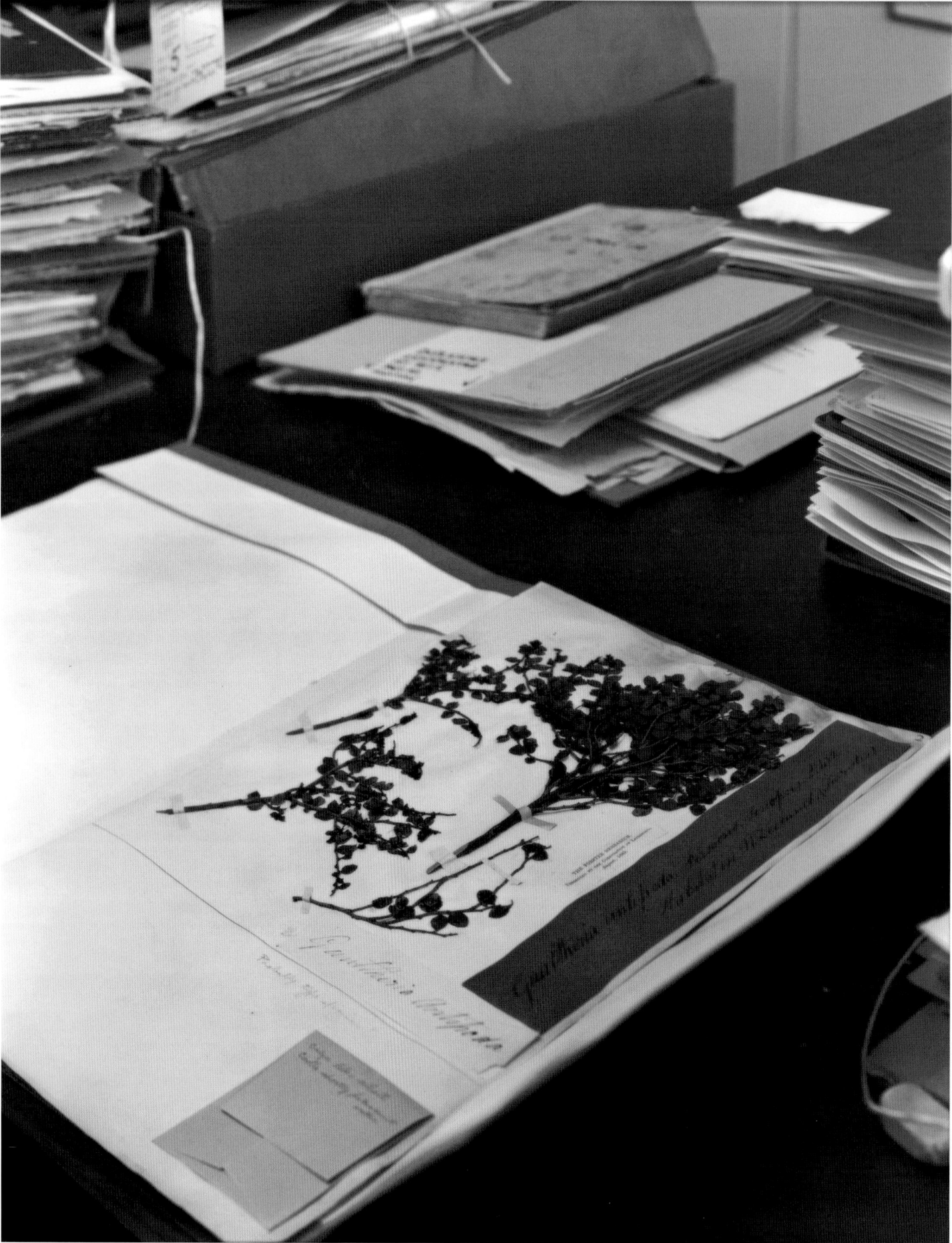

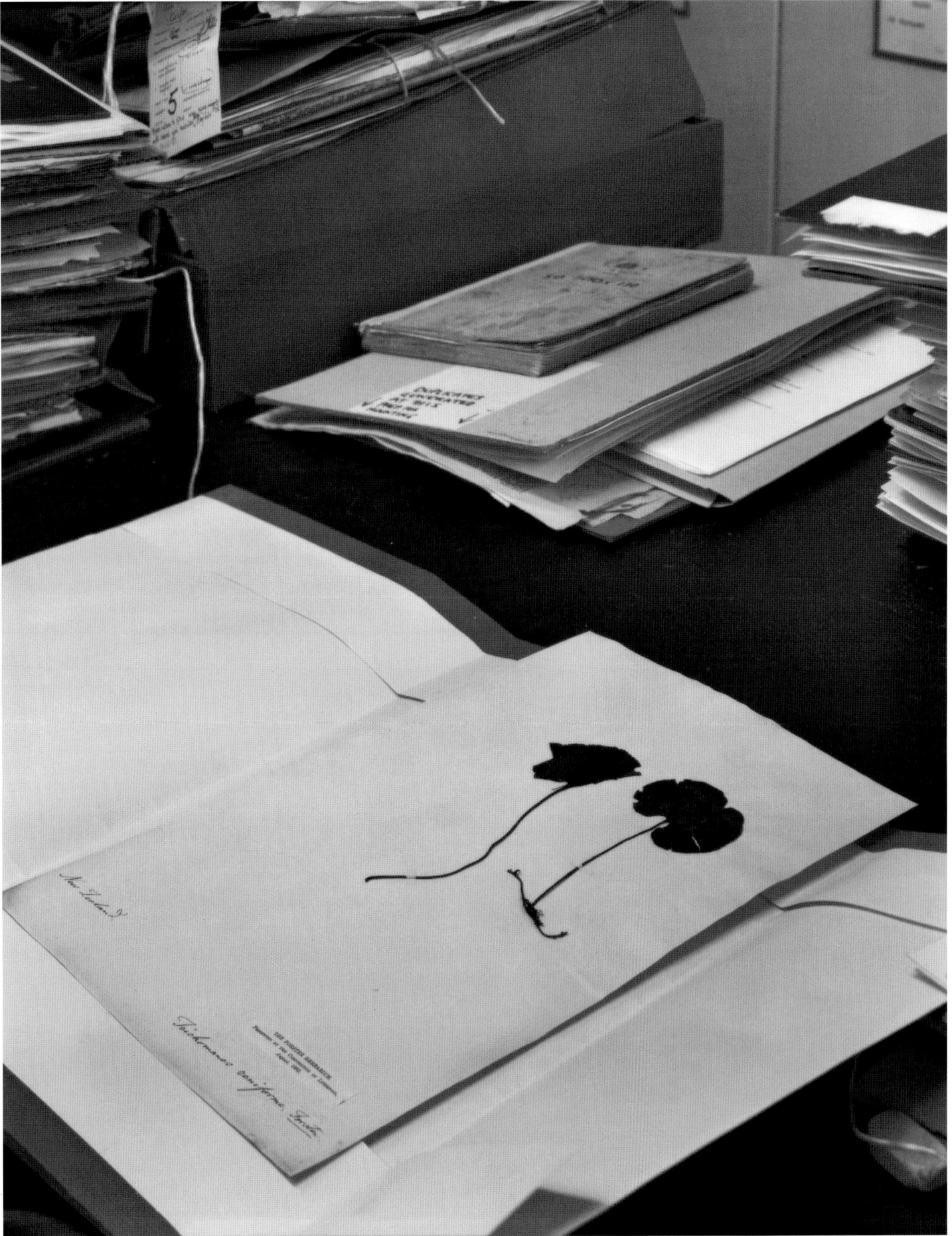

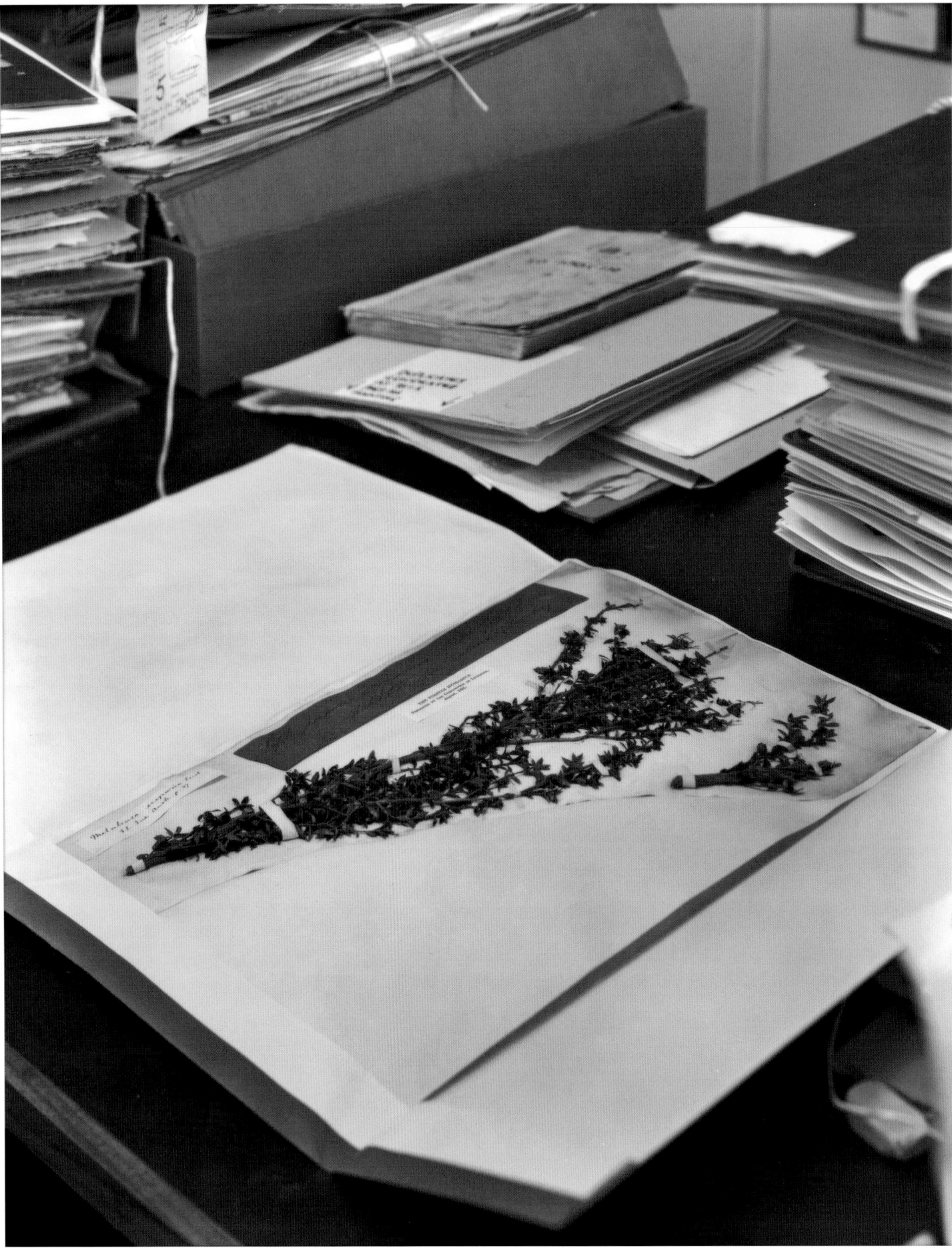

49 (a,b)
Exterior view, the Herbarium, Royal Botanic Gardens,
Kew, London, 3 December 1995

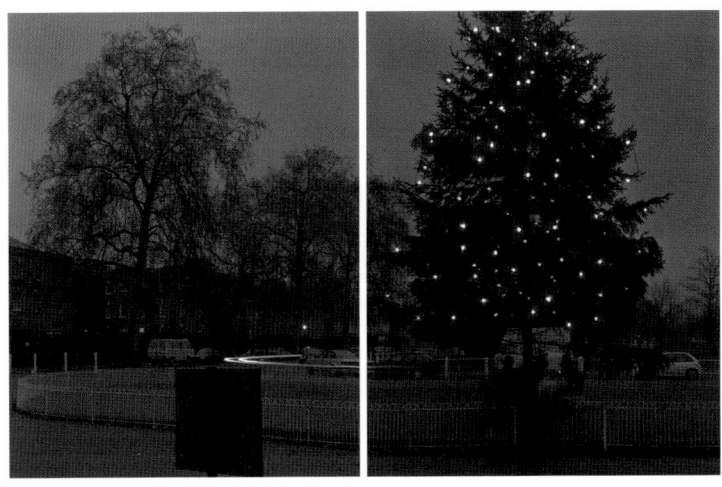

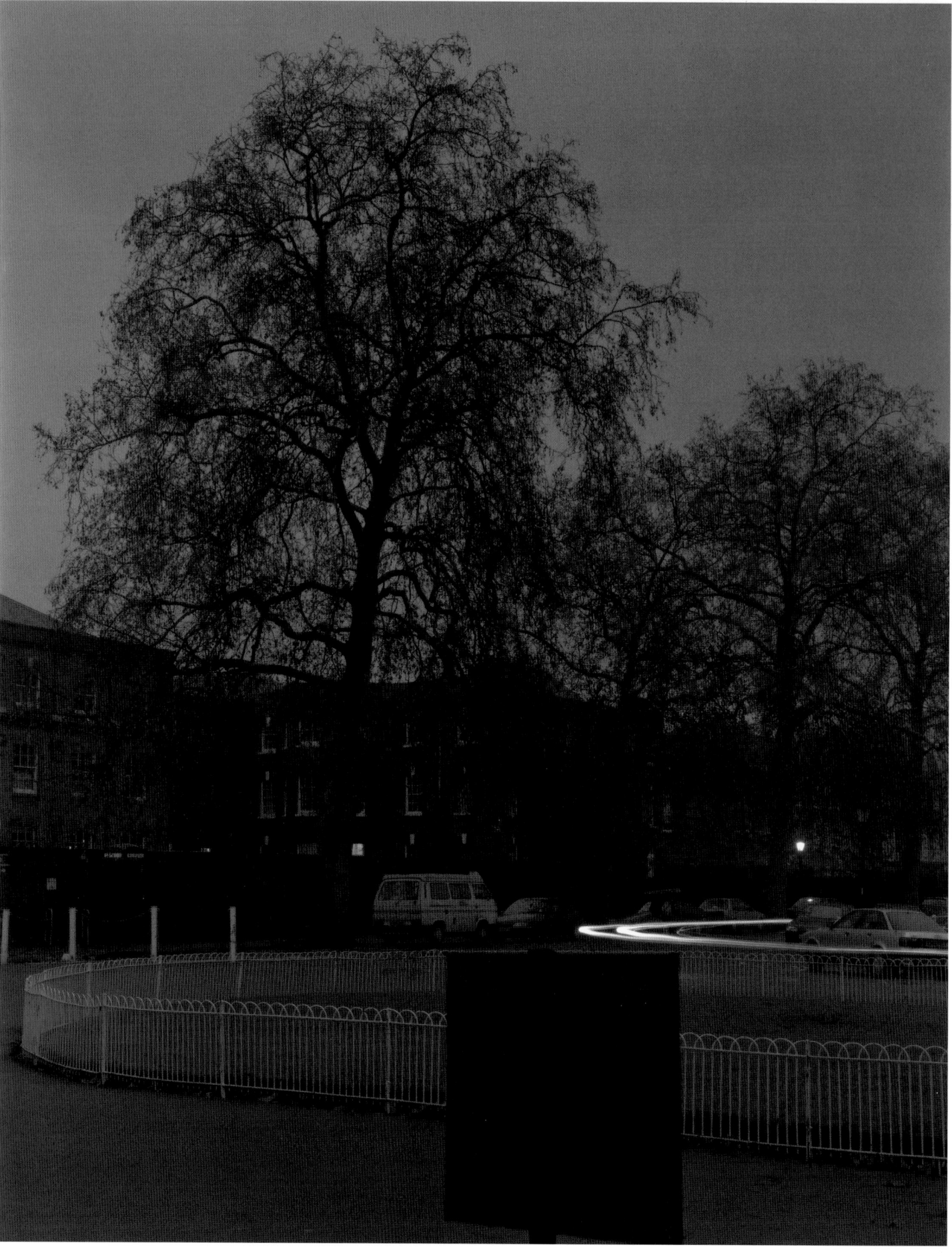

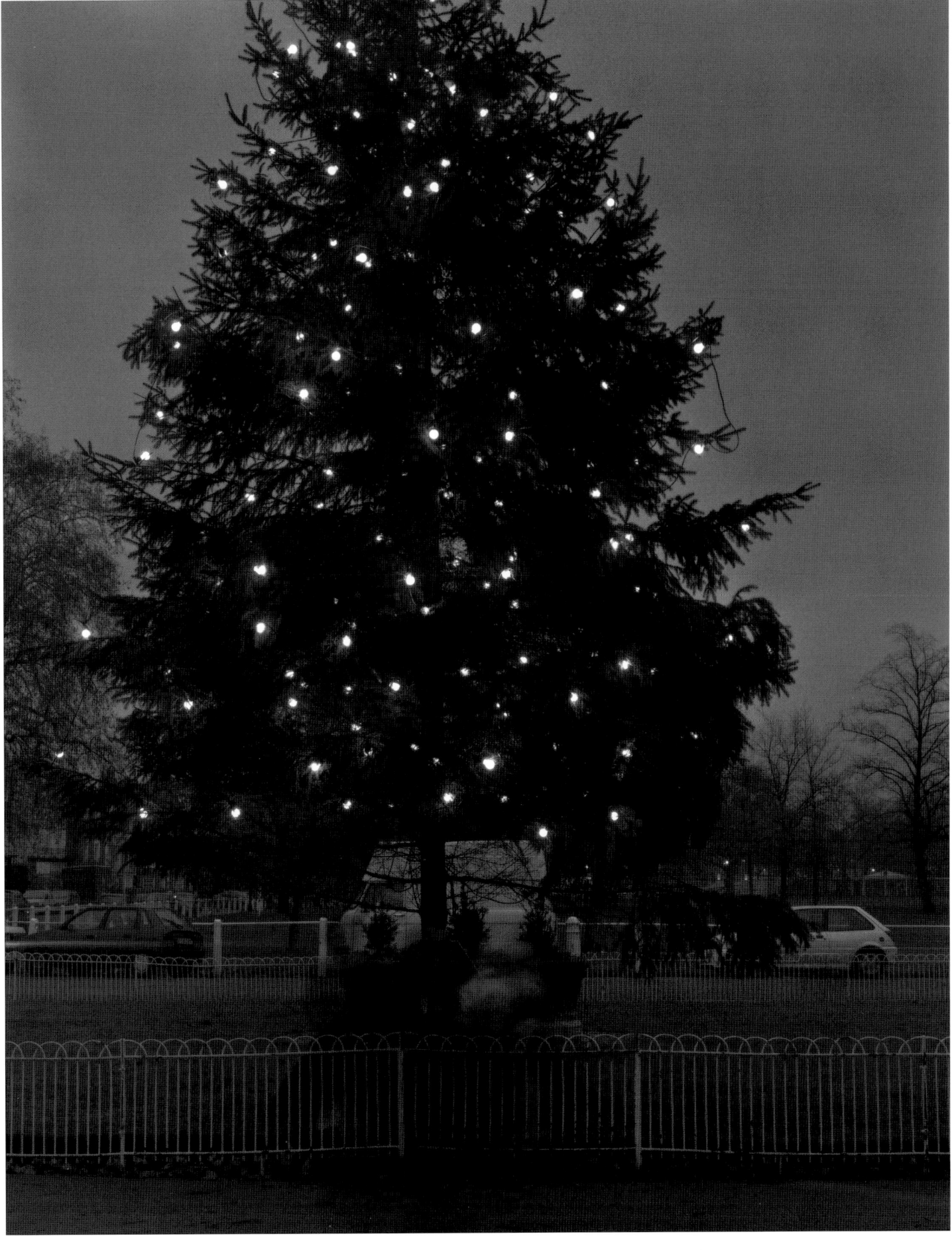

Notes

1   It has generally been assumed that the Dusky Sound Maori were a branch of Ngatimamoe, who had settled the South Island from the sixteenth century onward and had gradually been forced southward, eventually into Fiordland, by successive migrations and small incursions by Ngai Tahu. See Atholl Anderson's careful and thorough account, *The Welcome of Strangers: an ethnohistory of southern Maori, A.D. 1650–1850* (Dunedin, 1998), esp. pp. 51–56. It should be recalled that these larger tribal identifications were generally far less significant than subtribal affiliations: Anderson notes that Ngai Tahu was very much a retrospective tribal appellation (p. 26).

2   See Anne Salmond, *Two Worlds* (Auckland, 1991) and *Between Worlds* (Auckland, 1997). Harry Evison's important book, *Te Wai Pounamu* (Christchurch, 1993), is primarily concerned with nineteenth-century developments.

3   Cook, *Journals*, II, 112.

4   See Susanne and John Hill, *Richard Henry of Resolution Island* (Dunedin, 1987), for fuller details of his life and activities than are given by the Beggs.

5   Cook, *Journals*, II, 172.

6   George Forster, *A Voyage Round the World* (London, 1777), 138.

7   *The* Resolution *Journal of Johann Reinhold Forster, 1772–1775*, ed. Michael E. Hoare (London, 1982), II, 258. For further discussion of these confused identifications, see Nicholas Thomas, 'Liberty and License', chapter 3 in *In Oceania* (Durham, North Carolina, 1997).

8   *The Journals of Captain James Cook on his Voyages of Discovery. II. The Voyage of the* Resolution *and* Adventure, *1772–1775*, ed. J.C. Beaglehole, (Cambridge, 1961), 116-17, 122, n. 2.

9   James Cook, *A Voyage Towards the South Pole and Around the World* (London, 1777), I, 75.

10 George William Anderson, *A New, Authentic, and Complete Collection of Voyages Round the World* (London, 1784-86).

11 A.C. and N.C. Begg, *Dusky Bay: In the Steps of Captain Cook* (Christchurch, 1966), 113.

12 Begg and Begg, 113.

13 Begg and Begg, 126.

14 Begg and Begg, 127.

15 *The Bee* 3 (1791), 117.

16 *The* Endeavour *Journal of Joseph Banks* (Sydney, 1961), I, 403.

17 Cook, *Journals*, II, 175.

18 Wim Wenders, *The Logic of Images* (London, 1991), 73.

19 See Brigitta Hauser-Schäublin and Gundolf Krüger (eds) *James Cook: Gifts and Treasures from the South Seas* (Munich and New York, 1988).

Select Bibliography

Anderson, Atholl. (1998). *The Welcome of Strangers: an Ethnohistory of Southern Maori, AD 1650–1850*. Dunedin: University of Otago Press.

Anderson, George William. (1784–86). *A New, Authentic, and Complete Collection of Voyages Round the World*. London: Alexander Hogg.

Banks, Joseph. (1962). *The* Endeavour *Journal of Joseph Banks, 1768–1771*, ed. J.C. Beaglehole. Sydney: Angus & Robertson/Public Library of New South Wales.

Beattie, Herries. (1994). *Traditional Lifeways of the Southern Maori*, ed. Atholl Anderson. Dunedin: University of Otago Press.

Begg, A.C. and N.C. (1966). *Dusky Bay: In the Steps of Captain Cook*. Christchurch: Whitcombe and Tombs.

Cook, James. (1777). *A Voyage Towards the South Pole, and Round the World. Performed in His Majesty's ships the* Resolution *and* Adventure, *in the years 1772, 1773, 1774, 1775*. London: W. Strahan and T. Cadell.

_____ (1955–67). *The Journals of Captain James Cook on his Voyages of Discovery*, ed. J.C. Beaglehole. Cambridge: Hakluyt Society/Cambridge University Press.

Coombes, Annie E. (1994). *Re-inventing Africa*. New Haven: Yale University Press.

Coutts, P.J.F. (1969). 'The Maori of Dusky Sound: a review of the historical sources.' *Journal of the Polynesian Society* 78, 179-211.

Dening, Greg. (1980). *Islands and Beaches. Discourse on a Silent Land: Marquesas, 1774–1880*. Carlton, Victoria: Melbourne University Press.

_____ (1995). *Performances*. Carlton, Victoria: Melbourne University Press.

Desmond, Ray. (1995) *Kew: the History of the Royal Botanic Gardens*. London: Harvill Press/The Royal Botanic Gardens.

Forster, George. (1777). *A Voyage Round the World in his Brittanic Majesty's Sloop* Resolution. London: B. White.

_____ (1778). *A Letter to the Earl of Sandwich*. London: G. Robinson.

_____ (1999; orig. 1777). *A Voyage Round the World in his Brittanic Majesty's Sloop* Resolution, eds Nicholas Thomas and Oliver Berghof. Honolulu: University of Hawaii Press.

Forster, John Reinold (Johann Reinhold). (1982). *The* Resolution *Journal of Johann Reinhold Forster*, ed. Michael E. Hoare. London: Hakluyt Society.

_____ (1996; orig. 1778). *Observations made during a voyage round the world, on physical geography, natural history, and ethic philosophy*, eds Nicholas Thomas, Harriet Guest, and Michael Dettelbach. Honolulu: University of Hawaii Press.

Hauser-Schäublin, Brigitta, and Gundolf Krüger (eds) (1998). *James Cook: Gifts and Treasures from the South Seas*. Munich and New York: Prestel.

Hawkesworth, John. (1773). *An account of the voyages undertaken by the order of His Present Majesty, for making discoveries in the Southern Hemisphere, and successively performed by Commodore Byron, Captain Wallis, Captain Carteret, and Captain Cook*. Dublin: A. Leathley and others.

Jones, Peter Blundell. (1979). 'Scharoun's Staatsbibliothek: State Library, Berlin', *Architectural Review* 165, 330-41.

Joppien, Rüdiger, and Bernard Smith. (1985–87). *The Art of Captain Cook's Voyages*. New Haven: Yale University Press.

Salmond, Anne. (1991). *Two Worlds: First Meetings between Maori and Europeans 1642–1772.* Auckland: Viking.

_____ (1997). *Between Worlds: Early Exchanges between Maori and Europeans 1773–1815.* Auckland: Viking.

Schama, Simon. (1995). *Landscape and Memory.* London: HarperCollins.

Smith, Bernard. (1985). *European Vision and the South Pacific.* 2nd edn. New Haven: Yale University Press.

Thomas, Nicholas. (1997). *In Oceania: Visions, Artifacts, Histories.* Durham, North Carolina: Duke University Press.

Wenders, Wim. (1991). *The Logic of Images.* London: Faber and Faber.